DONALD P. GREEN
IAN SHAPIRO

PATHOLOGIES OF RATIONAL CHOICE THEORY

A CRITIQUE OF APPLICATIONS IN POLITICAL SCIENCE

YALE UNIVERSITY PRESS   NEW HAVEN AND LONDON

Designed by Nancy Ovedovitz and set in Times Roman type by The Composing Room of Michigan, Inc. Printed in the United States of America by Vail-Ballou Press, Binghamton, New York.

Library of Congress Cataloging-in-Publication Data

Green, Donald P., 1961–
Pathologies of rational choice theory : a critique of applications in political science / Donald P. Green and Ian Shapiro.
    p.   cm.
Includes bibliographical references and index.
ISBN 0-300-05914-0
1. Rational choice theory.   2. Political science—Methodology.
I. Shapiro, Ian.   II. Title.
JA73.G74   1994
320′.01′1—dc20   94-11070
                              CIP

A catalogue record for this book is available from the British Library.

The paper in this book meets the guidelines for permanence and durability of the Committee on Production Guidelines for Book Longevity of the Council on Library Resources.

10   9   8   7   6   5   4   3   2

For Ann and Judy

CONTENTS

PREFACE

Since the publication of Kenneth Arrow's *Social Choice and Individual Values* in 1951 there has been an explosion of rational choice scholarship in political science, but there exists in it a curious disjunction that provides both the occasion and motivation for this book. On the one hand, great strides have been made in the theoretical elaboration of rational actor models. Formidable analytical challenges have attracted a number of first-class minds; rational choice theories have grown in complexity and sophistication as a result. On the other hand, successful empirical applications of rational choice models have been few and far between. Most of the early rational choice work was either not empirical at all, or it was crude and impressionistic. What is surprising is how little things have changed in this regard since the 1950s.

When we began this study our goal was to understand and account for this relative dearth of sound empirical work. Early on we discovered that in the highly charged debates about the merits of rational choice theory protagonists tend to speak past one another. Practitioners operate within the confines of an esoteric technical vocabulary that is seldom understood by anyone else. Critics tend to ignore or heap scorn on the rational choice approach without understanding it fully. They dismiss its assumptions or scientific aspirations, or they get it wrong in elementary ways. Not surprisingly, practitioners generally ignore them.

We set out to write an appraisal that would address rational choice scholarship on its own terms. We did not challenge rational choice theorists' aspiration to study politics scientifically, nor did we take exception to the assumptions on which rational choice models have been based. We granted much of the rational choice critique of other modes of studying politics, and we looked to the literatures where rational choice models are reputed to have enjoyed their greatest successes: those growing out of the seminal works of Arrow, Anthony Downs, and Mancur Olson. Our question was, What has been learned about politics?

We focused our attention, therefore, on the empirical rational choice literatures and gradually came to the view that exceedingly little has been learned. Part of the difficulty stems from the sheer paucity of empirical applications; proponents of rational choice seem to be most interested in theory elaboration, leaving for later, or others, the messy business of empirical testing. But this is only part of the problem. On our reading, empirical failure is also importantly rooted in the aspiration of rational choice theorists to come up with universal theories of politics. As a consequence of this aspiration, we contend, the bulk of rational choice–inspired empirical work is marred by methodological defects.

Things will not improve, in our view, until this syndrome of methodological failings is understood and the universalist aspiration that gives rise to it is rethought. In the chapters that follow, we explain why this is so, indicate what kinds of changes are appropriate, and say something about how the changes that we recommend should shape future research. Thus, although much of our message may be construed as negative, we intend for this methodological critique to be part of a constructive effort designed to improve the quality of empirical research in political science.

The rational choice edifice is bewildering and perplexing to the uninitiated; lack of familiarity with its esoteric terminology and methods often leaves nonpractitioners unable to understand—let alone evaluate—the claims that are made on behalf of rational choice models. A secondary aim in our writing of this book is to remedy this state of affairs. None of the fundamental contentions of rational choice theory is inherently difficult to understand, and there is no good reason for rational choice to persist as an intimidating enigma to the nonpractitioner in political science. Consequently, although this is not a textbook—there are several such works by Luce and Raiffa (1957), Riker and Ordeshook (1973), Ordeshook (1986, 1992), Mueller (1989), Myerson (1991), and others—we have taken great care to explain basic rational choice concepts in nontechnical terms and to lay out our criticisms in ways that are intelligible to the nonspecialist.

A third aim of this work is to initiate a conversation between rational choice theorists and other students of politics. Critics tend to be ignored because their wholesale dismissals of the rational choice paradigm leave no room for constructive engagement or for synthesis between rational choice and other types of explanation in politics. By the same token, the isolated and inward-looking character of much rational choice theory is a source of many of its deficiencies. Rational choice theorizing is too much driven by controversies of its practitioners' own making and too little by the political phenomena that social scientists have traditionally sought to understand. In the spirit of initiating what we hope will be a continuing discussion, we have added a concluding chapter in which we respond to ten counterarguments that rational choice theorists have made to us either in conference settings or in personal correspondence.

A note on terminology. Throughout this book we employ the term *rational choice theory* loosely to include literature that sometimes travels by the names public choice theory, social choice theory, game theory, rational actor models, positive political economy, and the economic approach to politics, among others. We generally follow the definitions adopted by the practitioners under discussion, and where there is disagreement about the meaning of rational choice among practitioners, we discuss its source and implications. All quotations in the text are verbatim, and all uses of italics in quotations follow the original.

We have had a great deal of help from many quarters while working on this book. Special thanks are due Eric Schickler for his sterling service as a research assistant from the project's inception. We are also grateful to Clarissa Hayward and Adam Sheingate, who joined the project later. Colleagues, friends, and critics have read and commented on innumerable drafts of various chapters. Without in any way wishing to implicate them, we would like to thank Bob Abelson, Bruce Ackerman, Steve Brams, David Cameron, Jack Citrin, Bob Dahl, Robyn Dawes, David Epstein, Bob Erikson, John Ferejohn, Mo Fiorina, Alan Gerber, Mitch Green, Jeff Isaac, Danny Kahneman, Keith Krehbiel, Bob Lane, Joseph LaPalombara, David Lumsdaine, Sylvia Maxfield, David Mayhew, Sharyn O'Halloran, Barry O'Neill, Chick Perrow, David Plotke, Doug Rae, Susan Rose-Ackerman, Debra Satz, David Schmidtz, Norman Schofield, Jim Scott, Steve Skowronek, Rogers Smith, Edward Tufte, Mike Wallerstein, Alex Wendt, and the late Aaron Wildavsky.

Earlier versions of the manuscript were presented at the Yale Political Theory Workshop (February 1993); the annual meeting of the Public Choice Society in conjunction with the Economic Science Association, New Orleans (March 1993); the International Conference for the Advancement of Socioeconomics, New York City (March 1993); the sixty-eighth annual conference of the Western Economic Association, Lake Tahoe, Nevada (June 1993); and the annual meeting of the American Political Science Association, Washington, D.C. (September 1993). Numerous participants in these various forums—too many to list individually—have offered useful comments and suggestions; we are grateful to them all.

Financial support from Yale's Institution for Social and Policy Studies and the National Science Foundation (Grant SBR-9357937) is gratefully acknowledged. Gratitude is also due John S. Covell of Yale University Press for his interest in and support for the project from the beginning. Finally, both of our families must be thanked for their good-humored toleration of the daily irritations that accompanied the book's production.

PATHOLOGIES OF RATIONAL CHOICE THEORY

CHAPTER ONE

RATIONALITY IN POLITICS AND ECONOMICS

In politics, as in economics, people often compete for scarce resources. Since the 1950s this parallel between market competition for goods and political competition for the fruits of power has suggested to a growing number of social scientists that the methods of economics might usefully be applied to the study of politics. In one classic statement of this view in *The Calculus of Consent,* James Buchanan and Gordon Tullock (1962, 20) proposed that in studying politics one assumes, at least as a point of departure, that "the representative or the average individual acts on the basis of the same over-all value scale when he participates in market activity and in political activity." As Tullock (1976, 5) later elaborated this logic: "Voters and customers are essentially the same people. Mr. Smith buys and votes; he is the same man in the supermarket and in the voting booth." Buchanan and Tullock, and those who followed their lead in developing modern rational choice theory, hoped that by starting from this unitary view of human nature it would be possible to develop a "coherent and unified theoretical view of politics and economics" (Alt and Shepsle 1990, 1). In one assessment Ordeshook (1993, 76) noted that of all the accomplishments of modern rational choice theory "none is more important than that it has led to a reintegration of politics and economics under a common paradigm and deductive structure."

Although the interdisciplinary study of politics and economics is traceable to the eighteenth century at least, the characteristic mix of approaches that is the mark of modern rational choice theory is a creation of the 1950s.[1] At that time, rational choice

1. It does have earlier twentieth-century roots, however. As early as 1929 Harold Hotelling drew a parallel between market competition for consumers and party competition for votes. This way of thinking about democracy was reinforced in Joseph Schumpeter's 1942 classic *Capitalism, Socialism and Democracy,* in which he argued that democratic theory's traditional preoccupation with participation and the public good should be abandoned. He argued instead

theory was a small subfield in a political science discipline that was dominated by institutional analysis, behaviorist methods, and the group-based pluralist theory of politics.[2] Today, by contrast, rational choice theory has ventured well beyond its esoteric publications and audiences of the 1950s and 1960s. It is well represented in the principal journals and conferences of the discipline, and its proponents are highly sought by all major American political science departments. Rational choice theory has also expanded beyond political theory and American politics, first into the study of international relations and more recently into comparative politics. Indeed, scarcely an area of political science has remained untouched by its influence. A count of rational choice articles published in the *American Political Science Review* at five-year intervals since 1952, illustrated in figure 1.1, attests to the steady growth of rational choice theorizing. Invisible in 1952, rational choice scholarship some forty years later accounted for fifteen of forty-one articles in the discipline's leading journal.[3]

Many perceive this transformation of the study of politics to have been a triumph. For example, William Riker (1990, 177–78) insists that the use of rational choice theory accounts for the only genuine advances ever to occur in political science. Although others would not go this far, it has become standard to introduce anthologies and review essays by genuflecting in the direction of the theory's achievements. Jack Knight (1992, 1063) asserts that rational choice theory "has significantly advanced our understanding of the role of institutions in social life." Nowhere, says Gregory Kavka (1991, 371), has the expansion of economic models of rational choice been "more extensive, or successful, than in the field of politics." Kristen Monroe (1991, 2) describes rational choice as "one of the dominant paradigms of political and social science, offering insightful, rigorous and parsimonious explanations," and Peter Abell (1992, 203–4) urges sociologists to adopt rational choice theory partly because of its many achievements in political science, which are "barely necessary to mention."

Rational choice theorists are by no means the first to try to account for what happens in politics by assuming that both voters and politicians are rational maxi-

---

for a model in which political leaders and parties are treated as firms that produce a product—"governmental output"—competing for votes just as firms compete for market share.

2. For a description of the political science orthodoxies against which the early rational choice theorists were reacting see Schumpeter 1942, 250–68, and Olson 1965, 98–131.

3. This count is not exact, because some articles are difficult to classify. That technical nonrational choice articles can easily be confused with rational choice articles is illustrated by the fact that Herbert Simon (1992), in the course of complaining about Theodore Lowi misclassifying his work as rational choice, misidentifies Green 1992 as a piece of rational choice scholarship. Gaffes and marginal cases aside, the growth in rational choice scholarship in the discipline is beyond dispute.

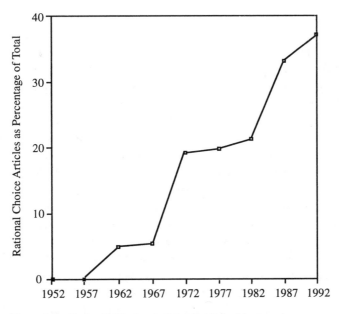

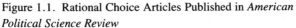

Figure 1.1. Rational Choice Articles Published in *American Political Science Review*

mizers of interest or utility, but most earlier treatments have been informal and impressionistic.[4] What sets contemporary rational choice scholarship apart is the systematic manner in which propositions about the microfoundations of political behavior are derived. In their efforts to explain political outcomes, rational choice theorists appeal to deductive accounts of incentives, constraints, and calculations that confront individuals. Systematic analytic inquiry into the strategic behavior of individuals has led rational choice theorists to approach traditional questions of political science in novel ways, and to ask previously unasked questions about the nature of political phenomena. They do not contend that traditional political scientists have studied the wrong phenomena; rather, their view is that traditional political scientists, by ignoring the logic of microfoundations, have studied the right phenomena in the wrong ways.

The advent of rational choice theory has recast much of the intellectual landscape in the discipline of political science. Since the 1950s rational choice models have generated a series of theorems about the logic of majority rule, for example, that have raised the possibility that democratic institutions might be profoundly dysfunctional

4. See Hans Morgenthau's *Politics Among Nations*, Charles Beard's *Economic Theory of the Constitution*, John Calhoun's *Disquisition of Government*, and *The Federalist Papers*, not to mention Marx's abundant corpus and Hobbes's *Leviathan*.

in ways that had not hitherto been appreciated. These analytic results have opened up at least three related lines of research. One strand of literature that developed is designed to plumb the incoherencies of democratic procedures and to devise institutional reforms that might in principle remedy them (Riker 1982). In a second line of research, the analytic results of the 1950s have been employed to account for a variety of features of the political landscape that had gone unexplained, or at any rate were not well explained by political scientists. Erratic patterns of policy making (Riker 1992), systemic inflation (Nordhaus 1975), deficit spending (Buchanan and Wagner 1977), and a continuously expanding public sector (Meltzer and Richard 1978, 1981; Peltzman 1980) have all been interpreted by reference to the arbitrary and manipulable character of democratic institutions. Finally, early rational choice findings about the logic of majority rule have prompted new types of reflection on the normative foundations of democracy. If apparent majorities are often chimerical, if minorities can manipulate democratic decision rules to generate the results they desire, and if there is no way to amalgamate individual desires into a "general will," as Rousseau had claimed in *The Social Contract,* then the nature and desirability of democracy require reevaluation (Buchanan and Tullock 1962; Brittan 1977; Riker 1982).

Rational choice scholarship has also brought a new look to the ways in which political scientists study the dynamics within democratic institutions. Seniority rules and committee assignments (McKelvey and Riezman 1992; Cox and McCubbins 1993), the methods by which elected officials control bureaucracies (McCubbins and Schwartz 1984; Weingast 1984), the internal structure and character of bureaucracies themselves (Moe 1989), and the macroeconomic policies of governments (Nordhaus 1975; Lindbeck 1976; Tufte 1978) have all been traced to the job-saving and turf-guarding impulses that are often characteristic of elected officials. And what goes for politicians also goes for political organizations and voters. In most rational choice accounts parties try to maximize their chances of electoral victory rather than any particular ideological agenda, and voters seek to maximize their individual interests through the political process. People who give time and money to political campaigns do so not merely because it fulfills a sense of civic obligation and a felt need to try to influence public policy, as many political scientists traditionally had thought (Hedges 1984). Rather, rational choice theorists contend, campaign contributions may frequently be understood as market transactions; they are "investments" made by donors in exchange for promised "favors" from political candidates once they are elected (Snyder 1990).

Although a good many of these claims might be compatible with arguments that have been made about politicians and voters in the past, rational choice theorists have worked out the microfoundations of these behaviors with a parsimony and rigor that has not hitherto been attempted by political scientists. By working through the logic of the incentives confronting political actors in a variety of structural settings, rational choice theorists have sought to enrich our understanding of the nature of politics and of the possibilities and limits of political reform.

THE EXPLANATORY POWER OF RATIONAL CHOICE THEORY

The aura of success that surrounds the rational choice movement has produced a circumstance in which political science journals "are replete with game-theoretic models of elections, committees, and war and deterrence; and press editors eagerly pursue half-completed manuscripts by practitioners in the field" (Ordeshook 1993, 74). Curiously, however, the stature of rational choice scholarship does not rest on a readily identifiable set of empirical successes. In 1978 McKelvey and Rosenthal (405–6) noted that although game theory had achieved a substantial impact on political science at the "conceptual level," only rarely had it led to "rigorous empirical analysis of real world political behavior." A year later Fiorina (1979, 48) quipped that contemplating the empirical achievements of rational choice theory "is a bit like dwelling on the rushing accomplishments of Joe Namath." Little appears to have changed in the interim. In his review of the literature on legislative politics Krehbiel (1988, 259) contends that "during the last decade, several breakthroughs have increased the usefulness and visibility of spatial models," but he concedes that empirical successes are as yet difficult to identify. Likewise, in Lalman, Oppenheimer, and Swistak's review chapter on rational choice theory's contribution to political science, analytic innovations overshadow empirical accomplishments (1993).[5]

Critics of rational choice theory often seem no more interested in addressing empirical applications. Most attacks focus on rational choice assumptions about human psychology and rationality or on what are taken to be rational choice theory's ideological ramifications. Four book-length anthologies written since 1986 attest to this tendency: In an entire issue of *Rationality and Society* (October 1992) devoted to a symposium on rational choice theory, not a single contributor from either side addressed the empirical successes and failures of rational choice models, even though the journal is advertised as having been created "to provide a forum for debate over the conceptual apparatus and empirical application of rational choice theory in the social sciences." The same is true of *Rational Choice Theory: Advocacy and Critique,* edited by Coleman and Fararo (1992), though it contains articles with such titles as "Rational Choice Theory: A Critical Assessment of its Explanatory Power" and "The Limits of Rational Choice Explanation." Essays in Jon Elster's collection

5. Lalman et al. do claim that "the body of formal results and their empirical tests have grown steadily" (82) and that "repeatedly, formal theory models have led to better specification of statistical models, even to the point of specifying the functional form to be estimated. Many new (at times nonobvious) relationships have been uncovered through the use of formal methods" (98). Unfortunately, these assertions are not elaborated further.

Rational Choice (1986a) and Kristen Monroe's *Economic Approach to Politics* (1991) address empirical issues, but none purports to be an empirical assessment of rational choice scholarship.

Our focus here is on the empirical power of rational choice theory. We contend that much of the fanfare with which the rational choice approach has been heralded in political science must be seen as premature once the question is asked: What has this literature contributed to our understanding of politics? We do not dispute that theoretical models of immense and increasing sophistication have been produced by practitioners of rational choice theory, but in our view the case has yet to be made that these models have advanced our understanding of how politics works in the real world. To date, a large proportion of the theoretical conjectures of rational choice theorists have not been tested empirically. Those tests that have been undertaken have either failed on their own terms or garnered theoretical support for propositions that, on reflection, can only be characterized as banal: they do little more than restate existing knowledge in rational choice terminology.

The discrepancy between the faith that practitioners place in rational choice theory and its failure to deliver empirically warrants closer inspection of rational choice theorizing as a scientific enterprise. In our view, the weaknesses of rational choice scholarship are rooted in the characteristic aspiration of rational choice theorists to come up with universal theories of politics. This aspiration leads many rational choice theorists to pursue ever more subtle forms of theory elaboration, with little attention to how these theories might be operationalized and tested—even in principle. When systematic empirical work is attempted by rational choice theorists, it is typically marred by a series of characteristic lapses that are traceable to the universalist ambitions that rational choice theorists mistakenly regard as the hallmark of good scientific practice. These pathologies manifest themselves at each stage of theory elaboration and empirical testing. Hypotheses are formulated in empirically intractable ways; evidence is selected and tested in a biased fashion; conclusions are drawn without serious attention to competing explanations; empirical anomalies and discordant facts are often either ignored or circumvented by way of post hoc alterations to deductive arguments. Collectively, the methodological defects of rational choice theorizing that we discuss in this book generate and reinforce a debilitating syndrome in which theories are elaborated and modified in order to save their universal character, rather than by reference to the requirements of viable empirical testing. When this syndrome is at work, data no longer test theories; instead, theories continually impeach and elude data. In short, empirical research becomes theory driven rather than problem driven, designed more to save or vindicate some variant of rational choice theory rather than to account for any specific set of political phenomena.

The upshot is that, valid as the rational choice criticisms of other modes of political science might be, rational choice scholarship has yet to get off the ground as a rigorous empirical enterprise. Indeed, many of the objections that rational choice theorists characteristically advance against rival modes of social science turn out to be applicable to their own empirical work. Rational choice theorists complain, for instance, that inductive theory building lacks "fecundity because it contains too few logical constraints," that explanatory categories can arbitrarily be "multiplied to fit all cases," and that it is impossible to tell "a consequential finding" from "an artifact" (Achen and Snidal 1989, 167–68). We demonstrate here that the bulk of empirical rational choice scholarship to date is similarly vulnerable. It is marred by unscientifically chosen samples, poorly conducted tests, and tendentious interpretations of results. As a consequence, despite its enormous and growing prestige in the discipline, rational choice theory has yet to deliver on its promise to advance the empirical study of politics.

SCOPE OF THE PRESENT CRITIQUE

Although we believe that this claim can be defended across the board, we sustain it here with respect to part of the literature only. This is unavoidable. The rate at which rational choice studies are being conducted and published is so rapid that anyone who sets out to conduct a fully comprehensive evaluation of the literature might never finish. Our focus here is on studies of American politics, where much of the most sophisticated rational choice work has been done, with particular attention to the collective action, legislative policy making, and party competition. These literatures have grown out of three classic texts: Kenneth Arrow's *Social Choice and Individual Values* (1951), Anthony Downs's *An Economic Theory of Democracy* (1957), and Mancur Olson's *The Logic of Collective Action* (1965).

Arrow's impossibility theorem rendered all democratic rules of collective decision potentially suspect. In response to Abram Bergson's influential analysis of social welfare functions (1938), which appeared to show that the state could maximize social welfare through objective aggregation of individual preferences, Arrow demonstrated that so long as minimal assumptions about rationality and the complexity of choice are granted, no social welfare function exists that is neither imposed nor dictatorial. This impossibility result, which was to earn Arrow a Nobel Prize, had an enormous impact on how rational choice theorists have thought about the basic characteristics of democracy and majority rule.

In particular, it set the terms of future inquiry into the potentially unstable character of majority coalitions. Arrow noticed that when three voters {I, II, III} attempt to decide among three outcomes {A, B, C} by majority vote, a voting cycle may result. Suppose, for example, that voter I prefers A to B and B to C; voter II prefers B to C and C to A; and voter III prefers C to A and A to B. If A is the status quo, it can be defeated by C, which in turn can be defeated by B, which in turn can be defeated by A. Majority rule, in this instance, is incapable if rendering a stable collective choice. Although the possibility of voting cycles had been known since the time of Condorcet, Arrow called attention to their broader significance for the study of politics.

An Economic Theory of Democracy (Downs 1957) is widely regarded as "one of the cornerstones for contemporary rational actor theory" (Monroe 1991, ix). For Downs, each party's platform represents a means by which office is won, not simply a list of party objectives. When two political parties jockey for position along an ideological continuum in an effort to garner voter support, Downs argued, their platforms tend to converge to the ideological position of the "median voter" (see Chapter 7). If the numbers of parties or ideological dimensions increase, or if voters abstain when each of the alternatives put before them is unappealing, however, the story becomes more complex. Much of the literature on party competition since the 1950s has been concerned with exploring these complexities, which attests to Downs's continuing influence on the study of American politics. Downs also reshaped the way in which political scientists viewed the nature of mass opinion and political participation. In contrast with the then prevailing lamentations about voter apathy and ignorance, Downs argued that the collective nature of electoral choice made it irrational for voters to expend resources gathering information about politics. Along similar lines, Downs suggested that voter turnout represents a collective action problem. Given the minuscule probability that a single individual's vote will influence the result of an election, why should a rational individual bother to vote? Downs's accounts of party competition, spatial voting, rational ignorance, and voter turnout have so reshaped the study of American politics that Mueller (1989, 4) attributes to *An Economic Theory of Democracy* "perhaps the greatest influence on political scientists" of any work of rational choice theory.

The Logic of Collective Action (Olson 1965) expanded the purview of rational choice theory beyond the actions of governments and political parties. Olson's focus was on the logical basis of interest group membership and participation. The reigning political scientists of his day had granted groups an almost primordial status. Some appealed, with Gaetano Mosca (1939, 163), to a natural human "instinct" for "herding together and fighting with other herds." Others followed Talcott Parsons and Robert Bales (1955, 9) in ascribing the formation of groups that are not rooted in kinship to the process of modernization. Whatever the justification, political scientists generally assumed organized groups to be the basic units of politics, entities that coalesced more or less inevitably around shared values and interests. This group theory of politics, associated with such names as Arthur Bentley, David Truman, and Earl Latham, was the central focus of Olson's critical attack. Challenging their assumption that private groups and associations operate according to principles that differ "from those that govern the relationships among firms in the marketplace or between taxpayers and the state" (1965, 16), Olson offered a radically different account of the logical basis of organized collective action. His central thesis was that "only a *separate and 'selective' incentive* will stimulate a rational individual in a latent group to act in a group-oriented way" (1965, 51); that is, an incentive that accrues exclusively to those who contribute to the group.

Like Downs, Olson was centrally concerned with the logic of free-riding. If an economic, political, or social good is provided regardless of whether one contributes to its provision, the rational individual will consume it without contributing. Olson's work elevated the free-rider problem to an issue of importance for political scientists, and this theme remains prominent in rational choice scholarship. In Mueller's estimation, "the free rider problem pervades all of collective choice. It necessitates the passage of laws, the raising of taxes, and the hiring of police. It deters citizens from becoming informed about public issues, and even from voting" (1989, 319). It is a mark of Olson's influence on the field that the entire chapter on the logic of collective action in Mueller's survey of rational choice theory is structured around Olson's work and responses to it.

Beyond their own seminal contributions, the rational choice literatures spawned by Arrow, Downs, and Olson are generally regarded as the most advanced and formidable in political science. Monroe (1991, 2) includes them in her account of the domains in which rational choice theories have offered "insightful, rigorous and parsimonious explanations." These works all feature on Ordeshook's list of the "centerpieces" of the rational choice "revolution" (1993, 72, 87, 92). Collectively these literatures occupy well over half of Mueller's 1989 textbook. If further evidence of the preeminent position of these literatures within rational choice scholarship were needed, it was supplied by Lalman, Oppenheimer, and Swistak in their 1993 survey of the contributions of rational choice theory to political science. The authors explicitly single out coalitional stability and collective action as the domains in which rational choice theory has made its most profound contributions.

Focusing centrally on these major literatures, we claim that to date few theoretical insights derived from rational choice theory have been subjected to serious empirical scrutiny and survived. Many empirical tests turn out on close inspection to have been so poorly conducted that they are useless in evaluating rational choice hypotheses. Tests that are properly conducted tend either to disprove these hypotheses or to lend support to propositions that are banal. Furthermore, rational choice hypotheses are too often formulated in ways that are inherently resistant to genuine empirical testing, raising serious questions about whether rational choice scholarship can properly be regarded as social science. The deficiencies of existing empirical research should concern proponents of rational choice theory more than appears to be the case. In the course of developing our critique, we indicate a variety of ways that rational choice theories might be reformulated to avoid the difficulties we identify.

LIMITS TO OUR ARGUMENT

It is important, at the outset, to call attention to what we are not arguing. First, this is not a critique that challenges the rational choice theorists' aspiration to study politics scientifically. On the contrary, we applaud the scientific motivation behind the rational choice research project. Its advocates correctly note that much of what passes for the scientific study of politics is anything but that, and they seek to remedy the situation. Whereas many other analysts of politics have given up on the traditional goals of science, rational choice theorists aim to produce "lawlike claims about measurable phenomena" and are committed to "developing theories that can explain and predict observed patterns of behavior and practice" (Ferejohn 1991, 280). Although we are less sanguine than most rational choice theorists about the likelihood of uncovering general laws about politics, we share their desire to study politics scientifically. We do argue in Chapter 2, however, that on any of the philosophy of science views commonly embraced by rational choice theorists, empirical testing must occupy a central role. Currently it does not.

Second, we have no objection to the formal, mathematical exposition that is characteristic of rational choice scholarship or to the development of a "coherent, parsimonious, and deductive theory" (Ordeshook 1993, 72). Stating a theory in the form of a deductive set of propositions has its uses; it can bring unnoticed contradictions in informally stated theories to the surface, and it can reveal the existence of analytical relations that had escaped notice. It will become plain in subsequent chapters, however, that formalism is no panacea for the ills of social science. Indeed, formal exposition does not even guarantee clear thinking. Formally rigorous theories can be inexact and ambiguous if their empirical referents are not well specified. Formalization, moreover, cannot be not an end in itself; however analytically tight and parsimonious a theory might be, its scientific value depends on how well it explains the relevant data. But we have no quarrel with formalism as such.

Third, ours is not a general attack on the rationality paradigm. Unlike other critics of rational choice theory, we are agnostic about whether rational individuals are the wellsprings from which political phenomena emerge. Nor do we assert that rational choice models are without heuristic value or deny their utility as a means of hypothesis-generation. We are open to the possibility that rationality will often be part of defensible explanations in political science. But this is quite different from saying that rational choice applications have made substantial empirical contributions to the study of politics; we contend that they have not.

Fourth, we do not claim that rational choice models are incapable of explaining political phenomena, only that few nontrivial applications of these models have been shown to withstand empirical scrutiny. It will become plain that we think there are good reasons for skepticism of the universalist ambitions that many rational choice theorists harbor, but we readily concede that certain rational choice applications might be sustainable. It is our contention here, however, that to date the empirical work that is alleged to provide support for rational choice models is deeply flawed and that the empirical work that has been done well tends to undermine the rational choice approach. Flawed empirical work arises not merely because of sloppiness (though, as is the case throughout social science, there is plenty of this), but because rational choice theorists tend to commit certain characteristic mistakes in formulating and testing empirical hypotheses. As a consequence, impressive as many of the analytic results of rational choice theory might be, it remains to be established that they tell us anything new and reliable about politics. If rational choice models are to be used and tested in a rigorous empirical fashion, their proponents will have to approach empirical questions differently. At various points throughout the book we offer specific suggestions on how this might be accomplished.

Fifth, our focus is on rational choice theory as an explanatory enterprise in political science. We shall have little to say about the ideological or prescriptive dimensions of rational choice. Our argument is not without normative implications, however. Prescriptive implications are sometimes drawn from explanatory rational choice arguments that rest on shaky empirical ground. For instance, a substantial rational choice literature has grown up on the phenomenon of "rent-seeking," in which monopoly interest groups induce governments to protect their dominant positions through the regulatory process. In fact there is mixed evidence on whether and how often rent-seeking behavior actually occurs. Yet at the end of his otherwise even-handed review of the rational choice literature on this subject, Mueller (1989, 245) concludes that "the best and simplest way to avoid the rent-seeking problem is to avoid establishing the institutions that create rents, that is, the regulations and regulatory agencies that lead to rent-seeking."

Too often prescriptive conclusions of this kind are floated on empirically dubious rational choice hypotheses, as when Riker and Weingast (1988, 378) argue that the susceptibility of majority rule to manipulation justifies robust court-enforced constitutional constraints on what legislatures may legitimately do, as was undertaken by the U.S. Supreme Court during the *Lochner* era. Riker and Weingast point to the analytic possibility of legislative instability in support of the proposition that "neither the Court nor legal scholarship has provided the theoretical underpinnings for the presumption of the adequacy of legislative judgment and, indeed, neither has even asked whether legislative judgment really works." It will become plain in subsequent chapters, however, that persuasive evidence has not been adduced to sustain Riker and Weingast's claim that the possibility of cycles is often realized in actual legislatures. When explanatory rational choice theorizing is used to advance prescriptive claims of this sort, it takes on an ideological character that is exposed by a critique of the questionable empirical foundations on which it rests.

PLAN OF THE BOOK

We begin, in Chapter 2, with an overview of the central features of rational choice theory, identifying points of agreement and disagreement among different practitioners. Chapter 3 is devoted to an account of the characteristic pathologies that afflict rational choice applications. This chapter supplies the basis for the critical reviews of the literature that follow in the next four chapters. Chapters 4 and 5 are concerned with collective action, the first focusing on voter turnout and the second on social dilemmas. Chapter 6 deals with cycling and legislative behavior, and Chapter 7 with spatial models of electoral competition. In Chapter 8 we conclude by responding to ten anticipated criticisms of our argument, initiating what we hope will be a continuing dialogue about the future of rational choice theory and political science.

CHAPTER TWO

THE NATURE OF RATIONAL
CHOICE THEORY

Before examining how rational choice theories are applied, it is necessary to say something about what rational choice theories are and how they are
distinctive. The rational choice approach to the study of politics, as Jackman (1993,
281), Grofman (1993b), and others have noted, is often caricatured by being reduced
to one or two of its characteristic assumptions and presented as a monolithic theory
that all practitioners are presumed to accept. A more accurate depiction is that most
practitioners agree on some, but not all, features of the definition of rational choice.
As a result, there is no single rational choice theory or unambiguous standard for
assigning the label "rational choice" to a theory. Our purpose in this chapter is to
describe the rational choice approach to the study of politics in a way that takes these
complexities into account. It is not part of our objective here to adjudicate disputes
among rational choice theorists as to how rationality is best understood. Rather, our
aim is to supply the reader with an understanding of the principal ways that rationality
has been characterized in the rational choice tradition and a sense of what is at stake in
the different characterizations from the standpoint of empirical testing.

We begin with an account of the less controversial assumptions that are generally
shared by rational choice theorists. These assumptions concern utility maximization,
the structure of preferences, decision making under conditions of uncertainty, and,
more broadly, the centrality of individuals in the explanation of collective outcomes.
Next we turn to the issues on which there is disagreement, notably the nature and
content of human goals and the amount of information rational agents are presumed to
possess and use. We conclude with some remarks about the different views of explanation that seem to guide rational choice theorizing, noting the implications of these
views for empirical research. This overview sets the stage for our discussion of
rational choice models of politics in subsequent chapters.

GENERALLY ACCEPTED ASSUMPTIONS

The first assumption about which there is widespread agreement among rational choice theorists is that rational action involves *utility maximization*. To say that a person maximizes utility is to say that when confronted with an array of options, she picks the one she believes best serves her objectives. As Olson (1965, 65) puts it, an individual's actions are rational when her objectives are "pursued by means that are efficient and effective for achieving these objectives," given her beliefs.

Rational behavior is typically identified with "maximization of some sort," as Arrow (1951, 3) puts it, even if there is scant agreement among rational choice theorists on just what is maximized and how, if at all, this utility should be measured.[1] Individuals are assumed to be uninterested in others' fortunes (or, indeed, their own) except insofar as those fortunes impinge on their particular maximizing strategies. Rational choice theorists need not dissent from the proposition that the welfare of others might affect an individual's conception of his or her preferences, as when an egalitarian wants the income of the poor to increase or an elitist wants the income of those around him to be comparatively lower. The maximizing assumption requires only that *some* schedule of preferences is maximized; it "does not specify any particular goal" (Riker 1990, 173).

Rational choice theorists agree, second, that certain *consistency* requirements must be part of the definition of rationality. These requirements are seen as essential to a science of rational action. "Unless economic units act in conformity with some rational pattern no general theory about what would follow from certain premises would be possible" (Rothschild 1946, 50). Following the lead of microeconomists, rational choice theorists of politics have sought to keep their consistency requirements minimal, but two appear to be widely accepted. First, it must be possible for all of an agent's available options to be rank-ordered. This is sometimes called the assumption of connectedness. It requires that an agent regard any two available outcomes as either unequal (that is, she prefers one to the other) or equal (she is indifferent). Connectedness does not require that numerical values attach to preferences for different options, that comparisons can be made across individuals, or that arithmetic functions can be performed on an individual's preference ranking. But it does assume the possibility of rank-ordered preferences over all available outcomes for every individual.

Rational choice theorists also assume that preference orderings are transitive. If A is preferred to B, and B is preferred to C, then this consistency rule requires that

---

1. There can be forms of strategic behavior that are not maximizing, as is illustrated in Herbert Simon's contention that people do not seek the best alternative in any feasible set (1955, 1956). Instead, he argued, they "satisfice"; they limit themselves to what seems to be "good enough" or satisfactory. See also Eckstein 1991.

A be preferred to C. Transitivity assumes nothing about the intensity of preferences or the amount by which the different outcomes are valued in comparison with one another. It does not even require that these amounts be known to the individual, much less that they be measurable by a third party. Transitivity requires only minimal consistency within preference orderings. When the connectedness and transitivity requirements are both met, we have what Arrow (1951, 13) described as a weak ordering of preferences. This is generally assumed by rational choice theorists to be axiomatic of rationality.[2]

Third, rational choice theorists routinely assume that each individual maximizes the *expected value* of his own payoff, measured on some utility scale (Luce and Raiffa 1957, 50). The focus on expected rather than actual utility is required by the fact that decision making often takes place under conditions of uncertainty. A farmer who chooses to plant one crop rather than another has to make assumptions about future weather, which he cannot forecast with certainty. It is usually assumed by rational choice theorists that numerical probabilities can be attached to different eventualities —for example, the value of an outcome for an agent weighted by the probability of achieving it (Elster 1986b; Harsanyi 1986).

If, for example, a person were neutral with respect to risk (though nothing in rational choice theory requires that he or she must be), the idea of expected utility maximization implies that the individual would be indifferent between having $5 or having a 50 percent chance of having $10. The assumption of expected utility maximization is usually justified by reference to von Neumann and Morgenstern's theorem (1947). Using weak assumptions about rational behavior, they demonstrated that for a decision maker whose choices among outcomes and gambles follow certain assumptions of consistency, there is a way to assign utility numbers to the various outcomes so that he or she would always select an option that maximizes expected utility (Myerson 1991, 2). "Expected utility," observes Fishburn (1988, 1), "has served for more than a generation as the preeminent model of rational preferences in decision making under conditions of risk."

A fourth assumption that commands widespread agreement among rational choice theorists is that the relevant maximizing agents are *individuals*. Unlike evolutionary biologists, for example, who have debated for decades over whether the basic unit of survival is the species, the group, the individual, the gene, or some other entity (see Gould 1992), rational choice theorists of politics generally agree that it is by reference to the maximizing actions of individual persons that collective outcomes must be explained. Buchanan and Tullock (1962, 13) declare that collective action is nothing

Check on this.

_____

2. As Arrow (1951, 12–13) puts it, if we define R as a single relation "preferred or indifferent to," then the idea of a weak ordering requires that we accept the following two axioms: *For all x and y, either xRy or yRx,* and *For all x, y, and z, xRy and yRz imply xRz.*

more than "the action of individuals when they choose to accomplish purposes collectively rather than individually," so that for them the state "is seen as nothing more than the set of processes, the machine, which allows such collective action to take place." Riker and Ordeshook (1973, 78–79) put it thus: "Society, not being human, cannot have preferences in any proper sense of 'have,' nor indeed can it order the preferences that it does not have." Consequently, they argue, we are bound to assume the existence of individual preference orderings and individual choices among alternatives as our basic theoretical building blocks in the study of politics. Likewise, Elster (1986b, 3) contends that because the mechanisms through which rational choice explanations operate are the preferences and beliefs of individuals, rational choice explanations cannot be predicated upon entities other than individuals. "A family may, after some discussion, decide on a way of spending its income," he notes, "but the decision is not based on 'its' goals and 'its' beliefs, since there are no such things." Riker (1990, 171) goes so far as to suggest that consistent generalization in the social sciences is possible only when "the central propositions are about rational decisions by individuals."[3]

The task for rational choice theorists, then, is to explain collective outcomes by reference to the maximizing actions of individuals. Indeed, Olson's original thesis about the logic of collective action stemmed from his observation that the then orthodox group theory of politics associated with the writings of Bentley, Truman, Latham, and others offered no account of why rational individuals would coalesce into groups to pursue their objectives. The group theorists had failed, in Olson's view, to see that rational individuals will "*not* voluntarily make any sacrifices to help their group attain its political (public or collective) objectives" (Olson 1965, 126). Even when the individual in question greatly values the good that a group provides, there will always be an incentive for that individual to free-ride, to avoid participating,

3. It is sometimes said that rational choice theory is not necessarily individualist in its assumptions, that political parties are assumed, for example, to be maximizing agents in theories of electoral competition, and that nation-states are treated as the basic maximizing units by game theorists of international relations. There are also versions of rational choice Marxism in which classes are regarded as the basic maximizing units (compare Przeworski 1991). But in such circumstances parties, nation-states, or classes are assumed to be unitary actors of whom preferences, goals, and strategies may meaningfully be predicated. Even in such applications, therefore, rational choice remains individualist in its basic ontology. For this reason, rational choice theories are sometimes criticized as misleading just because they ignore pertinent complexities that are internal to their primitives. For criticism of the Downsian model of party competition along these lines see Budge and Farlie 1977, 115. For criticism of the assumption that nation-states are monolithic "rational" individuals in many rational choice models of international relations see Maoz 1990, Bueno de Mesquita and Lalman 1992, and Russett 1994. For criticism of Przeworski's Marxism on analogous grounds see Swenson 1991a, 1991b and Shapiro 1993.

secure in the knowledge that this course of action will likely have no effect on whether the good is provided. The rational choice literature has generally followed Olson's individualist account; indeed, many of its central research questions would not arise were it not assumed that individuals are the basic maximizing units.

Finally, rational choice theorists generally assume that their models apply equally to all persons under study—that decisions, rules, and tastes are "stable over time and similar among people" (Stigler and Becker 1977, 76). Although nothing in the core assumptions of rational choice theory requires that the content or even strategic character of agents' preferences necessarily be identical for all agents, in practice to allow interpersonal variation may generate insuperable problems of tractability (Strom 1990, 126). "If utility functions and perceptions differ widely," Goetze and Galderisi note, "and if people have very different combinations of altruistic and self-interested motives then the construction of adequate explanatory models might be frustrated. Patterns of universal behavior may not [in that case] be discoverable" (1989, 38). To avoid this result, rational choice theorists generally assume away such differences, at least when constructing empirical applications. This *homogeneity* assumption is usually justified on grounds of theoretical parsimony. If an outcome can be accounted for only by assuming that in deciding how to vote some voters make sophisticated calculations about the likely votes of others while other voters do not, for example, "we are forced to say that *two* different models—the models of sincere and sophisticated voting—must be used simultaneously to explain what we observe, a decision that is, to say the least, scientifically unparsimonious and one which would call for an explanation as to why the behavior of some voters must be explained with one model and the behavior of other voters with another" (Enelow 1981, 1077–78; see, however, Denzau, Riker, and Shepsle 1985).

In sum, rational choice theorists generally agree on an instrumental conception of individual rationality, by reference to which people are thought to maximize their expected utilities in formally predictable ways. In empirical applications, the further assumption is generally shared that rationality is homogeneous across the individuals under study.

COMPETING VIEWS OF RATIONAL CHOICE

Yet there is more to any theory of rational behavior than the features just described. As we delve more deeply into the meaning of rationality, we find several areas of disagreement among rational choice theorists.

The first such area of dissensus concerns the robustness of assumptions about human goals. In what Ferejohn (1991, 282) dubs the "thin-rational" account, agents are assumed to be rational only in the sense that "they efficiently employ the means available to pursue their ends." In "thick-rational" accounts, by contrast, "the analyst posits not only rationality but some additional description of agent preferences and beliefs." Adherents to this view "generally assume that agents in a wide variety of situations value the same sorts of things: for example, wealth, income, power, or the perquisites of office." Utilitarianism and classical economics rested on thick-rational accounts for most of their histories, as did the embryonic rational choice arguments of Hobbes (who assumed that individuals maximize power) and Bentham (who assumed that they maximize pleasure). Neoclassical economics is, by contrast, thin-rational in its assumptions about consumers: they are presumed to maximize their utilities, but the content of those utilities is not specified. On the other hand, the neoclassical theory of the firm is thick-rational in Ferejohn's sense, since all firms are assumed to be maximizers of profits.

Some rational choice theorists of politics claim to assume only thin rationality. Riker (1990, 173) argues, for example, that so long as the consistency requirements of an Arrovian weak ordering are met, any choice—including suicide—can be interpreted as rational. He concedes that this makes the sense in which individuals are self-interested tautological, arguing that it is the formal structure of preferences, not their content, that does rational choice theory's explanatory work. Other rational choice theorists embrace models that assume more robust conceptions of self-interest that are incompatible with altruistic and consciously self-defeating behavior (compare Klosko 1987).

Riker is correct that some rational choice literatures in political science, notably the literatures on cycling and instability, depend almost entirely on thin rationality. As a result, these literatures keep controversial assumptions about human goals and motivation to a minimum. It will become plain, however, that what is gained by avoiding controversial assumptions about human nature can come at a considerable cost from the standpoint of measurement and empirical testing of rational choice hypotheses. If the content of preferences is not specified, it becomes enormously difficult to determine, for example, whether a changed outcome in the majority vote of a committee reflects the presence of stable but cyclical preferences among the voting members, changes in their preferences over time, or some other phenomenon.

In addition, it is sometimes unclear whether an account is thin-rational or thick-rational. Even if nothing is specified about the content of preferences, the researcher may make certain assumptions about the stability of preference orderings that are more robust than what mere thin rationality requires. For instance, an otherwise thin account may assume that people do not change their preferences toward the same set of available outcomes over time, or that the actors' tastes are not directly influenced by the choices offered them or by the behavior of others. In principle, theories range from thick to thin, but empirical applications seldom approximate the latter ideal type.

Much of the rational choice literature rests on unambiguously thick-rational as-sumptions. For instance, the literature on party competition typically assumes that parties try to maximize votes and, in so doing, maximize power; the rent-seeking literature assumes that interest groups try to maximize a variety of goals, from profits to environmental conservation; much of the law-and-economics literature assumes that judicial decisions maximize the production of wealth; and the literature on legislators and bureaucrats assumes that they try in various ways to maximize career advancement. These assumptions may be more controversial than thin-rational ac-counts, but prima facie they should be expected to present fewer difficulties from the standpoint of empirical testing, because there is less room for ambiguity in the definition and measurement of what allegedly is being maximized. However, we show in subsequent chapters that thick-rational accounts have often proved to be just as slippery as thin-rational accounts when tested empirically.

A second area of disagreement among rational choice theorists concerns the amount of relevant information that agents can normally be presumed to possess and act on. Conventional neoclassical models of market behavior assume both perfect information and consumers' ability to understand and use that information. These assumptions are unrealistic, all the more so in politics, where voters are reputed to be ill-informed about the leaders and policies among which they are presumed to choose. As a result, many rational choice theorists of politics have moved away from the assumption of perfect information, though they retain the assumption that actors make the most of the imperfect information they possess (see McKelvey and Or-deshook 1987).

Imperfect information arguably reflects the fact that acquiring information is of-ten time-consuming and costly. Taking the view that information-gathering resem-bles other economic investments, Downs (1957, 215) reasons that any seeker of information "continues to invest resources in procuring data until the marginal return from information equals its marginal cost." As Elster (1986, 19–20) notes, however, such logic leads to a conundrum: the agent has to assess the value of information that she does not yet have in order to determine whether it is worth taking the trouble to gather that information. A variant of this conundrum arises when rational choice theorists debate the rationality of "myopic" behavior, in which actors pursue immedi-ate rewards without regard for the possibility that this strategy may lead to undesired outcomes (Krehbiel and Rivers 1990; Austen-Smith 1991). If strategic foresight and planning are assumed to be costless, myopic action cannot be characterized as ratio-nal. But if one allows for cognitive costs (or distractions arising from the pursuit of objectives in other aspects of life), myopic strategies may be construed as rational, given an actor's shortsighted beliefs. Rational theories, in sum, encompass a range of assumptions about the knowledge actors have concerning the strategic choices before them.

RATIONAL CHOICE CONCEPTIONS OF EXPLANATION

Rational choice theorists see themselves as engaged in a common explanatory enterprise. As with the definition of rationality, however, they do not all characterize this enterprise in quite the same way. Yet most accounts of it share two basic features. One relates to the type of causal arguments that are considered; the other concerns the universalism to which rational choice theorists aspire.

Intentions as Causes Because rational choice theorists assume that social outcomes are the by-products of choices made by individuals, rational choice explanations are typically formulated by reference to individual intentions. According to Satz and Ferejohn (1993, 1–2), the most common philosophical interpretation of rational choice theory "conceives of it as a psychological theory wedded to a reductionist program in the social sciences, where the behavior of a social aggregation is explained in terms of the mental states (i.e., the desires and beliefs) of its component individuals and their interactions." Elster (1986b, 12) also argues that rational choice explanation is a "variety of intentional explanation." It requires not only that agents' "reasons be causes of the action which they rationalize," but also that agents' beliefs and desires, on which those reasons are based, be both rationally held and internally consistent. As Elster elaborates:

> Ideally, then, a rational-choice explanation of an action would satisfy three sets of requirements. First, there are three optimality conditions. The action is the best way for the agent to satisfy his desire, given his belief; the belief is the best he could form, given the evidence; the amount of evidence collected is itself optimal, given his desire. Next, there is a set of consistency conditions. Both the belief and the desire must be free of internal contradictions. The agent must not act on a desire that, in his own opinion, is less weighty than other desires which are reasons for not performing the action. Finally, there are [*sic*] a set of causal conditions. The action must not only be rationalized by the desire and the belief; it must also be caused by them and, moreover, caused 'in the right way' [it must have been intended by the agent to produce the effect it in fact produced]. Two similar causal conditions are imposed on the relation between belief and evidence. (16)

Not surprisingly, some rational choice theorists do not want to commit themselves to every aspect of so demanding an account. In the real world of politics, coming up with explanations that can be shown to meet the relevant optimality, consistency, and intentional conditions would be a tall order. It is evident, however, that neither the optimality requirement nor the consistency conditions (which guarantee an Arrovian weak ordering) can be relaxed without abandoning the entire rational choice venture. This leaves the rationality of the agent's beliefs and the intentional account of causation as the obvious candidates for less demanding kinds of formulation. Rational choice theorists have explored both possibilities.

There are good reasons for seeking to relax Elster's strong requirements about the rationality of an agent's beliefs, if only because of the enormous burdens that are otherwise placed on the researcher. One way to do this is to take the agent's beliefs as given. In effect this means that beliefs are subjected to requirements that are no more epistemologically demanding than are preferences in the model, thereby obviating any need for the researcher to broach questions that move beyond the subjective world of the agent under study. Another way is to remain agnostic about whether the content of a belief is true or false, requiring only that an agent's beliefs be rationally updated as he or she encounters new information.

Moves of this kind create problems of their own, however. As Downs (1957, 8) notes, "How can we distinguish between the mistakes of rational men and the normal behavior of irrational ones?" If one takes the agent's beliefs as given, it may be impossible to distinguish these two cases. If, on the other hand, the researcher does try to distinguish them empirically, substantial measurement problems have to be confronted. It is often difficult to know whether a person's beliefs are rationally held in Elster's sense, or even whether they have been rationally updated in the light of new information.

Demonstrating empirically the existence and causal efficacy of intentions is diffi-cult in the best of circumstances, and some rational choice theorists have flirted with abandoning the intentionality requirement entirely. Thus McKelvey and Ordeshook (1982, 312) argue that political candidates employ complex strategic decision rules, even if the "substantial numerical complexities" required by these strategies make it doubtful that the candidates "could ever compute and abide by such solutions." Likewise, Posner (1972, 1979, 1980) abandons the intentionality requirement when he argues that common law judges make decisions that maximize the efficient produc-tion of wealth, but he thinks that the judges are typically unaware of this result and that often they do not intend to produce it.[4]

This theoretical move obviates the need to identify intentional causal mechanisms, but at a considerable cost from the standpoint of empirical testing. It then becomes exceedingly difficult for the researcher to pin down what the causal mechanism involved is or to know what would count as evidence in support of its existence. Satz and Ferejohn (1993) try to sidestep these difficulties by distinguishing "internalist" from "externalist" rational choice explanations. Describing the conventional require-ment of intentional causal agency as an internalist interpretation, they contend that it is unnecessarily demanding for many of the questions social scientists study. This is an

---

4. Indeed, he goes so far as to excoriate one judge for trying to apply wealth-maximization theory in a particular case (Posner 1979, 298–99).

important move because Simon (1955, 1956), Kahneman and Tversky (1979, 1984), Abelson and Levi (1985), and others have shown that the psychology of choice often differs significantly from the deliberative processes of rational choosing. If rational choice theory "is taken to specify a psychological mechanism," Satz and Ferejohn (1993, 6) concede, "then these criticisms may be fatal." Accordingly, they propose that the theory should be thought of as illuminating "structures of social interaction in markets, governments, and other institutions." On an externalist understanding, rational choice theorists "are not interested in explaining a particular agent's behavior, but in the general regularities which govern the behavior of all agents." Satz and Ferejohn contend that these regularities reflect the fact that "it is not the agents' psychologies which primarily explain their behavior, but the environmental constraints they face." On this view, rational choice explanations are best thought of as accounting for environmental constraints and their effects; as such they "do not necessarily depend on psychological foundations" (7).

Satz and Ferejohn recognize that there are difficulties with unqualified forms of externalism. Although they want to insist that good rational choice explanations need not be derivable from postulates about psychological states of individuals, they do not deny the causal influence of mental states, and they concede that predicting an action is not the same as explaining it. Consequently, they argue that rational choice explanations must be compatible with, though not necessarily deducible from, maximizing assumptions about the intentions of individuals. The relevant agents' actions must be explicable *as if* they were maximizing utility.

Theorists who employ hypothetical assumptions of this kind often think by reference to evolutionary metaphors, since evolutionary theory is in substantial part a theory about the structural constraints within which organisms exist. As Satz and Ferejohn (1993, 17–18) put it, "Evolutionary biology views nature as a selective structure. The structure of nature selects types with certain properties: those who lack those properties do not reproduce. However, those properties are not necessarily the consequence of the intentional states of the organism. Nonetheless, these properties themselves can often be described in a decision theoretic way; we can predict the behavior of an organism by assuming that, within constraints, it will behave in ways that will maximize its expected reproductive output." Just as evolutionary theory is not a theory about the intentions of organisms, so rational choice models in the social sciences are best understood as a models of "powerful selective mechanisms."

The Satz-Ferejohn strategy for avoiding robust assumptions about the causal efficacy of intentions is intuitively appealing; yet it runs into difficulties that are especially troublesome from the standpoint of evaluating the theory's empirical power. It is notoriously difficult to test evolutionary theories empirically because they are compatible with so many outcomes. Granted, evolutionary theory does yield certain types of testable predictions. For instance, a version of evolutionary theory might generate the hypothesis that there was a gradual expansion in the cranial capacities of a particular species over a specified period of time. This, then, would lead to the prediction that newly discovered skulls from later in the specified period should be larger than those from earlier in the period. Such a prediction could be falsified by the discovery of larger earlier skulls, or smaller later skulls, of the relevant type (assuming that independent procedures for dating skulls were available). Typically, however, it is not possible to predict the development of a given organism or even species on the basis of an evolutionary hypothesis. More generally, it is often difficult to come up with testable predictions from evolutionary theory because the workings of natural selection are compatible with an organism's evolving in a myriad of directions, with its surviving or dying out or its evolution being critically shaped by random external events.

On the Satz-Ferejohn interpretation of individual maximization, evolutionary theory would predict, presumably, that lemmings will not jump off cliffs to their deaths or that human beings will not choose to go to certain death in war. Satz and Ferejohn might respond that they are not in the business of predicting particular outcomes or events, but once the move is made to abandon the "internal" reading of the microfoundations of rational choice hypotheses, it is difficult to see how such hypotheses *can* "illuminate structural relations and causes" (Satz and Ferejohn 1993, 26), except via testable predictions. Yet it will become plain in subsequent chapters that on an "external" reading rational choice hypotheses are compatible with so many divergent empirical outcomes that testing becomes problematic.

The differences between rational choice internalists and externalists, in the Satz-Ferejohn senses of these terms, should not be overstated. Both are methodological individualists in that they posit maximizing propensities of individuals in explanations of political behavior. Both accept the standard "thin" definition of strategic rationality by reference to an Arrovian weak ordering of preferences, and each can also embrace "thick" assumptions about rationality defined in terms of self-interest or some other variable that agents might be thought to maximize. What divides internalists from externalists is that internalists assume that something like Elster's intentionalist account of the psychological microfoundations of political action is true, whereas externalists say that one should proceed as if it were true and see what predictive success can be achieved. à la Friedman

Universalism and the Search for Equilibria A second assumption about explanation that commands widespread agreement among rational choice theorists concerns their universalist aspirations. Rational choice theorists "are committed to a principle of universality," Ferejohn (1991, 281) observes, according to which "[all] agents act always to maximize their well-being as they understand it, based on their beliefs, preferences, and strategic opportunities." Rational actor theory, Noll and Weingast

I reject this scientistic ambition wrt social behavior of self-conscious agents.

(1991, 239) note in a similar vein, "should seek consistency and universality." The rational choice commitment to universality results from its proponents' conception of scientific advance, which is thought to occur when generalizable results can be shown to follow from analytic propositions derived from axioms.

Rational choice theorists are skeptical that universal theories of politics can be developed through the inductive methods that have characterized political science through most of its history. "Deductive theoretical propositions are of interest," Achen and Snidal (1989, 168) contend, because they "interconnect with one another." Use of such theories prevents "arbitrary multiplication of explanatory categories" and ensures that surprises and insights flow from the theory rather than mercurial inventions that arise to cope with the idiosyncrasies of particular cases. Riker (1990, 177) insists that the failure of the social sciences to advance reflects the fact that they have "not been based on rational choice models." Bueno de Mesquita (1985, 129) links the scientific status of rational choice models to their lawlike character. "We must not be lulled by apparent empirical successes," he warns, "into believing that scientific knowledge can be attained without the abstract, rigorous exercise of logical proof." In the same spirit Achen and Snidal (1989, 168) argue that social scientists who work from the analysis of particular cases toward empirical generalizations (in their view commonly but mistakenly called "middle level theory") fail to see that this method "makes decisive theory-verification well-nigh impossible." Whatever the merits of inductive generalizations, they "are not a substitute for theorizing; empirical laws should not be mistaken for theoretical propositions."

For many rational choice theorists, the search for theoretical propositions is a search for equilibria. Ordeshook (1982, 25) notes, for example, that despite other methodological differences, rational choice theorists "share, knowingly or unknowingly, a common goal: to search for political equilibria." With characteristic decisiveness Riker (1980, 443) declares that in "the absence of such equilibria we cannot know much about the future at all." Though they interpret the concept of equilibrium in competing ways (see Ordeshook and Shepsle 1982), rational choice theorists insist that unless equilibria can be discovered, lawlike statements—from which predictive hypotheses are derived—cannot be developed. Ordeshook (1986, xiii) explicates the relationship between equilibria and lawlike statements as follows: "An equilibrium is a prediction, for a prespecified circumstance, about the choices of people and the corresponding outcomes. This prediction generally takes the form 'if the institutional context of choice is . . . and if people's preferences are . . . then the only choices and outcomes that can endure are . . . ' Thus, equilibria replace both journalistic interpretations of events and statistical correlations between environmental factors and political outcomes as explanations. In the deepest meaning of the word, the study of equilibria, in game theory, combined with substantive applications, is an attempt to provide *causal* explanations."

Concepts of equilibrium "are the link between our abstract models and the empirical world that we are trying to understand." But what does equilibrium mean in the study of politics? It is borrowed, with modification, from the natural sciences. "Physical equilibria occur when forces balance one another so that a process repeats itself (such as orbits) or comes to rest (as in completed reactions). The scientist explains such equilibria by showing that, in an equilibrium, the forces must in fact balance; or that, in a disequilibrium, the forces must fail to balance" (Riker 1990, 177). Whereas the physicist's equilibrium is the product of mechanical forces, that of the rational choice theorist stems from the purposive behavior of individuals: "What must be balanced is choices of actions—that is, intentions, which are thus analogous to physical forces. Social equilibria occur when actors choose in the most advantageous way, given the choices of others, and reach an outcome they would not wish to depart from. That is, they would not wish to have chosen differently because the outcome reached is the best they can achieve under the circumstances" (Riker 1990, 177).

The rational choice conception of equilibrium was influenced greatly by the work of John Nash (1950). A Nash equilibrium occurs if there is a potentially self-reinforcing agreement whereby each actor "does what is best for her given what others [would] do" (Przeworski 1991, 20). It can be understood intuitively as an agreement from which no party has an incentive to defect. Harsanyi (1986, 92) defines it more exactly: "A given strategy of a certain player is called a *best reply* to the other players' strategies if it maximizes this player's payoff so long as the other players' strategies are kept constant. A given combination of strategies (containing exactly one strategy for each player) is called an *equilibrium point* if every player's strategy is a best reply to all other players' strategies." When people can enter into binding agreements with others, "an equilibrium corresponds to an outcome in which no coalition has the incentive or the means for unilaterally insuring an improvement in the welfare of all of its members. In game-theory terms such an equilibrium is called a core and corresponds in simple voting games to a Condorcet winner" (Ordeshook 1982, 26).[5]

If a single equilibrium point exists for a given configuration of actors' preferences and set of institutional rules, then it is possible to derive predictive hypotheses about

---

5. The term *game* refers to a formal representation of a choice situation. This formal representation specifies the set of players, the strategic options available to them, the outcomes associated with each combination of players' moves, and the way the players rank the possible outcomes in terms of their preferences. See Luce and Raiffa 1957, chaps. 1 and 3. Noncooperative game theory concerns social interaction in which agreements and promises are not enforced by a third party, as distinct from cooperative game theory, in which there is usually communication among players, the opportunity to make binding agreements, and third-party enforcement. The presence of third-party enforcement means that there is no need for self-enforcing contracts in cooperative games. See Nash 1950; Harsanyi 1986, 92–93.

what actual agents will do, assuming that people behave rationally. If there are many possible equilibria, then rational choice models become more indeterminate; if there are no equilibria, then the political world threatens to be chaotic and inherently unpredictable in its basic structure. This is why so much of the theoretical rational choice literature revolves around trying to identify the necessary and sufficient conditions for the existence of equilibria.

The dominant view among rational choice theorists is that in politics unique equilibria can seldom be identified, though theorists differ on the significance of this fact. For those like Riker (1980, 443) it means that political science is "*the* dismal science." On his view, if determinate predictions cannot be derived from the laws in which equilibrium models are embedded, then the claim that rational choice models amount to anything more than mere empirical generalization has to be abandoned. Other rational choice theorists take less than an all-or-nothing view. Elster (1986b, 19) notes, for example, that when a model predicts multiple equilibria "it can still help us to eliminate some alternatives from consideration, even if it does not conform to the ideal of eliminating all options but one." Ordeshook (1986, 98) points out that the discovery that no equilibrium exists can be "a clue to what actions and outcomes we can anticipate," and a considerable rational choice literature has developed in an effort to model strategic behavior in such settings.[6]

Rational choice theorists who resist Riker's pure, all-or-nothing universalism do not entirely abandon universalist ambitions. The qualified forms of universalism that they adopt do vary, however. One account, advocated by Elster and Ferejohn, may be described as *partial universalism*. This is the view that rational individual maximization explains part, but not all, of what goes on in every domain of politics. There is disagreement, among those who adopt this view, over just how much explanatory work rationality should be expected to do in different circumstances. For Elster (1986, 27) rationality should play a "privileged, but not exclusive role" in explaining political outcomes. Ferejohn (1991, 284) makes a weaker claim, based on the acknowledgment that multiple equilibria are ubiquitous: "In a very wide class of situations of strategic interaction—indeed, in virtually any game that takes place over time or in which there is a nontrivial informational structure—almost any outcome can occur in some game-theoretical equilibrium. This indeterminacy, often called the 'folk theorem' by game theorists, suggests that unless we substantially enrich the concept of rationality itself, or supplement it with extra assumptions about human nature, rationality by itself cannot fully account for the selection of one outcome rather than another."

This leads Ferejohn to argue that rational choice theory should be complemented

---

6. See reviews in Ordeshook 1986 and McKelvey 1991. This issue is taken up again in Chapter 6.

by other partial theories, such as cultural theories. Because human actions are located at the boundaries of the sphere of action, which is constrained by the logic of rational calculation, and the sphere of meaning, which is constrained by "subtler ideational logics," they cannot be explained "without taking both spheres into account" (1991, 283–86). For Ferejohn, then, cultural theory supplements rational choice theory by enabling the researcher to discover which of the many possible equilibria rational choice theory predicts will actually occur. Just how much remains that is genuinely universal on this type of account is debatable. In subsequent chapters we note that rational choice theorists who have advocated partial universalism have left unexplored the extent to which a phenomenon is explained by individual maximization as opposed to habit, blunder, and the like. Nor have they devoted much attention to how individual maximization interacts with other independent variables, preferring instead to focus on the rationality components of partial universalist explanations.

A more radically revisionist approach is *segmented universalism,* the view that rational choice explanations are successful only in certain domains of political life. On this view, the systematic failure of rational choice theories in certain domains— such as in the explanation of voter turnout—suggests that rational choice theorists should try to develop accounts of the circumstances in which rational choice explanations will succeed. Satz and Ferejohn (1993, 3) suggest, for example, that "rational choice explanations are most plausible in settings in which individual action is severely constrained." Just as rational actor models do a better job of explaining the behavior of firms than of consumers in the economy, they contend, so these models should be expected to do a better job of explaining the behavior of parties than voters in politics. Another possibility is that rational choice models tend to be more successful in domains of politics that are comparatively similar to economics, so it would be reasonable to expect more success in accounting for bureaucratic capture than for ethnic riots (Schumpeter 1942; Green 1992). A third view, advanced by Maoz (1990, 318–21), is that rational choice models will be more successful in situations that do not involve extremely high or extremely low levels of stress. Low stress "can imply both low motivational drives and low practical constraints," suggesting that agents are "likely to resort to routine mechanisms for problem solving." Conversely, in high-stress circumstances typically "the motivational drive is extremely strong, and time pressure is acute." This increases the likelihood that "emotional factors and practical constraints inhibit analytic procedures" and prevent rational decision making. On this view, rational choice models should be expected to do best in situations of moderate stress. A fourth hypothesis, suggested by Elster (1986, 19–20), is that rational choice explanations are more likely to be correct when the options confronting an agent are fixed rather than when they hinge on the possible actions of others, and in less urgent decisions than in more urgent ones. Brennan and Buchanan (1984) embrace yet another logic when they argue that since the act of voting is not plausibly regarded as an investment—because of the infinitesimal chance that any one vote will affect the outcome—spatial models of voter preference do not fall within the domain of the theory. Aldrich (1993) and Fiorina (personal correspondence, 1993) generalize this argument, suggesting that rational choice models will be useful when the stakes are substantial and when the actions of the individual have a significant impact on the disposition of the stakes. If the outcome does not matter much or if the agent is unlikely to be able to influence it, then it would not be worthwhile to be strategically rational.

Defenders of segmented universalism might be thought to have abandoned universalism entirely; this would be a misperception. First, they often have in mind what Ferejohn describes as thick-rational interpretations when they acknowledge rational choice theory's limits. Thin-rational accounts, which are conceived of by Ferejohn, Riker, and others who defend them as tautologies applicable to all human action, continue to be maintained across the board. Second, most rational choice theorists who affirm segmented universalism back into this affirmation, domain by domain, as a result of empirical setbacks. They want to defend the most universal a variant of the theory possible, and they typically search for a variant that can explain what goes on in a particular recalcitrant domain rather than give up on explaining that domain. Third, some of the arguments for segmented universalism are themselves rooted in rational choice logic, most obviously Fiorina's conjecture that in certain circumstances it will not be strategically worthwhile to behave strategically, and Satz and Ferejohn's claim that relatively constrained conditions are more likely to prompt strategic action than relatively unconstrained conditions. It will become clear in subsequent chapters that conjectures of this sort have yet to be tested empirically and that the theoretical arguments that underpin them remain relatively underdeveloped.

Finally, some rational choice theorists have tempered their universalism by depicting rational choice as a *family of theories* rather than as a single theory. Different versions of the theory involve various claims about what is maximized, as we have seen. Apart from the distinction between thin and thick accounts of rationality, there are different thick-rational accounts in the literature. Votes, wealth, profits, power, influence, or some other entity can be maximized, depending on the stipulations of the theorist. Different rational choice theorists also work with various assumptions about what instrumental rationality entails. Some theorists try to account for agents' anticipation of the strategic behavior of other actors. This aspect of the picture is further complicated by the range of rational choice views concerning the attitudes of maximizing individuals toward one another—attitudes that range from mutual indifference to various kinds of interdependent utilities.

It is sometimes said, therefore, that rational choice theory is really a family of theories that share in common a commitment to the idea that the maximizing behavior of individuals explains political outcomes (see Becker 1976; Laver 1981; Elster

1986a; Riker 1990, 172–77). Indeed, some theorists appear to suggest that even the maximization hypothesis can be modified or abandoned in certain circumstances. Ferejohn and Fiorina (1993, 1) characterize their theory in which voters go to the polls in order to minimize the chances of experiencing that outcome they most regret (failing to cast the decisive ballot in an election) as a rational choice model, although Schwartz (1987) and others disagree. Both Lowi (1992) and Monroe (1991) regard Simon's model of satisficing behavior as a type of rational choice explanation, a characterization that Simon (1993) contests.

silly

Depending on one's interpretation of the relevant basis for family resemblance, adopting the family-of-theories view might amount to anything from a mild qualification of universalism to complete abandonment of it. At the latter extreme, note that Wittgenstein (1963, 31–32) coined the term *family resemblance* as part of his attack on universals, pointing out that words like *game* refer to classes of related phenomena that share no single defining feature. It is doubtful, however, that any rational choice theorist would want to go that far; such a move would be at odds with the frequently trumpeted aspiration to come up with a theory that could credibly be described as more systematic and less ad hoc than the going alternatives in political science. Our impression is that rational choice theorists tend to prefer some members of the family to others, creating a hierarchy that ranges from versions of the theory that are implausible but interesting to versions that are plausible but banal.

The versions of rational choice theory that are most arresting, and usually most coveted by rational choice theorists, are thin-rational accounts that produce counterintuitive results regardless of agents' tastes and preferences or their knowledge about one another's likely behavior (Stigler and Becker 1977). Arrow's impossibility theorem rests on such an account, but results like his are few and far between. More common are thick-rational accounts that posit self-interest as the basic political motivator. Among these, rational choice theorists most often try to vindicate those that posit the self-conscious maximization of money, power, or influence under conditions of full information. It was because Olson offered a theory of this kind that *The Logic of Collective Action* attracted so much attention. When such explanations fail, rational choice theorists typically move to imperfect information models as the first line of defense (Harsanyi 1986; Coughlin 1992). If this fails, the next step often involves turning to thick-rational accounts that appeal to motives other than narrow self-interest, as in Riker and Ordeshook's contention (1968) that voters go to the polls to maximize the psychic benefits of fulfilling their civic obligations. *But what then is left of rational choice distinctiveness? this is just a new way of stating precisely the sort of explanation rational choice theory claimed it could overcome.*

If these levies around the definition of rationality do not hold, other characterizations of human motivation wait in reserve, as we point out in Chapters 4 through 7. Although results that vindicate the strategic capacities of utility-maximizing individuals are generally preferred, when these do not pan out theorists turn to more realistic decision-theoretic models that make less taxing assumptions about people's cognitive capacities. When agents apparently fail to maximize even under these conditions, satisficing and minimax regret strategies wait in the wings. And when the possibility of agents' demonstrating even quasi-rational behavior no longer seems viable, there is always the last-resort expedient of turning from "internalist" to "externalist" accounts of causation, thereby opening up the porous world of evolutionary metaphors. Rational choice theorists do not explicitly defend this hierarchy among rational choice family members. Rather, their preferences among the different variants may be inferred from the pattern according to which empirical literatures develop: a research program is founded upon an arresting proposition at or near the top of this hierarchy, but as anomalies arise subsequent work gravitates downward.

ASSUMPTIONS ABOUT SCIENTIFIC METHOD

The rational choice penchant for holding onto some form of universalism, no matter how qualified, is linked to a particular view of the scientific method. The aspiration to deduce true explanations from axioms makes sense by reference to the deductive nomological conception of explanation, which requires that empirical laws include only general terms, referring to "general kinds, not to individuals," and that, "taken together, the laws must entail that when initial conditions of the general kinds described are realized, an event of the kind to be explained *always* occurs" (Miller 1987, 19).

In spite of the commitment to develop general laws, much rational choice research does not fit comfortably within the strictures of this model. The reason is that much rational choice research is based on what Moe (1979, 215–16) describes as "core statements"—axioms, postulates, and assumptions about people and the contexts in which they act—that are concededly unrealistic. These usually include several of the following: that people always act rationally (according to the specified definition); that people base their actions on certain types of information, sometimes "perfect information"; that people update their beliefs in accordance with Bayes' Rule; that people evaluate their options on the basis of values specified in the theory (usually nonaltruistic values or utility schedules that exhibit such mathematical properties as transitivity, ordinality, etc.); that the relevant political "commodities" are homogeneous and infinitely divisible; and that preferences remain fixed for the duration of the time frame in question. Although some rational choice models are more unrealistic than others, they are, as Moe notes, usually "not even close to descriptive accuracy."

The use of explanations based on unrealistic assumptions is usually justified by reference to a model of explanation different from the deductive nomological one. On this view, which Milton Friedman (1953, 3–43) developed partly as a critique of the covering-law model, science does not necessarily advance via the development of lawlike generalizations; valid theories may just as reasonably emanate from a superstition or a scientist's dream as from a theorem. Indeed, noting that wildly implausible and contradictory theories (measured against the existing stock of knowledge of the day) have sometimes survived and become accepted, Friedman argued that paying too much attention either to realism or to consistent generalization of a theory was likely to produce an illicit conservative bias in theory building. On the Friedman-instrumental view, the decisive test of a theory is its predictive or explanatory power, not its internal structure or its concurrence with received wisdom.

The Friedman-instrumental view can justify building rational choice hypotheses on unrealistic assumptions, but at the cost of undermining the claims of Achen and Snidal, Bueno de Mesquita, Noll and Weingast, and others who insist that scientific advance comes only with developing theory—that is, establishing the existence of covering-laws. As Moe (1979, 215–39) and Miller (1987, 18–19) have noted, the covering-law model gets its distinctiveness and power from its requirement that covering-laws be both general and empirical—subject, that is, to disconfirmation through observation. This reality check is essential to ensuring that covering-laws are not mere flights of intellectual fancy; if they turn out to be at variance with the observed data, they must be abandoned, or modified and then subjected to new empirical tests.

Given the competing rationales behind the covering-law and instrumental views, it is not legitimate both to justify the unrealism of rational choice explanations on instrumental grounds and to appeal to the covering-law model in defense of axiomatic proofs. Either the development of general theory is justified on covering-law grounds (in which case it cannot legitimately be based on unrealistic assumptions), or the unrealism is justified on instrumental grounds (in which case the particular mode of theory building is beside the point; testable predictions are what matter).

This leaves two options for those who want to pursue rational choice theory as part of the endeavor of advancing the empirical study of politics. One option is to modify the assumptions on which the theory rests to make them more realistic (thereby remaining within the strictures of the covering-law model); this is the tack advocated by Austen-Smith (1984), Krehbiel (1988), Ferejohn (1991), Noll and Weingast (1991), and Johnson (1991). Striving for realism raises the demand for empirical testing and the standards that a theory must meet to be successful. The other possibility is to abandon the covering-law model, justifying the unrealism of the theory on instrumental grounds. This is a view from which rational choice theorists often shy away in their explicit pronouncements on method, since it calls into question the value of much of their work, the bulk of which is not empirical at all. Often, however, rational choice work derives its intellectual appeal from its putative ability to make predictions about politics from a small handful of unrealistic assumptions about motivations, information, and incentive structures. On this description, it is difficult to make sense of the rational choice venture in anything other than Friedman-instrumental terms.

In the end, whether rational choice theory is thought of in covering-law or Friedman-instrumental terms, empirical testing cannot be escaped. On either view, a theory of politics has no payoff if its hypotheses do not survive empirical scrutiny. In this light, it is surprising that both defenders and critics of rational choice theory have paid so little attention to empirical testing. It is to that subject that we now turn.

CHAPTER THREE

METHODOLOGICAL PATHOLOGIES

Whatever may be said on behalf of the analytic elegance or heuristic value of rational choice theories, empirical applications have tended to suffer from two classes of methodological infirmities. The first encompasses what may be described as pedestrian methodological defects. Scholars working within the rational choice tradition from time to time misapply statistical techniques, overlook problems of measurement error, or rely excessively on inferences drawn from a small number of case studies. Although potentially serious, methodological shortcomings of this kind come with the territory in political science and are not the main focus of our critique.

More interesting is the syndrome of fundamental and recurrent methodological failings rooted in the universalist aspirations that motivate so much rational choice theorizing. These concern the ways hypotheses are conceptualized, the manner in which they are transformed into testable propositions, and the interpretation of empirical results when tests are conducted. We contend that these (often mutually reinforcing) mistakes stem from a method-driven rather than problem-driven approach to research, in which practitioners are more eager to vindicate one or another universalist model than to understand and explain actual political outcomes. More than anything else, it is this aspiration that leads to the errors that we describe here as the pathologies of rational choice theory. We make good on the claim that these are *characteristic* failings in Chapters 4 through 7, where we review in systematic fashion rational choice literatures on turnout, collective action, legislative behavior, and electoral competition. In this chapter we describe and illustrate these methodological failings, explaining why they are at odds with basic requirements of sound empirical research.[1]

1. It is not our position that every attempt to test rational choice models empirically goes

POST HOC THEORY DEVELOPMENT

Many of the methodological failings of applied rational choice scholarship are traceable to a style of theorizing that places great emphasis on the development of post hoc accounts of known facts. Can a rational choice hypothesis explain
the existence of seniority systems in Congress? The growth of deficit spending by
governments? Why people vote for third parties? To answer such questions the
theorist engages in a thought experiment designed to generate an explanation of a
given phenomenon that is consistent with rational choice assumptions, somehow
specified. Fiorina and Shepsle (1982, 63) offer a lucid description of this approach:

> Our position is that scientific progress reflects (1) the scholarly *choice* of models
> that (2) possess equilibria that (3) correspond to observed regularities. This
> entails neither constructing equilibrium models *ex ante,* generalizing and refin-
> ing subject to the constraint that equilibrium be preserved . . . nor retaining
> disequilibrium models only to be tongue-tied when asked to say something
> positive about the world. . . . To travel the first path is to say little that applies to
> the world of phenomena, and to travel the second is to say little, period. Instead,
> we recommend a third path, one termed "retroduction." . . . Put simply, the
> retroductive process begins with an empirical regularity X and poses the ques-
> tion, "How might the world be structured so that X is an anticipated feature of
> that world?" The answers (and there should be several) are models, all of which
> have in common the regularity X as a logical implication.

To be sure, striving to explain observed empirical regularities is preferable to
fashioning theories according to the dictates of "neatness, or other aesthetic criteria"
that otherwise guide rational choice theorizing in both political science and economics (Fiorina and Shepsle 1982, 63). But given the lack of specificity about what it
means to be a rational actor, it is not obvious what sorts of behaviors, in principle,
could fail to be explained by some variant of rational choice theory. Rational choice
theorists have at their disposal a variety of assumptions about actors' objectives
(wealth, power, moral satisfaction, etc.) and the extent to which individuals derive
utility from the well-being of others, as well as the sorts of information and beliefs
actors possess, their tastes for risk, the rate at which they discount future rewards,
whether their decisions are informed by reasoning about strategic behavior of others,
and, if so, the decision rules used when actors face conditions of uncertainty.[2] As

---

awry. But as we point out in the chapters that follow, in those rare cases when appropriate tests
are appropriately conducted, the results seldom sustain any novel or counterintuitive propositions.

    2. Although rational choice theory is often advertised as a unified approach to the study
of social, economic, and political behavior, we saw in Chapter 2 that there seem to be
few constraints on the assumptions that underlie empirical accounts, and sometimes quite

Ordeshook (1993, 95) points out, those who craft post hoc explanations have not necessarily achieved much: "Even if such models fit the data up to an acceptable level of statistical accuracy, we must contend with the fact that we can establish nearly any reasonable outcome as an equilibrium to some model, provided only that model is sufficiently complex. . . . Designing assumptions so that a model's predictions fit the data is, in fact, little more than an exercise in curve fitting, albeit of a slightly more complicated sort than the type we generally hold in disrepute."

One indication of the ease with which post hoc accounts may be generated is that a great many sufficient explanations arise to explain phenomena such as nonzero voter turnout or differences between the platforms of the two American parties. Another indication is that sufficient explanations pop up to explain certain "stylized facts" that, on reflection, are not facts at all. McKelvey and Riezman (1992, 951), for example, set for themselves the task of explaining both why incumbent legislators tend to be reelected by wide margins and why legislatures have seniority systems. But neither of these premises holds for legislators or legislatures generally. The reelection rates of U.S. senators and representatives contrast sharply, and the strength of the seniority system in Congress has varied over time. Furthermore, statistical studies of Congressional elections (Feldman and Jondrow 1984; Ragsdale and Cook 1987) detect no evidence of the putative causal connection between seniority and incumbent electoral fortunes. Under these circumstances, it is difficult to know what to make of McKelvey and Riezman's analytic result that in equilibrium legislators adopt a seniority system and voters unanimously reelect all incumbents.[3]

One might at this point object that what we are calling post hoc theorizing might well be characterized as puzzle-solving, a legitimate scientific activity. It could be argued, for example, that the fact that voters go to the polls in large numbers despite the theoretical prediction that rational citizens abstain leads to the discovery of civic-mindedness. Our reservation about such "discoveries" (if they may be described as such) is that retroduction merely establishes the proposition that it is not impossible that some rational choice hypotheses might be true. Often rational choice theorists seem to regard this as the end of the exercise; that the post hoc account they propose indeed vindicates the approach of looking at politics as though it were populated by actors who approach "every situation with one eye on the gains to be had, the other eye on costs, a delicate ability to balance them, and a strong desire to follow wherever rationality leads" (Downs 1957, 7–8). Data that inspire a theory cannot, however, properly be used to test it, particularly when many post hoc accounts furnish the same prediction. Unless a given retroductive account is used to generate hypotheses that

contradictory motives are imputed to agents, depending on the domain of application (Mueller 1979).

3. McKelvey and Riezman (1992, 958) caution that their model implies more than one equilibrium. An alternative equilibrium is one in which "seniority is rejected by the legislature and all legislators are defeated for reelection."

survive when tested against other phenomena, little of empirical significance has been established.

For example, many rational choice theorists have sought to explain why, as Schumpeter (1942, 261) put it, "normally, the great political questions take their place in the psychic economy of the typical citizen with those leisure-hour interests that have not attained the rank of hobbies." The hypothesis of "rational ignorance" (Downs 1957) holds that citizens know little beyond what they can learn costlessly, because they have no incentive to expend resources to become knowledgeable about political affairs. In light of the small probability that any voter's ballot will prove decisive in an election, the rational citizen reasons that the benefits of casting a well-informed vote will not offset the expenditure of time and money spent gathering information. As we note in Chapter 5, this argument is widely touted as a successful explanation of what is taken to be widespread voter ignorance. But since other post hoc explanations for voter ignorance are imaginable, one must ask: Why should we put stock in *this* explanation? What else does this account tell us about the conditions under which voters will or will not invest in costly information?

Post hoc theories are not only tested inadequately, the manner in which they are developed tends to be in tension with the enterprise of empirical testing. To the extent that theorists exploit the ambiguity in the meaning of rationality to transform successive disconfirming instances into data consistent with a newly recast theory, one must question whether the succession of theories is susceptible to empirical evaluation in any meaningful sense. As we will see in subsequent chapters, rational choice theorists seldom set forth a clear statement of what datum or data, if observed, would warrant rejection of the particular hypotheses they set forth or, more generally, their conviction that politics flows from the maximizing behavior of rational actors.[4]

These problems of empirical evaluation are compounded by the fact that rational choice models of a given phenomenon are difficult to evaluate vis-à-vis alternative theoretical perspectives that are not rooted in the assumption of utility maximization. In principle as well as in practice, rational choice models may be constructed from a wide assortment of assumptions about beliefs, tastes, and environmental constraints. Not surprisingly, rational choice models may generate diametrically opposing predictions. Some rational choice accounts, for example, predict that collective political action will collapse under the weight of the free-rider problem; others suggest that such movements may be sustained by solidary incentives. Some variants of rational

---

4. It is not hard to understand why rational choice theorists might be reluctant to relinquish the propositions that they advance. Leaving aside rare instances in which theorems rest on flawed proofs (e.g., Austen-Smith and Riker 1987), these propositions *are* true as analytic statements. Rational choice theorists, therefore, often regard empirical setbacks as indicating a given theorem's limited range of application. As we point out in Chapters 5 to 7, theorists in this position often cling to the notion that the forms identified in a theorem are fundamental and operative, even if they are offset in specific applications.

choice theory predict that candidates in a two-party system will adopt identical platforms, while others assert that candidates will adopt divergent political stances. That constructions of rational choice theory predict X and Not-X creates vexing problems for those seeking to compare the performance of rational choice models against competing perspectives. The predictions of one rational choice model will invariably overlap with those derived from another kind of theory.

Alternative theoretical accounts, it should be noted, occupy a small pedestal in the rational choice pantheon. The drive for sufficient accounts of political phenomena often impels rational choice theorists to focus instead on what the theory *does* seem to explain. As Russell (1979, 11) notes, this style of analysis is often accompanied by a striking disregard for alternative explanations, leaving open the question of whether the data conform equally well to the predictions of competing theoretical accounts. Sometimes the failure to consider the relative strength of rational choice versus alternative explanations stems from mere sloppiness or parochialism. More often, however, it results from a faulty approach to theorizing that stresses the formulation of sufficient explanations. Ironically, the insistence on pressing one form of explanation to the exclusion of others has the effect of diminishing the persuasiveness of rational choice accounts.[5]

Because of the lack of interest in competing explanations, research is seldom designed with an eye toward rejecting a credible null hypothesis, a conjecture accorded presumption of truth by the researcher, in favor of a rational choice–derived alternative. The null hypothesis that the researcher seeks to reject is frequently rather prosaic—for example, the hypothesis that experimental electors vote randomly (McKelvey and Ordeshook 1984) or that behavior is unresponsive to changes in price (Wittman 1975).[6] Just as overcoming an adversary like Grenada does little to attest to the military might of the United States, one's views of politics are not much influenced by the fact that a rational choice proposition vanquishes a trivial or implausible null hypothesis. This is not a critical failing, but we should accord explanatory power to rational choice theories in proportion to the credibility of the null hypotheses over which they triumph. More often than not, rational choice scholars consider either untenable alternative explanations or none at all.

In sum, when post hoc theorizing is used to come up with possible rational choice

5. Olson's rational choice explanation for the economic decline of Britain (1982), for example, surely would have been more compelling had he compared (or even mentioned) any of the more than half-dozen competing explanations (see Cameron 1988). Much the same may be said of the large literature that places the blame for inflation and the growth of government at the doorstep of democratic institutions and the incentives they engender (see Barry 1984; Mueller 1989, chap. 17).

6. Wittman (1975, 738) offers (though does not test) the hypothesis that those given paid time off work in order to vote will be more likely to do so. He also suggests that turnout will be higher, all things being equal, among citizens in good health.

explanations of observed phenomena or to reformulate rational choice hypotheses in ways that evade or appear to account for anomalous instances, the rational choice theorist may believe that the theoretical approach has in some significant way been "saved." In reality, the specific hypotheses in question have yet to be tested.

This critique of post hoc theorizing is not meant to foreclose the possibility of genuine theoretical innovation. Our point is not that theoretical predictions can never be changed to accommodate new evidence. Rather it is that the "innovations" that typically emerge do not involve new predictions as such; they involve mere redescription of the processes by which a previously known outcome obtains. Having recast their hypotheses to encompass known facts—and, in particular, anomalies—rational choice theorists typically fail to take the next step: proposing a coherent test to gauge the empirical adequacy of the newly revised hypothesis. Even less often do they take the step after that: gauging the empirical power of their preferred theoretical formulation against that of alternative explanatory accounts.

FORMULATING TESTS

To test a theory, one needs to know in advance what the theory predicts. From time to time, certain rational choice theorists have expressed discomfort with the lack of attention devoted to this aspect of applied rational choice scholarship. For instance, in 1978 Fiorina and Plott observed that "game theoretic and social choice–theoretic models . . . are developed and advocated without a hint of possible operational definitions—one can find proof upon proof, but one searches in vain for a detailed discussion of exactly how and when a model should be applied" (575–76). Concerns of this kind, however, have had surprisingly little impact on the evolution of rational choice scholarship, and the imbalance between analytic exposition and application remains marked.

Those who seek to derive testable propositions from rational choice models frequently find, moreover, that these theories are constructed in ways that insulate them against untoward encounters with evidence. This problem turns up in various forms. Those who advance models so parsimonious or abstract that recognizable features of politics are all but absent (for example, models of policy making that omit mention of political parties and treat each branch of government as unitary actors [Banks 1989; Spiller and Spitzer 1992]) deflect empirical scrutiny by describing their theories as simplifications or first cuts at thorny theoretical issues. Others assert that their models capture general truths that need not coincide with specific applications, as when Calvert (1985, 87) defends a model of candidate strategy "because it reveals the properties that underlie all electoral competition, even though these properties may be counteracted by the particular conditions of a real world situation" (see also Strom 1990, 11).

Arguably the most important source of slipperiness in model building is the multiplication of unobservable terms, which causes the complexity of a theory to outstrip the capacity of the data to render an informative test. This general problem is compounded by the specific difficulties that attend the ambiguous translation from equilibrium models to empirical tests.

Slippery Predictions Rational choice explanations typically comprise an array of unobservable entities. Tastes, beliefs, decision rules, and, at a higher order of abstraction, equilibria, form the essential ingredients of most rational choice models. The problem is not the positing of unobservable terms per se, but rather the ratio of latent constructs to observable measures in rational choice accounts.[7] As this ratio grows, it becomes increasingly difficult to establish whether a set of data confirms or disconfirms a rational choice explanation.

Consider, by way of illustration, a game in which two players must divide $14 between them. If the players can agree on how to allocate the money, then that agreement becomes binding; if no agreement is reached, then player 1 receives $12, and player 2 receives nothing. "Cooperative game theory," note Hoffman and Spitzer, "predicts that the subjects will cooperate and divide the rewards $13 to $1 (the Nash bargaining solution: an even division of the $2 gain from trade). Under no circumstances should [player 1] settle for less than $12, according to game theory" (1985, 259). Suppose that after repeated observations of this game actually being played, one encountered a substantial number of resolutions in which the players divided the $14 evenly.[8] What may be inferred from this pattern of results? That the dollar amounts were too small to induce preferences over and above preexisting tastes for fairness? That despite the proscription of threats, player 1 feared physical retaliation from player 2? Mistaken understanding of the game? A temporary departure from equilibrium that would be rectified through greater exposure to the real world of cutthroat negotiations?

As this example indicates, rational choice hypotheses that meet with unanticipated facts may be resuscitated by recourse to a variety of unobservable thought processes

7. The problem is exacerbated to some degree by the skepticism with which rational choice scholars regard "psychological" measures of tastes and beliefs. Although tastes and beliefs figure prominently in rational choice explanations, many scholars working within this tradition question the validity of measures other than behavior—actual choices—as indications of preference. As we note in the chapters that follow, however, this skepticism about soft data has not prevented rational choice theorists from voicing speculations about psychological processes based on no data.

8. Indeed, Hoffman and Spitzer (1985, 260) report that all of their experimental subjects do precisely that when the roles of players 1 and 2 are assigned by coin flip. Under these conditions, the subject in the role of player 1 always "agreed to take $5 *less* than the $12 that he could have obtained *without* the other subject's cooperation." See also Hoffman and Spitzer 1982.

for which there are insufficient direct or indirect measures. When faced with discordant results, it may be difficult, therefore, to distinguish empirically among three different claims about the principal unobservable term, equilibrium:

- The preferences assumed by the model are accurately represented in the setting one observes, but some or all of the actors lack the strategic acumen to play the game as rational choice recommends, and hence predicts.
- The model accurately captures the actors' objectives, but, perhaps owing to the particular characteristics of the equilibrium itself, there is a temporary departure from this predicted outcome.[9]
- The model does not capture one or more features of the observed game, and the outcomes conform to the equilibria (or lack thereof) associated with some other game.

The propagation of theoretical terms that are either unmeasurable or difficult to measure creates a situation akin to underidentification in statistical models involving latent variables (Bollen 1989). Under these circumstances, data cannot furnish a convincing test. When any hypothesis fails, the researcher is always in a position to argue that a successful prediction was thwarted by an offsetting tendency or temporary aberration. In this respect, empirical discussions in rational choice scholarship are reminiscent of debates about the declining rate of profit that once preoccupied Marxists. Having convinced themselves by analytic argument that the rate of profit in capitalism must fall over time but failing to find evidence to support this contention, Marxists for decades devoted their energies to identifying masking, fleeting, and countervailing tendencies that obscure this alleged phenomenon. Declining profitability was believed to be going on just beneath the surface on the strength of a theory that insisted that this must be so (compare Roemer 1979a; Van Parijs 1980).

The underidentification problem may be addressed in two ways. One is to set limits on the range of theoretical arguments that may be used in the construction or resuscitation of a theory. This kind of restriction, however, proves difficult to maintain against the impulse to defend the universal applicability of the rational choice approach. Often these restrictions are endorsed by such figures as Downs (1957) and Olson (1965), who introduce rational choice inquiry into a given domain of politics. But over time these constraints are relaxed by subsequent authors seeking to preserve a model in the face of discordant evidence. Another approach is to gather additional data so as to give the number of measures a sporting chance to catch up with the

9. Fiorina and Shepsle (1982) offer a lucid typology for various kinds of equilibria. Some, like "black holes," attract and retain outcomes in a social system. Others are retentive but not attractive, or vice versa. In the latter cases, it may be impossible to determine empirically whether a system is temporarily or permanently out of equilibrium.

number of theoretical terms. Rational choice scholars tend to shy away from this approach, perhaps a tacit admission that the formal precision of rational choice models greatly outstrips political scientists' capacity to measure.

Vaguely Operationalized Predictions A second common pathology related to hypothesis testing concerns the fit between the hypotheses advanced and the empirical tests used to evaluate them. Since equilibrium analysis is at the heart of much rational choice scholarship, many rational choice propositions are stated in the form of point predictions. Sometimes that point prediction is a rate or proportion, as in the case of Olson's conjecture that in the absence of selective incentives or coercion, members of large groups will not engage in collective action to advance their joint interests (1965). In other cases, the point prediction involves a particular outcome, as in the case of a specific majority rule equilibrium point in a cooperative bargaining game. Such propositions are invariably false to some degree; strategic blunders sometimes occur, producing nonequilibrium outcomes. The argument then shifts to the often expressed "hope that enough people act rationally enough of the time in their political behavior for economic theories of politics to yield descriptions, explanations, and predictions which are frequently useful approximations to the truth" (Kavka 1991, 372).[10]

It is unclear whether a rigorous test of a point prediction can be constructed in the form of an approximation. If several millions of dollars in small contributions are collected by referendum campaigns, is that evidence in support of the free-rider hypothesis (Lowenstein 1982, 572–73), given the paltry ratio of contributions to public concern over the outcome of these elections, or against it (Tillock and Morrison 1979), given the presumed irrationality of absorbing personal costs on behalf of a broadly diffused public good?

The match between theory and evidence becomes more ambiguous when rational choice hypotheses move seamlessly between point predictions and marginal predictions. The former concerns the location of an equilibrium under static conditions; the latter—derived from "comparative statics" analysis—concerns the direction in which an equilibrium is expected to move in response to exogenous changes in goals, beliefs, or environmental constraints. It is logically possible that only one sort of prediction will survive empirical testing, but the availability of two standards of evaluation affords defenders of a model more opportunity to claim support for its predictions. In particular, predictions at the margin are often hailed when static predictions fall into trouble. Whatever the defects of rational choice explanations of why citizens bother to go to the polls, Grofman (1993a) argues, rational choice theory does predict correctly that people are less inclined to vote in bad weather.

10. As we note in Chapter 5, when empirical failures occur, this "approximation" notion accompanies attribution of anomalies to the behavior of an irrational few.

We have no objection to the use of comparative statics to generate hypotheses. To the contrary, we find tests that focus on change at the margin much more amenable to traditional quasi-experimental methodology than those involving point predictions. Our concern is with the notion that the rationality of certain actions can be rescued on the grounds that the actors are to some degree responsive to changes in costs or benefits. Take, for example, the study of why politically inexperienced candidates challenge incumbent members of the House of Representatives. The behavior of these challengers is something of a mystery, since their chances of defeating an incumbent are nothing short of dismal. Like most puzzles of this sort, the behavior of challengers may been explained by reference to such ancillary factors as self-delusion, eagerness to promote legal practices while on the campaign trail, belief that *somebody* should contest the incumbent, and so forth. Banks and Kiewiet (1989, 1007) try to salvage the notion that rational, election-seeking behavior accounts for the decisions of weak challengers by arguing that "weak challengers can maximize their probability of getting elected to Congress by running now against the incumbent" rather than waiting for an open-seat contest in which they may have to defeat other strong opponents in both the primary and general elections. As the authors note dryly, "This probability may not be very high, but they are maximizing it." The study of whether weak challengers are *more* attracted to races against incumbents or to open-seat contests may be a worthy endeavor in its own right, but it is unclear how the results speak to the question of whether weak challengers are rational to oppose House incumbents, so long as rationality requires that the benefits of doing so outweigh the costs (1000).

SELECTING AND INTERPRETING EVIDENCE

Another set of characteristic pathologies concerns the manner in which rational choice hypotheses are tested. The first has to do with the biased fashion in which evidence is selected. The second deals with subtler ways in which evidence is projected from theory rather than gathered independently from it. The last involves the strategic retreat from domains in which the theory is found to perform poorly. All three methodological defects undermine the theoretical claims they are intended to support, as it is the structured search for disconfirming evidence that is essential to scientific testing.

Searching for Confirming Evidence When reading applied rational choice scholarship, one is struck by the extent to which advocates of rational choice models permit their theoretical commitments to contaminate the sampling of evidence. The procedure of adducing instances that confirm a hypothesis is perhaps most transparent in such domains as regulation and bureaucratic politics, where the ideological stakes are high. This practice, reminiscent of advertisements that show one brand's achieve-ments while mentioning neither its failings nor the comparable achievements of its competitors, is not limited to these ideologically charged domains, however. In its more qualitative manifestations, rational choice scholarship tends to ruminate over confirming illustrations combed from the political landscape, memorable moments in history, and biblical texts (Brams 1980, 1993; Riker 1982, 1986). Elsewhere, this pathology leads researchers to dwell on instances of successful prediction, be they the phenomena of strategic counteramendments by committee leaders on the House floor (Weingast 1989, 810) or the suboptimal provision of collective goods (Olson 1965). The tendency to adduce confirming instances also manifests itself, though in subtler form, in quantitative research that goes through the motions of contrasting treatment and control conditions en route to a conclusion that follows trivially from the research design. McCubbins (1991, 107), for example, finds that time-series analyses of federal data for the period 1929 to 1988 "strongly support" his game theoretic account of how divided party control of Congress leads to budget deficits. Granted, his statistical estimates suggest that "since 1929, divided government has yielded sizable increases in the national debt" (102), but the period studied contains just two such episodes: the advent of supply-side economics under Ronald Reagan, and the drought of federal revenues during the waning days of the Hoover administration.

A variant of this methodological problem surfaces in studies that use laboratory behavior to support rational choice propositions but fail to build a control group into the experimental design. As we argue in detail in Chapter 6, successful experiments of this sort at most suggest that a laboratory setting can be constructed to approximate the conditions presupposed by a theorem; a researcher seeking to defend a rational choice hypothesis need only engineer a confirming illustration. Generated without a control group, the results give no indication of whether the observed outcome would have obtained anyway for reasons unrelated to the theory in question, nor does the experiment tell us whether this theory predicts successfully under other circum-stances. Experiments crafted in this way illustrate rather than test.

Projecting Evidence from Theory A profound desire to establish rational choice theory's breadth of application from time to time opens the door to a tendentious reading of the empirical record. Sometimes this is a simple matter of authors imagin-ing a datum consistent with economic logic (for example, bad weather depresses voter turnout) and assuming this datum to be empirically verified. At other times, one finds rational choice theorists asserting almost by way of afterthought that some eccentric feature of a model mirrors reality. For example, McKelvey and Riezman's legislative model (1992) hinges on the assumption that those with seniority are more likely to be recognized on the floor in the initial round of voting but not in subsequent rounds. The authors insist that this characterization provides a "realistic description

of the seniority system for the U.S. Congress" because seniority-influenced committees get first crack at making proposals, and "once the bills go to the floor, the
committees lose most of their power" (958). Suffice it to say that this is a rather sparse
depiction of the process by which legislation is proposed and amended in Congress
(Weingast 1989).

Even when a full-blown empirical study is undertaken, the theoretical convictions
of the authors may guide what they infer from a set of observations and how they
reconstruct the data for presentation. For example, an obscure set of House votes on
the Powell Amendment to a 1956 measure authorizing school construction has been
offered up time and again as evidence of how legislators vote to strengthen a proposal
they dislike in an effort to make the amended bill unpalatable (Riker 1965, 1982,
1986; Denzau, Riker, and Shepsle 1985). A dispassionate examination of the historical record, however, shows that the facts surrounding the Powell Amendment are at
best ambiguous with respect to the phenomenon of strategic voting (Krehbiel and
Rivers 1990). Indeed, the omissions and factual distortions that Krehbiel and Rivers
detect in previous accounts (556–60, 574) suggest that earlier writers were unable to
assimilate data that did not conform to their theoretical expectations.

Arbitrary Domain Restriction On occasion, rational choice theorists will concede
that there are domains—such as voter turnout and organized collective action—in
which no plausible variant of the theory appears to work. Some theorists are then
inclined to withdraw, choosing to concentrate on applications in which these theories
appear to have better success. For instance, in trying to make the case that his wealth-
maximization hypothesis explains the evolution of the criminal law, Posner (1985) is
forced to come to accept that he cannot explain the existence of laws against such
"victimless crimes" as prostitution and drug abuse. He therefore abandons this domain, insisting nonetheless that wealth-maximization provides a powerful explanation of the rest of the criminal law.

Such a move might at first sight seem reasonable, even modest, but there is more at
stake here than meets the eye. Suppose it transpired one day that red apples did not fall
to the ground as other heavy bodies do. One would not be much impressed by the
physicist who said of the theory of gravity that, though it seems not to work for red
apples, it does a good job of explaining why other things fall to the ground and that
consequently from now on he was going to restrict his attention to those other things
when using the theory.

What we are calling arbitrary restriction to domains where a theory seems to work
is not to be confused with two nonarbitrary forms of domain restriction that scientists
engage in routinely. First, as Moe points out (1979, 235), testing of all scientific
theories involves the insertion of ceteris paribus clauses designed to exclude omitted
factors, so that a proper test of the hypothesis that objects of unequal mass fall to earth

at the same rate presupposes wind resistance to be held constant.[11] Second, theories may properly include an account of what are conventionally termed "interaction effects," factors that limit or enhance the influence of the independent variables of theoretical interest. Indeed, the value of a theory in the eyes of those who wish to understand and influence politics may hinge on a clear account of the conditions under which it is held to apply. Arbitrary domain restriction occurs when an empirically testable set of limiting conditions is lacking but retreat is sounded anyway. There is, in other words, a critical difference between specifying the relevant domain in advance by reference to limiting conditions and specifying as the relevant domain: "wherever the theory seems to work."[12]

The problem of arbitrary domain restriction is thus the obverse of the tendency to adduce confirming instances. The latter involves fishing for supportive evidence; the former, draining lakes that contain problematic data. While the practice of adducing confirming instances produces misleading tests, arbitrary domain restriction renders problematic the enterprise of testing. If the appropriate domain within which a theory is to be tested is defined by reference to whether the theory works in that domain, testing becomes pointless.

Posner, in our example, pushes the case for wealth-maximization as far as he can and cuts and runs when he has to. Yet he neither considers any alternative explanation nor sees the need to offer an account of why the theory breaks down in the domain of victimless crimes. For domain restriction to be adequate, the relevant domain must be

---

11. It is important to note that ceteris paribus provisos must refer to confounding factors, such as wind resistance, whose effects are in principle testable. One cannot take the position that only when all the logical assumptions of a theorem are satisfied empirically do the theorem's empirical predictions follow.

12. In much the same vein, arguments about when and where to apply a theory must be advanced in a consistent fashion. For example, in an effort to bolster their claim that House "leaders will be chosen in such a fashion that their personal reelection is not too incompatible with the duties of office," Cox and McCubbins (1993, 130) point out that one rational choice argument, based on the idea of the "uncovered set" (see Chapters 6 and 7), predicts "definite limits to the policy platforms that those seeking leadership positions will adopt" and, in particular, rules out successful bids by noncentrist candidates (130). Although Cox and McCubbins wish to embrace this prediction, they note that it is open to the objection that decisions enacted by majority rule are inherently unstable, that "there will always be some majority, all of [w]hose members could be made better off if its policies were changed" (131). Cox and McCubbins respond that this objection about the inherent vulnerability of House speakers rests on the assumption that actors incur no transaction costs when identifying or forming new majority coalitions. When these costs are taken into account, they contend, the instability problem no longer applies to the choice of speaker. They neglect to mention, however, that their preferred predictions based on the uncovered set also presuppose the absence of transaction costs.

specified independently of whether the theory explains the phenomenon within it. Furthermore, the hypothesis about the limiting conditions of rational choice explanations must itself stand up to empirical testing. As we noted in Chapter 2, rational choice theorists such as Brennan and Buchanan, Fiorina, and Satz and Ferejohn have suggested some hypotheses about the conditions under which rational choice explanations are likely to apply. It will become plain in subsequent chapters, however, that these recommendations have not yet had much impact on the design and application of rational choice models.

CONCLUDING COMMENTS

Although widespread among empirical applications, the methodological problems identified in this chapter are not inextricable features of rational choice theorizing. Indeed, the larger message of this book is not that rational choice models of politics should simply be abandoned. Rather, the rational choice approach must be rethought fundamentally, and its relations with the existing stock of knowledge and theory in the social sciences should be reevaluated. It is therefore necessary to understand what the recurrent methodological problems are, why they turn up, and how they might be remedied. In this spirit, we turn to the literatures on turnout, collective action, legislative behavior, and electoral competition.

CHAPTER FOUR

THE PARADOX OF
VOTER TURNOUT

At the foundation of democratic politics stands the act of voting, accompanied by a paradox. Starting with Anthony Downs (1957), rational choice theorists have characterized voter turnout as a collective action problem in which individuals are asked to sacrifice time and transportation costs on behalf of a public good, the election of a particular candidate or party. Although rational citizens may care a great deal about which person or group wins the election, an analysis of the instrumental value of voting suggests that they will nevertheless balk at the prospect of contributing to a collective cause since it is readily apparent that any one vote has an infinitesimal probability of altering the election outcome. Why take the time to vote when the election outcome will be unaffected by one's ballot? Unless rational citizens find the act of voting gratifying—because, say, they enjoy democratic participation or seek the status rewards of being seen at the polls—they will abstain and foist the costs of voting onto others.

In situations where voting is optional and altruism rare, the equilibrium posited for voter turnout in large electorates is one in which very few people, if any, bother to go to the polls. Many scholars, including several working within the rational choice tradition (Tullock 1967; Hardin 1982; Brennan and Buchanan 1984; Satz and Ferejohn 1993), therefore view voter turnout as a case in which rational choice theory fails empirically. For our purposes, the case of voter turnout is interesting not because it is a failure but because it illustrates the characteristic ways that rational choice theorists have reacted to discrepancies between theory and observation. In their resolute determination to declare some variant of rational choice theory victorious over the evidence (or, alternatively, to declare peace with honor through artful domain restriction), rational choice theorists have trotted out an astonishing variety of conjectures about the costs and benefits of voting, in the process generating an enormous literature, possibly larger in terms of academic citations and sheer bibliographic length than any other rational choice literature in American politics. Moreover, it is a literature that has enjoyed something of a renaissance in leading political science journals (Uhlaner 1989; Morton 1991; Fedderson 1992; Knack 1992; Aldrich 1993; Filer et al. 1993; see also Grofman 1993a).

In spite of its size and the prestige of the academic publications in which this literature has developed, rational choice scholarship has contributed fewer substantive insights than examples of defective social science research. Choosing voter turnout as our starting point enables us to illustrate many of the pathologies described in the previous chapter, in particular what we have labeled post hoc theorizing, slippery predictions, and an inability to formulate a cogent null hypothesis. The literature on voter turnout also has the advantage of being relatively intuitive and nontechnical. The essential formal ingredients of the rational choice account, with which we begin this chapter, amount to a few elementary expressions. Following a brief overview of the standard rational choice models, we organize the literature according to its two objectives, to grapple with the phenomenon of large absolute numbers of voters and to explain fluctuation in turnout rates by reference to changes in the costs and benefits of voting.

DECISION-THEORETIC MODELS OF VOTING

The rational choice model that has come to dominate accounts of voter turnout characterizes each citizen's decision calculus as a balance of four quantities. The first is B, the benefits a voter derives from seeing his or her preferred candidate win. Sometimes these benefits are conceptualized as tangible gains, such as financial rewards, while other times they are defined to include intangible forms of ideological gratification. For concreteness, one might imagine B to represent the amount of money one would willingly give up in order to determine unilaterally the election outcome (Schwartz 1987). Note that B is a collective good in the sense that no citizen may be excluded from enjoying his or her favored candidate's victory, regardless of whether he or she voted. The rational voter, however, recognizes that the opportunity to cast the decisive ballot is at best an uncertain prospect and assigns to it the probability weight p. The decision-theoretic model, in contrast with the game-theoretic approach discussed below, assumes that p is a fixed quantity rather than a parameter that arises endogenously from the strategic interaction of citizens deciding whether to vote.[1]

In addition to the expected electoral consequences of one's ballot, the model

---

1. Holding p constant, however, gives rise to a paradox: if every voter abstains because no single vote is thought to be decisive (p is very small), then any voter's ballot will be decisive ($p = 1$). See Meehl 1977.

includes the benefits and costs of the voting act. The "selective incentives" of voting (D) represent the utility one receives as a direct consequence of casting a ballot. Tellingly, it is not easy to think of contemporary illustrations of selective incentives that do not take the form of psychic gratification. Grasping a bit, we note that such states as California furnish voters with ballot stubs, which from time to time have served as discount coupons in local fast-food promotions. In this instance, the economic value of the ballot stub is a selective benefit of voting. On the other side of the ledger, the cost of voting (C) includes a myriad of inconveniences, ranging from transportation expenses to foregone opportunities to earn wages (Tollison and Willett 1973). Furthermore, if the act of voting is defined to include voter registration in advance of the election, costs may include the nuisance of figuring out when and where to register (Rosenstone and Wolfinger 1978) or the risk that, having registered, one's name will be selected for jury duty (Knack 1993b).

According to this formulation, the citizen weighs the opposite sides of the balance sheet and votes if the sum of selective incentives and expected collective benefits exceeds the cost of voting. That is, the citizen goes to the polls if

$$pB + D > C. \tag{4.1}$$

The essential ingredients of the paradox of voter turnout lie in the product term, pB. As Beck (1975), Margolis (1977), and Chamberlain and Rothschild (1981) have suggested, even in situations in which the outcome of a race between two candidates is believed to be quite close, the probability of casting the decisive vote amid a large number of ballots is minuscule.[2] Suppose, for the sake of argument, that the odds of casting the decisive vote are as high as 1 in 100,000. As Schwartz (1987) notes, even

2. A few words should be said about the statistical models used to calculate the probability of casting a decisive vote in two-candidate elections (see Chamberlain and Rothschild 1981). These models assume that x voters cast ballots and that each voter decides for whom to vote based on an independent flip of a coin that comes up heads with probability p. This model may be said to be unrealistic in two ways. First, it is odd to suppose that each voter enters the voting booth with the same probability of voting for a given candidate. This assumption tends to understate the odds of a tie or one-vote victory (consider the alternative limiting case of two evenly sized parties that vote deterministically for their preferred candidate, producing a deadlock with probability 1). On the other hand, these models also assume the turnout x to be fixed, whereas common sense suggests that not only is any one voter's turnout decision probabilistic, but the probability of voting need not be independent across voters (who may be exposed to the same get-out-the vote efforts). These nuances greatly complicate the task of calculating the probability of casting a decisive vote. Statistical models aside, the fact remains that in presidential elections, which have always been the mainstay of empirical tests of the rational choice model, thousands of votes separate the winner and loser in small states; tens of thousands in large states.

for a voter willing to exchange as much as $10,000 for the privilege of unilaterally determining the election outcome, the expected value of voting is no more than a dime. Increase the size of the hypothetical electorate or decrease the closeness of the election outcome and even this deeply committed citizen would find the expected value of voting to be worth less than a penny. To the extent, therefore, that voters sacrifice time and energy to go to the polls, the costs of voting will dissuade citizens from casting ballots (Downs 1957; Tullock 1967, 108–14; Frohlich and Oppenheimer 1978, 97–116).

THEORY MEETS DATA

"Unfortunately for theory," laments Carole Uhlaner (1989, 390), "people do vote." Indeed, in any given national election, tens of millions go to the polls, and sparse though voter turnout may be in many local elections, it is still far from zero. Only a few rational choice theorists, to our knowledge, have had the temerity to adduce theory-confirming instances of elections that ended in a tie or attracted zero turnout (Sanders 1980; Ledyard 1984; Owen and Grofman 1984). Most readily admit that the absolute number of voters exceeds what any simple version of the theory would predict and that voter turnout does not seem destined to converge to an equilibrium at or near zero. Moreover, in experimental settings where voters are assigned carefully controlled monetary rewards depending on which candidate prevails, most voters opt to pay a poll tax even when it exceeds the financial stake they have in the election outcome (Plott 1991). The divergence between the observed rate of turnout and the expected equilibrium presents a prima facie problem at least, since irrationality would appear to be an irreducible ingredient of voter participation.

How have rational choice theorists responded to this anomaly? For the most part, scholarship has taken the form of post hoc theorizing designed explicitly to "reinterpret the voting calculus so that [the act of voting] can fit comfortably into a rationalistic theory of political behavior" (Riker and Ordeshook 1968, 25). Rather than concede that actual voters do not fit the description of the free-rider envisioned in economic theories, many rational choice theorists have turned the anomaly on its head and asked: What must be true of the data in order for some rational choice model of voter turnout to be valid? How might the benefits of voting outweigh its costs for large numbers of citizens?

From the start rational choice theorists have had difficulty formulating a satisfactory post hoc model of turnout. Because the probability of casting a decisive vote is so small, rational choice scholarship has time and again appealed to instrumental objectives other than contributing to an electoral coalition. In an effort to escape the conclusion that the equilibrium level of turnout is near zero while at the same time retaining the view of voting as goal-directed activity, Downs (1957) speculated that voters go to the polls because they fear the collapse of democracy in the event of widespread abstention. As Downs's critics have pointed out, this is not only an implausible account but one that flies in the face of the logic of collective action on which the paradox of voter turnout rests. The maintenance of democratic institutions is itself a public good to which any one voter's contribution is negligible. Why not stay home and let others save democracy? As Barry (1978), Tullock (1967), and Meehl (1977) have noted, Downs merely substitutes the paradox of civic-minded participation for the paradox of voter turnout.

Riker and Ordeshook (1968, 1973), in the most frequently cited attempt to patch the rational choice model of turnout, took the speculation in a different direction, arguing that Downs's original model, which omitted the D term in equation (4.1), had underestimated the selective rewards of voting. What are these selective incentives? In his initial formulation of his theory of mass decision making, Downs sought to restrict attention to tangible costs and benefits, such as money or opportunity costs. Riker and Ordeshook, on the other hand, widened the purview of the theory to include the psychic gratification a citizen derives from going to the polls. These include five sources of "satisfaction": those of "complying with the ethic of voting," "affirming allegiance to the political system," "affirming a partisan preference," "deciding . . . for those who enjoy the act of informing themselves," and "affirming one's efficacy in the political system" (1973, 63).[3] This conception of gratification, as Niemi (1976, 117) points out in a sympathetic exegesis, is defined with sufficient breadth to encompass even the value of avoiding having to say "'no' when asked whether or not you voted." Voting, in other words, is an act of consumption, and citizens go to the polls because the utility they derive automatically from affirmation and compliance outweighs the voting costs they expect to incur.

Although Riker and Ordeshook (1968) examine some survey data they neither estimate the costs of voting nor attempt to weigh these costs against the psychic rewards of fulfilling one's obligation to vote. Consequently, the argument concerning the balance of costs and benefits is scarcely more than a tautology. What convinces Riker and Ordeshook that selective benefits, such as civic duty, are sufficient to offset the costs of voting? Simply that people would not vote if the benefits of doing so were less than the costs. Indeed, they point out that the very fact of significant voter turnout led them to discover the importance of civic-mindedness in the first place, lest voter turnout be consigned to the "mysterious and inexplicable world of the irrational" (25–26). Having merely *stipulated* that the act of voting is more gratifying than costly,

3. Note that in the rational choice system, sacrifices of utility tend to be ruled out by construction. The very fact that one complies with an obligation is generally taken to "reveal" that the utility of compliance outweighs that of noncompliance. This view, of course, begs the question of whether some voters make genuine sacrifices when they vote instead of engaging in more preferred activities.

these authors solve the paradox of voter turnout by reducing it to the same logical status as the paradox of attendance at free concerts or the paradox of strolls along public beaches.

Many rational choice scholars plainly regard this theory-saving maneuver as an embarrassment, because tastes for doing one's civic duty are exogenous appendages to the rational choice model.[4] Aside from being a post hoc explanation (and an empirically slippery conjecture in any event), the notion that civic duty shapes voter participation raises more empirical problems than it solves. For one, it is unclear why civic duty should fluctuate from one sort of election to another within the same region, producing sharply different turnouts for Presidential elections, national off-year elections, statewide elections, and local elections.[5]

Second, it is a peculiar brand of civic duty that explains why people turn out to vote by the tens of millions but also accounts for the comparative dearth of letter writing to local officials (Verba and Nie 1972) or of enthusiasm for jury service (Knack 1993b). If the fulfillment of one's civic obligations or the expression of one's partisan identity are indeed consumption goods that citizens wish to enjoy, it is not clear why there should be pent-up demand for voting in national elections, given the myriad of opportunities to do one's duty or show one's colors. Nor does it seem to be the case that consuming more of these goods—whether by displaying lawn signs, contributing to campaigns, or voting in primary elections—diminishes one's thirst for the kinds of gratification that voting supposedly provides (see Margolis 1982).

Although perhaps uncomfortable with the retreat to psychic gratification as an explanation, rational choice theorists are drawn to the idea that side-payments attract voters to the polls. Uhlaner (1989, 419), for example, argues that "group leaders can provide additional benefits for voting (and costs for abstention) that increase the advantage of voting and bring more group members to the polls." It pays for leaders to enhance turnout because, "although the vote of a single individual has little influence on who wins, an increase of a few percentage points in some group's turnout may well change an election outcome," enabling the leader to extract concessions from candi-

---

4. In framing his economic model of voter turnout, Downs (1957, 276) hoped to circumvent explanations that referred to psychic benefits, arguing that "if it is rational to vote for prestige, why is it not rational to vote so as to please one's employer or one's sweetheart? Soon all behavior whatsoever becomes rational because it is a means to some end the actor values. To avoid this sterile conclusion, we have regarded only actions leading to strictly political or economic ends as rational."

5. Niemi (1976) claims that local elections are more costly to the voter because polling hours are sometimes shorter, it is more difficult to remember whether it is election day, and it is harder to make up one's mind concerning the obscure contests on local ballots. None of these arguments is tested empirically, however. Indeed, it is not clear that the last of these arguments is consistent with rational choice conjectures regarding "rational ignorance" (see Chapter 5).

dates (392). Leaving aside the fact that it is unclear from her description which social or political groups and leaders she has in mind, Uhlaner offers no persuasive evidence to suggest that selective incentives—as opposed to collective benefits, which would simply give way to a free-rider problem within the group—do in fact bring people to the polls.[6] As it happens, the lone illustration that she presents with accompanying data (the putative increase in turnout among union members in the dog days of 1982) is striking if only because the group mobilization interpretation she offers is not supported by her own statistical evidence.[7]

Other rational choice scholars know better than to let data clutter up a good story about side-payments. Building on the startling premise that "often it is obvious to others whether one has voted and how," Schwartz (1987, 104–5) asserts that "because voting is not perfectly secret, political leaders and party organizations, from the precinct on up, can offer selective incentives to individual voters. These include such tangible benefits as patronage, sidewalk maintenance, and zoning variances, as well as greater overall influence and access to public decision-making processes." Schwartz, though obviously concerned with the empirical strength of his theory vis-à-vis others, presents no evidence to suggest that voter preferences are indeed monitored or that such side-payments are exchanged for votes or that these transactions occur with sufficient frequency to explain the level of turnout in national elections.[8]

If one were to exclude selective benefits from the model on the grounds that they are either ad hoc or unsupported by evidence, the model of turnout reduces to the inequality originally suggested by Downs, in which one votes if

$$pB > C. \tag{4.2}$$

Expressing the model this way naturally leads defenders of rational choice theorizing to adopt a two-pronged strategy: downplay the cost of voting while emphasizing the collective benefits of one's vote. Olson (1965, 164) calls voting costs "insignificant and imperceptible" to many citizens, while Smith (1975, 65), Niemi (1976), Hinich (1981), Palfrey and Rosenthal (1985), Schwartz (1987), and Aldrich (1993) contend that the opportunity and transportation costs of voting (and by extension, registration) are overblown. In a twist on the usual economic logic of opportunity costs, Niemi

6. See also Morton 1991 for a group-based analysis that neither specifies what is meant by a group nor indicates how the free-rider problem within the group is resolved.

7. Our reanalysis of Uhlaner's data for 1980–84 using probit (available from the authors on request) turns up no evidence of the interaction she claims exists between union membership and the 1982 election, even when the analysis is restricted to non-Republicans ($p > 0.10$).

8. A useful field exercise for those convinced of the public nature of one's voting habits is to measure the time it takes to ascertain the turnout history of a stranger living in one's neighborhood.

(1976, 115) asserts that "virtually everyone takes time out during the day for non-working things, ranging from a few cocktails before lunch, to coffee breaks, to a beer on the way home, to reading to their kids, to reading the newspaper, and so on. It seems likely that time to vote is taken out of these kinds of activities." Taking this argument one step further, Palfrey and Rosenthal (1985) infer the costlessness of voting from a thought experiment in which they imagine the "near universal" turnout rates that would occur if voters were paid $20 to go to the polls.[9] In effect, these authors rely on their theoretical convictions to furnish the evidence necessary to make the theory work.

We have more to say about the effects of registration requirements and other tangible costs, but for the time being we note that the implication of this tendentious argument about the "tremendously exaggerated" cost of voting (Niemi 1976, 115) is that the calculus of voting boils down to

$$pB > \epsilon, \tag{4.3}$$

in which ϵ is a very small quantity. Now any appreciable collective benefit from voting will make turnout rational. Collective benefits, however, are so heavily discounted by the vanishingly small probability that one vote will be decisive that even the low hurdle of equation (4.3) can be surmounted only with some difficulty. One way to preserve the inequality expressed in the equation is to argue that p is not as small as intuition suggests. Here, such authors as Riker and Ordeshook (1968) play one of the wild cards in their deck, asserting that voters *misperceive* the likelihood that their vote will be decisive and act rationally based on their grossly inflated probability assessment. It is noteworthy that Riker and Ordeshook and others since have never supplied any evidence to suggest that citizens indeed harbor such beliefs.[10] At most, those advancing the misperception thesis have cited survey data in which some respondents describe the upcoming election as "extremely close." This is a far cry, as Cyr (1975, 25) and Aldrich (1993, 259) note, from asking respondents to estimate the odds that some upcoming election will be decided by a single vote. It is

9. The design of this thought experiment, however, evidently omits consideration of the unintended effects of side-payments. A body of actual experimentation suggests that the use of extrinsic rewards at times decreases intrinsic motivation, as when students are paid to get good grades or when bystanders are paid to perform good deeds (see Lane 1991). It is possible that paying citizens to vote would undermine the sense of civic duty that Riker and Ordeshook (1968) contend is critical to voter turnout.

10. Nor have they supplied any systematic evidence to support their notion that there is widespread exposure to and acceptance of propaganda emphasizing that each vote matters (see also Brunk 1980). Nonetheless, there seems to be a strong, if implicit, faith in Downs's dictum that "citizens who behave irrationally do so partly because someone who stands to gain thereby urges them on" (1957, 10).

even a farther cry from asserting that millions of voters imagine themselves in the role of tie breaker.[11]

Grasping efforts to resuscitate models of turnout by reference to widespread misperception were greeted no more favorably, both within rational choice circles and without, than were gambits involving civic duty. As Schwartz (1987, 108) notes, this misperception merely transforms the paradox of not voting into the paradox of foolish voters. Yet in their determination to construct an account of turnout that characterized the activity in instrumental terms, rational choice theorists have gradually depleted the supply of conjectures that can be advanced about the four explanatory variables depicted in equation (4.1). As this paradox grew in notoriety, solutions grew increasingly imaginative. Strom (1975; see also Tideman 1985), for example, asserts that the voter's expected utility calculus includes not only the utility one might gain from casting the decisive vote but also the disutility one would experience from failing to do so on account of abstaining.[12] Apparently not convinced by Strom's doubling of the infinitesimal value of voting, Hinich (1981) advanced precisely the opposite ad hoc account, namely, that people derive utility from contributing to a successful collective effort. Hinich claims that citizens seek to participate in the victory of a candidate, happily offering up superfluous ballots in an effort to bask in the glory of the victor. Missing from these explanations is an empirical demonstration that regret-avoidance or bandwagon incentives are sufficiently widespread and sizable to account for observed rates of voter turnout. Like so many rational choice theories, these essays go no further than to imagine data consistent with a conceivable rational choice account.

Another creative approach is to speculate about how a single vote *could* be pivotal. One may sidestep the thorny problem of casting the decisive ballot by assuming that

11. Dennis (1991, 44–47) makes a rare effort to measure perceived decisiveness but stops short of asking directly whether a particular election is likely to be decided by one vote. Instead, he presents a sample of Wisconsin adults with agree/disagree statements like "I sometimes don't vote when the outcome of an election is not going to be close," and "Whether I vote or not has virtually no effect on who gets elected."

12. Although not a rational choice model in the sense that it does not presuppose utility maximization (Schwartz 1987), the minimax regret argument advanced by Ferejohn and Fiorina (1974, 1975) antedates Strom's model. Ferejohn and Fiorina suggest that voters minimize the probability of their greatest regret, waking up the day after the election to find that their candidate had lost by one vote. Whether losing an election represents a greater regret than other outcomes—getting hit by a car on the way to the polls, say—has been questioned by many, and the model has been so thoroughly dissected that we have elected not to discuss it (see Beck 1975; Stevens 1975; Tullock 1975; Schwartz 1987; Aldrich 1993). By the same token, we have not taken up the solution proposed by Grafstein (1991), who argues that a "legitimate" rational choice model based on evidential decision theory can explain positive turnout, because the decision calculus envisioned by Grafstein is regarded as the antithesis of rational choice by some (Quattrone and Tversky 1988).

citizens seek merely to bolster their party's demonstrated electoral support by a single vote, enhancing that coalition's mandate to pursue its policy objectives (Stigler 1972). Absent from this account, however, is evidence that a single vote contributes anything appreciable to a party's legislative power.[13] An alternative scenario in which single ballots prove influential is offered by Schwartz (1987, 105), who argues that while a given vote "has practically no chance of determining which candidate wins the election, it has, at least by comparison, a non-negligible chance of determining which candidate carries her precinct, and that might well determine whether and at what levels her precinct receives certain distributive benefits—road repairs, snow removal, police patrols, and the like, as well as general receptivity to precinct concerns and complaints." Why candidates, and by extension voters trying to avoid their wrath, would care about winning an absolute majority in a given precinct (absent some institutional structure analogous to the Electoral College) is unclear, since presumably a vote is a vote regardless of where it comes from.[14]

This criticism applies with even greater force to elections in which a ballot question is at stake. Ultimately, each citizen can cast just one vote (perhaps *against* the powers that be), and it is hard to imagine this ballot proving decisive in any public official's allocative decisions. As it happens, intuition is all the reader has to go on, because Schwartz provides no evidence to suggest that fine-tuned patronage of this sort exists, let alone in a form sufficiently widespread nationwide to engender the sort of strategic calculations he imputes to voters.

GAME THEORY TO THE RESCUE?

In the hierarchy of rational choice models, game theoretic accounts, which allow for the possibility that people take into account the strategic decisions confronting others, seem to trump decision theoretic accounts, which present choices to individuals assuming the behavior of others to be given. Game theoretic models allow for more subtle rational calculation of costs and benefits; thus, if game theory were to succeed where earlier models had failed, it would be something of a coup.

---

13. Political scientists are divided, in fact, over the question of whether the size of a winning coalition affects the success with which executives pursue their policy objectives (see Michelson 1994).

14. Schwartz offers a host of other possible "subelectorates": ward, city, legislative district, neighborhoods, sections of town, labor unions, racial minorities, and income categories. Augmenting the slipperiness of his predictions, he notes that "the winning candidate (or the party in power) might reward a subelectorate for meeting some strategically assigned quota, for exceeding some predicted vote total by a specified amount, or for being pivotal in the election. There might be more than one point at which an additional vote would secure a noticeable jump in subelectorate benefits" (107).

That rational choice theorists would play the game-theory card to explain voter turnout may have been inevitable in any event given the awkward structure of the model in equation (4.1): the probability of casting a decisive ballot, which appears as an independent variable, is in turn a consequence of the decision to vote. If many people vote, one's chances of being decisive are trivial; if this reasoning leads others not to vote, then one's own vote will prove decisive (Meehl 1977).

During the 1980s there was a glimmer of hope that game theoretic models in which voters simultaneously decide whether to vote based on their strategic anticipation of others' actions could produce an equilibrium result in which many people turned out. Rather than take p as given (and infinitesimal), these scholars sought to investigate what would happen if the value of p were determined endogenously by the interaction of strategically minded voters, each confronting a similar decision. Palfrey and Rosenthal (1983) initially found that this theoretical development paid dividends.[15] Their model, in which voters possess complete information about the preferences and voting costs of other voters, generates certain equilibria in which high rates of turnout occurred. Ledyard (1981, 1984), using a somewhat different model, suggested that positive turnout results even when some uncertainty exists, although he was unable to ascertain just how positive these rates of turnout would be.[16] This seemed to be the breakthrough that rational choice was waiting for: a model that could accommodate significant voter participation without resorting to post hoc conjectures about civic duty and whatnot.

It was soon discovered, however, that once one allowed for either the possibility that voters may be uncertain about the voting costs of other citizens or that voters lack perfect information about the precise level of support for two competing candidates, the high turnout equilibrium result collapsed. The game-theoretic model might have survived by dint of Friedman-instrumentalist argumentation about the role of unrealistic assumptions in a predictive theory had it not turned out that the equilibrium disintegrates in the presence of a "relatively small degree of strategic uncertainty"

15. Palfrey and Rosenthal's model, like Ledyard's (see below), presupposes that the competing candidates offer distinct platforms, an issue to which we shall return in Chapter 7. As Morton (1991), among others, has noted, when candidates propose identical platforms, models which assume that voters evaluate candidates based on policy concerns predict zero turnout as long as $C > D$.

16. Over the years, many scholars (e.g., Schram [1991]) have announced with great satisfaction that their models of rational behavior predict "positive turnout." This seems to be an especially popular claim to make in abstracts to articles (e.g., Fedderson 1992; Morton 1991). Of course, the domain of positive numbers (integers, really) encompasses quite a wide range of potentially observable outcomes. Notably, authors seem reluctant to commit to any such very positive number as 104,000,000, roughly the number of voters nationwide who cast ballots in the 1992 national election. Perhaps this is because it is not clear from the models themselves whether voters will outnumber, say, exit pollsters.

(Palfrey and Rosenthal 1985, 73).[17] In an abrupt turnabout from their earlier findings, Palfrey and Rosenthal reluctantly adopted the standard fallback position of rational choice theorists, noting that "in very large electorates the only voters are citizens with net positive benefits from the act of voting, citizens whose sense of duty outweighs any cost in voting. We have come full circle and are once again beset by the paradox of not voting" (64). Game-theoretic solutions to the turnout problem have not resurfaced since this retreat was sounded almost a decade ago.

PEACE WITH HONOR VIA ARBITRARY DOMAIN RESTRICTION

The unpersuasiveness of the various attempts to formulate a general equilibrium model in which voters go to the polls in great numbers has led some rational choice theorists to expel the pesky turnout problem. In his recent review of the turnout literature, Aldrich (1993, 261) argues that turnout falls outside the boundaries of rational choice. According to Aldrich, the decision to vote, in contrast to such activities as contributing money to a campaign, is characteristically a "low-cost, low-benefit" affair. This is precisely the sort of behavior that rational choice is ill suited to explain, he maintains, and rational choice theory should not be impugned on account of its inability to make sense of voter turnout.

This argument represents an instance of arbitrary domain restriction in two senses. In the first place, there is nothing in rational choice theory that specifies the level at which costs or benefits are sufficiently small to render the theory inapplicable. Aldrich's intuition about the tractability of the phenomenon of turnout is precisely opposite that of rational choice theorists who have over the years asserted that turnout presents no insurmountable anomaly for rational choice (for example, Riker and Ordeshook [1968]; Strom [1975]; Schwartz [1987]; Uhlaner [1989]) and who, like Morton (1991, 759), have asked: "If we cannot explain individual voter turnout, then how can the rational choice approach be useful in examining political equilibrium?" It seems clear that turnout was banished from rational choice theory only when it became apparent that no satisfying theoretical solution could be worked out.

Second, Aldrich's attempt to pigeonhole turnout as a special case of collective action in which costs and benefits are low grossly underestimates the challenge that turnout poses for rational choice theory. Can it be said of Latin American elections, in which voters spend hours in polling lines, sometimes amid threats of violence, that turnout is a low-cost activity? What of the more than 100,000 African-Americans who persevered through the intimidation and poll taxes of the Jim Crow South and

17. An example of this retreat within the confines of a single essay may be found in Owen and Grofman's analysis of mixed strategies (1984), which initially asserts that the paradox of voter turnout is "easy enough to solve" (315), but a few turgid pages later concedes that voting makes sense only in elections that are believed to be extremely close (318).

voted in the national elections of the 1950s?[18] And if we reason that turnout promises low benefits to the voter because he or she cannot plausibly expect to shape the election outcome, it is unclear what distinguishes turnout from $100 contributions to political parties or other costly but ineffectual activities that Aldrich seems to regard as susceptible to rational choice theorizing. Like those who would have rational choice theory explain turnout, Aldrich, in his attempt to retreat from voting, fails to undertake the kinds of empirical investigation that would put his thesis to the test.

FROM WHY PEOPLE VOTE TO WHY TURNOUT RATES CHANGE

Thus far we have considered the question, What is the equilibrium rate of turnout predicted by a rational choice analysis? In the initial formulation of the paradox, the answer was zero or virtually so. No one could expect to sway the election unless he or she could be certain that only a handful of the millions of eligible voters would make it to the polls—a belief that would be absurd for any citizen deciding whether to vote during the waning hours of an election day. The null hypothesis that people cast ineffectual votes in large numbers obviously could not be rejected, and with successive emendations rational choice accounts were tailored to observed patterns of turnout in which millions made it to the polls. Notably, these reformulations, for all of their formal sophistication, were unable to specify what the newly predicted turnout equilibrium might be or, more to the point, what rate of turnout would be *inconsistent* with a rational choice analysis.

In addition, rational choice theorists have had difficulty demonstrating the role of strategic thinking in the turnout decision. Game-theoretic explanations, such as that offered by Palfrey and Rosenthal (1983), collapsed under their own weight, while the your-vote-does-matter arguments of Schwartz (1987) or Stigler (1972) were neither intuitively plausible nor supported by any systematic empirical investigation. Rational choice theorists have continually retreated to the fallback position articulated by Riker and Ordeshook (1968, 1973) that the psychic benefits of doing one's civic duty explain turnout (Palfrey and Rosenthal 1985; Plott 1991). It should be underscored, however, that since these psychic benefits are rarely measured and never in terms commensurate with the costs of voting, this hypothesis remains little more than an untested (and perhaps untestable) conjecture.

Now it may be argued that such *variables* as the perceived closeness of the election or the degree to which one feels a sense of civic duty have been shown to affect the rate

18. It was difficult to ascertain precisely how many African-Americans voted in the South in any given election during this period. Our rough estimate was pieced together from survey data reported in Campbell et al. 1960 (297) and 1950 Census data. A similar point could have been made with regard to registration figures for the pre-Voting Rights Act South (U.S. Commission on Civil Rights 1965, 1968).

of voter turnout *at the margin* (Grofman 1993a). Leaving aside for the moment whether these claims are substantiated empirically, it is important to recognize the subtle but important distinction between arguments of this sort and the equilibrium analyses discussed above. It is one thing to argue, for instance, that the rewards of civic duty are sufficient to make the ratio of benefits to costs greater than one; it is quite another to contend that increasing one's sense of civic duty leads to a concomitant increase in the likelihood that one will vote. It is logically possible that only one of these two conjectures could hold empirically.

A simple hypothetical example illustrates this point. Recall that the rational choice model of the decision to vote presented in equation (4.1) included four variables: the net benefits associated with the victory of one's preferred candidate, the probability of casting a decisive ballot, the costs of voting, and the selective benefits of voting. Suppose we gather a sample of eight eligible voters. For the purposes of this example, let us assume that costs (C) are constant for our hypothetical citizens. For concreteness, we will assign this cost "9 utiles" in our numerical example. We further assume that all of the citizens in our sample believe their probability of casting the decisive vote to be ϵ, a trivially small number. Thus, although some of our citizens care a great deal about which candidate prevails, the improbability of casting a pivotal ballot renders pb_i less than 1 utile for each person. What remains are the selective benefits associated with voting, which we assume vary from one person to the next.

Table 4.1 presents the costs, benefits, expectations, and turnout decisions of eight

Table 4.1. Hypothetical Illustration of the Distinction Between Rational Turnout and the Marginal Effects of Changing Selective Benefits of Voting

Voter	Expected Probability of Casting Decisive Vote (p)	Collective Benefits (b)	Selective Benefits (utiles) (D)	Costs (utiles) (C)	Do They Vote?	Is it Rational to Vote?
Anthony	ϵ	b_1	1	9	No	No
Bruce	ϵ	b_2	2	9	No	No
Carole	ϵ	b_3	3	9	Yes	No
Duncan	ϵ	b_4	4	9	No	No
Edward	ϵ	b_5	5	9	No	No
Frances	ϵ	b_6	6	9	Yes	No
Gordon	ϵ	b_7	7	9	Yes	No
Harold	ϵ	b_8	8	9	Yes	No

Note: Assume that $b_i\epsilon < 1$ for all i voters.

hypothetical citizens. It is apparent from the table that the probability of voting rises dramatically as selective benefits increase. If subjected to a standard statistical analysis, these data would reveal an "effect" of citizen duty. But is voting rational, in the sense of equation (4.1)? The answer is no: the expected value of voting is always negative, and hence the predicted equilibrium is that none of these citizens goes to the polls. Finding that the variables in the canonical rational choice model exert a *marginal* influence on turnout does not imply that voters act rationally in the sense of equation (4.1). Indeed, marginal effects need not even imply that *most* voters act rationally; the implication of table 4.1 remains unchanged if we increase the proportion of citizens whose costs and benefits resemble those of the hypothetical voters named "Gordon" and "Harold."[19]

The distinction between showing that costs and benefits affect behavior at the margin and showing that voters reap a net gain from going to the polls may seem an arcane point. It turns out, however, to be critical to understanding a flaw in much of the argumentation in the turnout literature. Even if it were found that the closeness of a state or national election enhances turnout by increasing any single voter's chance of casting a pivotal ballot, as Frohlich et al. (1978), Silberman and Durden (1975), and Barzel and Silberberg (1973) contend, it would not follow that the expected benefits of voting are sufficient to explain why people incur the costs. In any large electorate, the odds of casting a decisive vote are, at best, extremely long; to say that a voter is more likely to cast a pivotal vote in a close national election is, in Schwartz's words (1987, 118), tantamount to "saying that tall men are more likely than short men to bump their heads on the moon." Similarly, if those with a strong sense of civic obligation vote at higher rates than those without this sense of duty, as Riker and Ordeshook (1968) allege, it does not follow that the gains from fulfilling one's obligation are great enough to offset the costs. The way these questions of sufficiency could be answered would be to measure directly the costs and benefits of voting (perhaps using the demand-revelation techniques that have been developed in the field of economics) and compare them; the marginal effects of such variables as closeness are in some sense beside the point.

This is not to say, however, that estimating marginal effects is uninformative. It may in the end be a more informative enterprise but one that is directed at a different sort of theoretical question, namely: What sorts of factors affect the equilibrium rate

19. It is also possible to construct the obverse example, in which the rational voting model is true for all voters in the sense that equation (4.1) is satisfied for everyone, but where the marginal influence of cost is estimated by linear regression to be very small. Consider the case in which net voting costs (x) are uniformly distributed from -100 to $+100$ (but $x \neq 0$), and the probability of voting is

$$\frac{1}{1 + e(-x^{-1})} \cdot$$

of voter turnout? Presumably, one cannot arrive at this "comparative statics" question through rational choice theorizing until one has resolved the issue of why the apparent equilibrium rate of turnout in the United States seems to hover at about 50 percent rather than zero. But having discussed this issue at some length already, let us set it aside and consider what rational choice theory has to say about marginal effects and the source of variation in observed rates of voter turnout.

The expected utility framework underlying equation (4.1) seems to imply two testable hypotheses about marginal effects (compare Ferejohn and Fiorina 1974, 1975). First, the collective benefits associated with an election outcome should not matter when the probability of casting the decisive vote is virtually indistinguishable from zero. Consider one of the highest-stakes elections: ballot measures designed to make fundamental shifts in the tax code. What difference should it make if such tax reduction measures as California's Proposition 13 offer one group of citizens tens of thousands of dollars in property tax relief while offering another group next to nothing? When the vote is expected to be lopsided—as was Proposition 13, which won by a 2-to-1 margin—the chance of casting a decisive vote is absurdly small, probably less than that of suffering a severe accident en route to the polls. Since this minute probability is multiplied by the collective benefits at stake to yield expected utility, even several orders of magnitude difference in B between the big winners and big losers washes out. Those who stand to gain or lose from an election outcome nonetheless have an incentive to shirk the costs of voting onto others.

As Brennan and Buchanan (1984) point out, rational choice theorists have some-times been reluctant to concede that collective benefits should not influence turnout in large electorates. Asserting what amounts to the opposite of this hypothesis, some have characterized voting as an "investment" (Fiorina 1976), suggesting that such tangible interests as "property and income subject to taxation" (Stigler 1975, 744) will drive voters to the polls. Wittman, for example, argues that "a statewide referendum on giving veterans certain benefits could be used to test hypotheses concerning rational voting. Presumably those areas with large percentages of either active or retired armed forces personnel would tend to have both a greater probability of voting and a higher probability of voting in favor than other areas with similar demographic characteristics except armed forces experience" (1975, 737). To be sure, hypotheses of this kind have a rational choice ring to them insofar as they presuppose a form of instrumental calculation (see Smith 1975; Filer et al. 1993). But viewed against the backdrop of the free-rider problem, they seem inconsistent with the rational choice perspective on collective action unless one is prepared to argue that voters place unreasonably high odds on casting the decisive ballot.

A second and less murky hypothesis is that the marginal effects of collective benefits should increase as the perceived closeness of the election increases. If one accepts the premise that the closer the election, the greater one's likelihood of casting a decisive ballot (p), then the expected utility model predicts that the closer the election, the greater the causal influence of B. We should therefore find an interaction between perceived closeness and citizens' stakes in an election outcome: as noted above, collective benefits should be all but irrelevant to the decisions of those who regard the contest as likely to end in a lopsided victory but increasingly influential as voters come to regard the election as a dead heat.

Empirical tests of rational choice models are divided between two methods of testing hypotheses about the interplay between collective benefits and the probability of casting a pivotal vote. One method uses aggregate data and compares the closeness and collective benefits of different elections; each observation in this type of analysis is a single election. The other method uses survey data and compares individuals with different perceptions about the closeness of an election and different interests in the election outcome. For most applications, the latter approach is more informative for three reasons. Those who use aggregate data rely on the closeness of the election outcome as the indicator of perceived closeness. Not only might actual closeness and perceived closeness differ, but any apparent "effect" of actual closeness on aggregate turnout may reflect forces having nothing to do with strategic thinking on the part of individual voters—such as the increased campaign effort that accompanies close contests and stimulates voter turnout (Gosnell 1927; Cox and Munger 1989). Second, analysis of statewide or countywide turnout patterns runs afoul of the general problem of statistical inference from aggregate data, in which the independent variables are group means (for example, the percentage of a group with high school diplomas), but the parameters of interest refer to individual-level decisions. For decades this kind of ecological analysis has been known to produce severely biased inferences (Robinson 1950; Palmquist 1993), but this critique has seldom been leveled at voter turnout research (see, however, Grofman 1993a). To make matters worse, aggregate regression analyses generally ignore the interaction between perceived closeness and benefits as it applies to the turnout decisions of individuals, perhaps a tacit admission that ecological regression would not work to recover the parameters associated with this interaction anyway. Even if it were found that "high-stakes elections" attract the greatest number of voters, it need not follow that *at the individual level* the marginal effect of one's stake in the election increases with the perceived closeness of the contest.[20]

20. Cox (1988) adds to this list an econometric objection about the use of measures of closeness other than the absolute gap in votes between the winning and losing candidates. Leaving aside these objections, we note for the sake of completeness that the literature seems to suggest that closeness matters in congressional, gubernatorial, and presidential elections (Barzel and Silberberg 1973; Silberman and Durden 1975; Dawson and Zinser 1976; Gray 1976; Patterson and Caldiera 1983; Crain, Leavens, and Abbot 1987), though some discrepant results turn up (Foster 1984; Ostrosky 1984). Suffice it to say that many of the essays that find closeness

Restricting our attention to tests of rational choice models in which the individual is the unit of analysis, the evidence turns out to be inconsistent with both expected utility hypotheses. Data presented by Riker and Ordeshook (1968) on turnout in presidential elections show that collective benefits affected turnout in 1952, 1956, and 1960 even among those who did not regard the election as close.[21]

Although this sort of analysis has been criticized on the grounds that national elections feature a wide assortment of contests, any one of which might draw voters to the polls (Wittman 1975; Hansen, Palfrey, and Rosenthal 1987; Wolfinger 1993), the conclusions do not change when we focus on special elections or elections dominated by a single ballot proposition. In a special citywide referendum on busing in Boston during 1974, for example, homeowners and the parents of children who attended public schools were significantly more likely to go to the polls despite the transparent lopsidedness of the contest (Green and Cowden 1992). Other survey data on participation in local school elections reveal similar patterns, suggesting that measures of personal concern or interest affect turnout even when the outcome is a foregone conclusion.

Another setback for the expected utility model is the weak or nonexistent interaction between perceived closeness and collective benefits. Ferejohn and Fiorina's examination of the turnout decision among registered voters showed that collective benefits are not more influential among those who believe the election to be very close (1975). Although Frohlich et al. (1978) claim to find such an interaction for the 1964

---

to be influential advertise their results as evidence for rational choice theories of voter turnout. The best of these works is probably a study of Oregon school district elections, which finds turnout to be inversely proportional to the number of registered voters in a district (Hanson et al. 1987). Unfortunately, this study does not compare district turnout rates for state or national elections in order to test the extent to which the prospect of casting the pivotal vote indeed lures voters in small school districts. Lest it be said that this book critiques only the weakest pieces of rational choice scholarship, we have omitted mention of many ecological studies that are on par with Kau and Rubin's demonstration that the Electoral College depresses turnout because populous states tend to have fewer electors per capita and thus their voters have less "voting power" (1976).

21. Collective benefits were measured according to whether one said that one cared about how the election turned out. Other measures of "benefits," as Aldrich notes (1976), produce similar or weaker results. Interestingly, some lukewarm support for the Downsian model was found by Campbell et al. (1960, 99–100), who note a slight increase in the effect of B when the election is perceived to be close. The authors note, however, that closeness of the national election (the survey measure that Riker and Ordeshook would later use) exerts more statistical influence than the more theoretically meaningful statewide closeness measure. Extending this analysis for the 1964 and 1972 elections, Aldrich (1976) obtains very similar results even when, for 1972, he uses a survey measure of perceived closeness of the contest in a respondent's state. Rational voters evidently do not find it in their interests to investigate the operation of the Electoral College.

election, Aldrich (1976) and Cyr (1975) show this effect to be faint and not replicated in other presidential elections. Voter turnout, like other forms of collective action to be discussed in the next chapter, tends not to follow the contours of an expected utility formulation.

What do rational choice theorists make of these results? Some concede that there is "very little evidence favoring an expected utility model" (Aldrich 1976, 732) and suggest that citizens instead follow such a quasi-rational decision rule as minimizing their maximum regret (see footnote 12). Others contend that the lack of interaction between election closeness and collective benefits, far from being a blow to expected utility, is really a strike in favor of Stigler's notion (1972) that citizens wish to make a nonprobabilistic contribution (of one vote) to an electoral coalition (Thompson 1982).

Most of the commentary about the variables p and B, however, is beside the point, addressing the separate marginal effects each exerts on voter turnout rather than their interaction. Riker and Ordeshook (1968) trumpet the fact that perceived closeness is a predictor of voter turnout, noting that people have been subjected to "propaganda" that leads them to overestimate their chances of casting a decisive vote (see also Brunk 1980; Thompson 1982). But when perceived closeness fails as a predictor, the notion that individuals might actually believe in their minuscule chances of casting a decisive vote is derided as illusory (Ashenfelter and Kelley 1975) or preposterous (Schwartz 1987). Either way, a version of rational choice theory finds support: if the closeness of an election is not related to turnout, models based on the formal mathematics of the odds of casting a decisive ballot are confirmed (Foster 1984); if closeness matters, voters have proved themselves to be good rational actors but poor statisticians (Barzel and Silberberg 1973; Silberman and Durden 1975; Frohlich et al. 1978; Filer and Kenny 1980). The prodigious literature on the effects of closeness, in sum, speaks obliquely to the underlying theory in question and offers a set of predictions that exhausts the range of possible empirical observations.

VOTING COSTS AND SELECTIVE INCENTIVES

Let us now consider the role that costs play in shaping voter turnout.[22] Here, the evidence seems to suggest that such factors as poll taxes, literacy requirements, and stringent registration requirements diminish voter turnout (Ashenfelter and Kelley 1975; Rosenstone and Wolfinger 1978).[23] These effects, while important

22. We exclude from our discussion Frohlich et al. 1978, Sanders 1980, or Schram 1991, which discuss the effects of costs but do not measure them directly.

23. For example, the expected turnout rate in states with closing dates fifty days prior to the election, such as Arizona or Georgia, is considerably lower than in a state such as North Dakota, which has day-of-the-election registration. It is not immediately apparent, however,

for policy making, are from a theoretical standpoint neither overwhelming nor surprising. As Ashenfelter and Kelley (1975) themselves note, it is surely banal to assert that cost reduces turnout to some degree. Granted, the poll tax and the one-party system that accompanied it depressed turnout. But such less severe (and time-bound) disincentives as short polling hours, irregular times during which one may register to vote, and the threat of being selected for jury service as a result of registering have much less influence on voting or registration rates (Ashenfelter and Kelley 1975; Knack 1993b; Rosenstone and Wolfinger 1978). Weaker still is the influence exerted by cost factors that vary across elections. Although, as Knack points out, it is often asserted as an article of faith that inclement weather depresses voter turnout, the effects of temperature and precipitation in fact prove to be small and statistically elusive (Traugott 1974; Knack 1994).

When one compares turnout rates across different types of individuals, evidence about costs becomes murkier, and predictions grow correspondingly more slippery. A recurrent finding for nearly a half-century is that American turnout increases with income (Press and Traugott 1992). Some have argued that personal income should be positively related to voting insofar as affluent people have more leisure time to devote to such activities as voting (Downs 1957; Russell 1972) or becoming informed (Sanders 1980). On the other hand, the economic logic of substitution suggests that high-income people have correspondingly higher opportunity costs in the form of foregone wages or comparably valued leisure time (Tollison and Willett 1973). Splitting the difference between these contrasting predictions while still generating the known result that turnout increases with income, Frey (1971) speculates that those with higher wages are more likely to have occupations that enable them to "work" (that is, reflect) while waiting in line at the polls.[24] Fraser (1972) and Niemi (1976), however, regard the time demands of voting to be so trivial as to render both income and substitution effects irrelevant. Rounding out the field are Filer et al. (1993), who interpret the positive income effect in terms of expected value, arguing that the fundamentally redistributive character of politics affects the assets of the rich more profoundly. It would appear, then, that most any observed relation between income and voter turnout may be said to be consistent with a rational choice interpretation.

The obverse of voting costs are the selective benefits of voting. We have already remarked about the absence of any systematic evidence to suggest that people vote because they think that it will buy them influence with local officials (Schwartz 1987)

---

that the correlation between stringent deadlines and cross-sectional voting rates ought to be interpreted as showing the effects of costs. It could well be that states in which feelings of "civic duty" run high are those in which policy steps are taken to make registration requirements less difficult.

24. Curiously, from the standpoint of this argument, the newly unemployed do not show a surge in their voting or in other forms of political participation (Schlozman and Verba 1979).

THE PARADOX OF VOTER TURNOUT 67

or curry favor with friends (Niemi 1976). Equally thin is the literature on whether these sorts of strategic objectives affect turnout rates at the margin. Knack (1992) presents some evidence purporting to show that the social pressure one spouse exerts on the other changes the probability that the latter will vote, but the design of this study is not compelling.[25] And as noted earlier, Uhlaner's demonstration of the effects of interest group encouragement to voters ironically reveals little indication that labor union members go to the polls when trade unionism is on the line (1989).

The main contender supported by data is the notion that people vote at greater rates when they think that they have an obligation to do so or when they wish to affirm their partisan identity (Riker and Ordeshook 1968, 1973). In defense of this claim, Riker and Ordeshook show that those who disagree with such statements as "It isn't so important to vote when you know your party doesn't have a chance to win" or "So many other people vote in the national elections that it doesn't matter much to me whether I vote or not" are more likely to vote (compare Aldrich 1976, 728).[26] Wolfinger (1993) criticizes the validity of these measures persuasively, arguing that they do not seem to tap the kinds of consumption benefits that Riker and Ordeshook postulate. Certainly, it is no small irony, given the importance of expected utility reasoning for rational choice theorists, that the ethos tapped by these survey items holds that one should vote regardless of whether one's ballot is likely to be influential.

It might be said that although the finding of higher rates of turnout among those with a stronger sense of civic duty strains the theoretical coherence of rational choice theory, it nonetheless represents an empirical discovery generated by rational choice scholarship.[27] Perhaps it may be said that the role of civic duty became a more actively debated issue in the wake of rational choice theorizing (Ordeshook 1986, 50), but credit for the empirical research itself cannot properly be assigned to rational

25. Because Knack relies on a nonexperimental cross-sectional study, he is restricted in the allowance he can make for the myriad of omitted factors that might make norm-enforcing couples more likely to vote. The particular statistical analysis that Knack employs, as it happens, takes no account of the general level of political communication between spouses.

26. Other survey measures in the civic duty scale used by Riker and Ordeshook include "A good many local elections aren't important enough to bother with" and "If a person doesn't care how an election comes out he shouldn't vote in it" (Campbell, Gurin, and Miller 1954, 194). Note that all of the questions in this scale are worded so that disagreement represents an expression of civic duty. Because respondents with more education are less likely to acquiesce to such agree-disagree survey questions, it is unclear how much of the civic duty "effect" on turnout is in fact attributable to education.

27. One should not be too hasty to declare the endorsement of civic norms a causal anteced- ent of voting intentions. As Wittman (1975, 740) has suggested, an alternative hypothesis not entertained by those investigating the statistical link between duty and turnout is that those with a positive attitude toward voting are more likely both to vote and to endorse favorable statements about voting.

choice scholarship. Just as the effects of perceived closeness on voter turnout had been assessed by such authors as Gosnell (1927, 3) or Campbell et al. (1960, 99–100) long before this activity became fashionable in rational choice circles, so too with civic duty. Employing the very survey measures that Riker and Ordeshook were later to use, the authors of *The Voter Decides* concluded that "the more strongly a person feels a sense of obligation to discharge his civic duties, the more likely he is to be politically active" (Campbell, Gurin, and Miller 1954, 199). Riker and Ordeshook's innovation over previous social-psychological work was to repackage this conclusion and claim for rational choice the empirical finding that people vote when they believe they should vote. To this day commentators who do not cite Riker and Ordeshook's work (for example, Knack [1992]) take this finding to be evidence for a "sociologi-cal" interpretation of voting.

CONCLUDING REMARKS

Readers interested in the determinants of voter turnout, in sum, will derive little insight from the empirical work in the rational choice tradition. Enduring research questions, such as why education exerts such a profound statistical influence on the voting behavior of Americans, are seldom addressed in illuminating ways. Some commentators (Sanders [1980]; Schram [1991]) speculate that education re-duces the tangible costs of voting (or voter registration) but furnish no systematic empirical assessment of the costs of voting and how they impinge on those with differing levels of education.[28] Others contend that education imparts a sense of civic duty and enhances interest in politics; here rational choice theory contributes nothing, because it is silent about the process by which people develop tastes and identities. Occasionally, rational choice theorists come to grips with the strong correlation between education and turnout by reference to instrumental reasoning about side-payments, but such attempts border on the ludicrous. Schwartz (1987, 116), for example, asserts that "education often . . . helps one appreciate the complex and subtle ways in which subelectorate voting [that is, the vote outcome in one's precinct] affects the delivery of policy benefits." And during unguarded moments, rational

28. There are two variants of the argument that education lowers voting costs, one suggest-ing that education helps one negotiate the bureaucratic steps necessary to register and find out when and where to vote (but see Nagler 1991), the other asserting that education renders less costly the task of understanding the issues at stake in an election. Although Downs (1957, 265) argues that information costs contribute to abstention (see also Aldrich 1993, 248, 263; Filer et al. 1993, 80), this contention is not consistent with rational choice theory as it is ordinarily conceived. As Frohlich et al. point out, "To argue that the cost of information constitutes a barrier to voting flies directly in the face of the Downsian conclusion that it is often rational to vote in relative ignorance" (1978, 182). See Chapter 5.

choice theorists tacitly admit that the effects of education are somewhat anomalous. Brunk (1980, 562), on the basis of an experiment in which a lecture on Downs apparently diminished students' intention to vote, asserts that the positive relation between education and voting may eventually be reversed "since those who are better educated will be more likely to encounter theories of rational participation."

The phenomenon of voter turnout may, in the end, say more about rational choice theory than the reverse. The inability to state and maintain a hypothesis about what any variant of rational choice theory does *not* predict shows up both in theorizing about the equilibrium rate of turnout in large electorates and in the marginal effects of explanatory variables. What observation would in principle be inconsistent with a theoretical framework that allows for post hoc insertion of idiosyncratic tastes, beliefs, and probability assessments as explanatory devices? Voting for presidential candidates in Guam, which in 1992 (because of a typhoon) took place a week after the rest of the United States had cast their ballots? No, doubtless a tale could be woven about how some combination of civic duty and the allure of other Guamanian contests drew several thousand citizens to the polls. Perhaps the fact that the act of voting seems to be habit-forming? No, it could be said that the voting experience relieves apprehensions a person might have about going to the polls. The positive effect of campaign appeals and door-to-door canvassing on turnout? Again, it may be argued that such appeals enhance one's sense of civic duty or reduce the information costs of voting or instill a fear of reprisal at the hands of angry activists prone to lash out at the uncooperative. Grafstein (1991, 989) remarks that "rational choice theory has had a difficult time getting voters to the polls." To this we would add that rational choice models would increase their theoretical import if they had *more* difficulty doing so.

Rational choice theorizing about voter turnout could be improved through several changes in approach. The coherence and explanatory power of these models could be enhanced if the commitment to universalism were discarded in favor of what we have termed partial universalism, or the view that rational maximizing is but one of several factors at work in the turnout decision and that the influence of strategic considerations is likely to vary across people and decision contexts. Although a synthesis of different theoretical perspectives entails a sacrifice in terms of theoretical parsimony, it offers a number of advantages. First, the coherence of rational choice theory would be improved by placing such phenomena as adherence to norms of civic duty or expression of partisan enthusiasm into a separate explanatory category from that of the more manifestly instrumental motives, such as the desire to reap the expected benefits of casting the decisive vote or the aversion to wasting time waiting in line. Sharpening the theoretical boundaries in this way helps reduce the conceptual strain that occurs when seemingly habitual, expressive, or rule-directed behaviors are forced into an interpretive scheme that recognizes only utility maximization. Second, a more synoptic view of the causal process that governs the decision to vote could enable rational choice scholars to move beyond interminable post hoc theorizing about why so many people vote to more nuanced and informative research. The phenomenon of voter turnout clearly contains many interesting facets that could be informed by rational choice theorizing, but not rational choice theorizing alone. For example, Knack (1994) finds that although weather does not affect the odds of voting among those with a strong sense of civic duty, those who do not endorse these norms are significantly influenced by whether it rains on election day. The interaction between one's normative mindset and the role that costs play in the decision process, which has been observed in other contexts (Green 1992), suggests a more complex psychology of choice than that assumed by conventional rational choice or social-psychological models. Freeing rational choice theorizing from the requirement that each facet of the explanation be consistent with utility maximization and the convention that a single (read parsimonious) decision calculus applies to all citizens provides researchers with greater latitude to anticipate such novel facts as these.

Rational choice scholarship would profit not only from a change in theoretical orientation but also from a change in the way scholars collect and analyze data on voter turnout. Very few studies of turnout decisions *among individuals* have been conducted by rational choice modelers themselves. The data analysis that is conducted, therefore, relies on survey measures that were developed by social-psychologists for very different purposes. To advance the study of how costs and benefits influence behavior, much more attention must be focused on the measurement of these theoretical terms, and rational choice theorists themselves must be at the forefront of these efforts.[29] If the strides made through social-psychological inquiry during the 1950s and 1960s are any indication, a closer connection with data may make for more trenchant theorizing.

In the short run, empirical rational choice scholarship in this area could be rejuvenated by applied statistical studies of the influence of various policy interventions. If rational choice provides one advantage over competing explanatory approaches, it is the ability to make clear predictions about the effects of increasing or decreasing the costs of voting. How would voter turnout change if absentee ballots were routinely distributed to eligible voters? What if voting were a week-long affair, or if ballots could be cast at a host of locations, such as supermarkets? What if voter registration forms were mailed periodically to unregistered voters? Perhaps if close empirical research guided by rational choice insights were to achieve some predictive successes (for example, in anticipating the consequences of the recently enacted registration bill due to take effect in 1995), scholarship in this area might be weaned away from

29. A survey effort designed to test rational choice theories of turnout undertaken by Jack Dennis (1991), however praiseworthy as one of the few efforts of its kind, suffers from serious conceptual problems that might have been alleviated had the work involved rational choice collaborators. See critical comments in Knack 1993a.

ethereal speculation about why rational citizens vote and refocused on questions of a more down-to-earth nature.

At present, empirical successes inspired by rational choice theory are difficult to identify, and consequently empirical investigations of voter turnout seldom do more than mention rational choice theory in passing (for example, Teixeira 1987, Wolfinger and Rosenstone 1980). Perhaps this state of affairs reflects the fact that most rational choice theorists are interested in turnout only insofar as this phenomenon represents what some regard as "the paradox that ate rational choice theory" (Fiorina 1990, 334). Whatever the case may be, there is a sense among some rational choice scholars that voter turnout is a distinctively recalcitrant area of application, unrepresentative of the empirical success rational choice theory has enjoyed elsewhere. Unaccompanied by a compelling account of why the act of going to the polls should fall outside the purview of rational choice theory, this view is merely an outgrowth of arbitrary domain restriction and may be criticized as such. All the same, we are not convinced that this point should be conceded. The literature on turnout *is* representative of a broad class of applications of rational choice theory in American politics. That empirical scholarship on voter turnout *seems* unusually problematic reflects an inflated appraisal of other applications, which have received less critical attention. As we turn our attention to collective action, legislative politics, and candidate competition, we again find it difficult to identify instances in which rational choice theorizing has contributed to the stock of empirically based knowledge about American politics.

CHAPTER FIVE

SOCIAL DILEMMAS AND FREE-RIDING

Rational choice theorizing in political science and economics often concerns the special problems that arise when people have opportunities to get something for nothing. The defining metaphor in this line of analysis is the public pasture, open and free of charge to all, which is gradually overgrazed to the point of ruination by "rational herdsmen" whose marginal benefits from bringing an additional animal to the pasture outweigh the marginal costs of using the unsupervised commons. Each "rational herdsman," explains Garrett Hardin (1968, 1244), "concludes that the only sensible course for him to pursue is to add another animal to his herd. And another; and another. . . . A conclusion reached by each and every rational herdsman sharing a commons." Eventually, pursuit of self-interest destroys the unregulated pasture, leaving the herders worse off than they might have otherwise been.

The "tragedy of the commons" parable about how rational self-interest leads to the suboptimal provision or protection of collective goods has been told innumerable times with reference to economic phenomena.[1] Whales are hunted, lobsters trapped, bison slaughtered, trees felled, and water diverted all because cheap, unregulated access to these resources encourages economic agents to exploit them to the point where marginal returns are equal to marginal costs—that is, where there are little or

1. Pure public goods, such as the victory of a particular candidate, clean air, or national defense, are nonrival in the sense that "each individual's consumption of such a good leads to no subtraction from any other individual's consumption of that good" (Samuelson 1954, 387) and nonexcludable insofar as "they must be available to everyone if they are available to anyone" (Olson 1965, 14). There are, to be sure, gradations of public goods. Everyone has the *right* to obtain admission to a national park, for example, but access is limited to those who pay a user fee. A highway bridge may be nonrival in principle, but crowding may occur in fact. These kinds of nuances will not concern us here because our attention will be focused on the political objectives pursued through broad-based collective action, which more or less conform to the definition of pure public goods.

no resources left to extract. Some draw from this parable the inference that the commons creates the tragedy and recommend privatization; others, that unregulated access is at fault and recommend public administration of the commons.[2] Whatever their policy inclinations, most economists regard the depletion of unregulated common resources as inevitable given the profit motive.

As we move from the realm of economics to that of politics, the collective goods problem often shifts from one of extracting resources from a common pool to one of contributing to a common fund.[3] A corresponding parable, described by Cheung (1983), depicts a gang of Chinese laborers manually tugging barges up the Yangtze River. Although the laborers are paid according to the number of barges that reach their destination, this incentive system is insufficient to entice the laborers to pull. No single laborer's efforts have more than a trivial effect on the progress of the barge, and the success of the team effort is a collective good to which each laborer is entitled regardless of effort. Left to pursue their own interests, therefore, the workers fail to pull the barge and therefore receive no pay. The barge moves only after the laborers themselves consent to the hiring of a taskmaster to whip them.

One implication of the barge parable is that agents or institutions can intervene to distribute incentives in such a way as to overcome the collective action problem. It has been suggested, for example, that the state may have originated as a solution to a collective action problem in which each person shared an interest in the rule of law but no one had an incentive to relinquish unilaterally complete freedom of action (Nozick 1974). In a similar vein, it has been suggested that the leadership posts in Congress are created and structured so as to reconcile each party member's common interest in that party's legislative success with his or her individual incentive to avoid the sacrifices necessary to pass legislation (Cox and McCubbins 1993). A second implication is that, absent institutions that alter the system of incentives, collective efforts that hinge on voluntary contributions collapse when the actors involved make self-interested calculations. Note that the parable offers, in essence, a "thick" theory of rational behavior in which the laborers seek wages while avoiding physical exertion—plausible but potentially false premises about motivation (compare Lane 1991).

Also implicit in the story is the assumption that whether laborers pull their lines reflects the motive force of palpable incentives or disincentives, rather than of such norms as "doing one's share," "every little bit counts," or "cheaters never prosper." The lash, not a sermon on personal responsibility, is what stirs the workers to action. This perspective on the collapse of voluntary collective undertakings informs an array

2. Still others reject the implications of the parable and argue that the commons can be preserved through informal regulation. See Hechter 1987 and discussion in Ostrom et al. 1992.

3. These situations are often referred to as the take-some and give-some social dilemmas (Dawes 1991).

of applications in political science that ranges from the alleged dearth of mass participation in interest groups to widespread ignorance about political affairs.

Voter abstention, which we discussed in Chapter 4, also belongs to this large class
of collective action problems, but there is a widespread impression that rational
choice models fare better in explaining collective endeavors other than voting (Olson
1965, 164; Aldrich 1993, 265). Russell Hardin (1982, 11), for example, asserts, "The
logic of collective action . . . yields a notoriously poor explanation of voting behavior, since it suggests that almost no one would voluntarily vote in, say, American
national elections. It helps us understand why half of eligible Americans do not vote,
but it does little to help us understand the other half. The logic of collective action is,
however, unquestionably successful in predicting negligible voluntary activity in
many fields, such as the contemporary environmental movement."

In this chapter we question the success with which rational choice theory explains
voluntary political activity other than voting. We focus primarily on the empirical
work that has been used to buttress Mancur Olson's claims about the conditions under
which individuals contribute to collective political causes, in particular, interest
groups and social movements. After reviewing the nonexperimental and experimental evidence on how people behave when confronted with social dilemmas, we
comment on the empirical status of Downs's "rational ignorance" hypothesis, which
maintains that citizens have an incentive to expend minimal resources to obtain
information about public affairs. Our review of the literature suggests that the quality
of applied rational choice scholarship does not improve as we move from voter
turnout to collective action more generally, nor do hypotheses derived from rational
choice theory fare significantly better when tested empirically. The principal difference that we detect between the two literatures is that rational choice commentary on
nonelectoral political behavior rests on fewer systematic empirical inquiries.

SOCIAL DILEMMAS

The essence of a social dilemma is that individuals' pursuit of gain leads
to a suboptimal collective outcome. Many political phenomena, from obedience to
weakly enforced laws to pork-barrel spending legislation, have been characterized in
these terms. Chief among them, however, is mass collective action—letter writing,
campaign contributions, picketing, attendance at political meetings, and kindred
activities on behalf of a social cause. As Olson (1965) argues, any one individual's
contribution to a joint effort of this sort will typically have a negligible effect on the
likelihood that the group's goals will be realized. One person's expenditure of several
hours attending a tedious protest meeting is no more likely to alter the fate of court-
ordered school desegregation than a single ballot is to sway an election. Furthermore,
to the extent that protest proves successful in changing policy, the individual will be

entitled to enjoy the fruits of collective action regardless of whether he or she contributed. The decision problem thus resembles the turnout choice characterized in equation (4.1). Participation in the group endeavor under these circumstances will only be rational if the selective incentives to participate outweigh the expected costs.

Many forms of collective action, including voter turnout, share the general characteristics of a Prisoner's Dilemma game (Hardin 1971).[4] The scenario from which this game takes its name is the following:

> Two suspects are taken into custody and separated. The district attorney is certain that they are guilty of a specific crime, but he does not have adequate evidence to convict them at trial. He points out to each prisoner that each has two alternatives: to confess to the crime the police are sure they have done, or not to confess. If they both do not confess, then the district attorney states he will book them on some very minor trumped-up charge such as petty larceny and illegal possession of a weapon, and they will both receive minor punishment; if they both confess they will be prosecuted, but he will recommend less than the most severe sentence; but if one confesses and the other does not, then the confessor will receive lenient treatment for turning state's evidence whereas the latter will get "the book" slapped at him. . . . The problem for each prisoner is to decide whether to confess or not. (Luce and Raiffa 1957, 95)

The abstract form of this game is depicted in table 5.1. The first entry in each cell of this table is prisoner 1's payoff; the second, prisoner 2's payoff. Each player has two options: *cooperate* with the other prisoner and keep quiet, or *defect* to the prosecutor and testify. If neither prisoner testifies then both receive the minor sentences (a_1, a_2). But if prisoner 1 testifies and prisoner 2 does not, then prisoner 1 goes free (c_1) and prisoner 2 gets the so-called "sucker's payoff" (b_2). If both testify, then the two respective payoffs are (d_1, d_2). The key assumptions about the payoffs are that $c_k > a_k$ (playing the other prisoner for a sucker leads to a more desired outcome than what one would receive if neither prisoner squeals) and that $d_k > b_k$ (being played for a sucker is a worse outcome than taking the fall together). From these assumptions it follows that *no matter what the other prisoner does*, it is always rational to testify. In the language of game theory, it is said that defection represents a "dominant strategy." Moreover, when it is assumed that $a_k > d_k$ (that is, the minor sentences that result if

4. Note that collective action problems could arise from games other than the Prisoner's Dilemma. In an Assurance game, defection is no longer a dominant strategy; players are better off cooperating if others do likewise. In a Chicken game, each player is better off playing the strategy opposite that played by the opponent. Strictly speaking, collective action problems arise whenever rational maximizers generate a collective outcome that is Pareto inferior to the status quo ante (Taylor 1987, 19). We focus on the Prisoner's Dilemma because it serves as the starting point for many analyses of collective action.

Table 5.1. Structure of a Prisoner's Dilemma

| | | Prisoner 2 | |
		Cooperate (do not testify)	Defect (testify)
Prisoner 1	Cooperate (do not testify)	(a_1, a_2)	(b_1, c_2)
	Defect (testify)	(c_1, b_2)	(d_1, d_2)

Terms
a_k: conviction on petty charge
b_k: conviction, maximum sentence
c_k: released
d_k: conviction, lenient sentence

Assumptions basic to Prisoner's Dilemma
Prefer c_k to a_k; and
Prefer d_k to b_k

Auxiliary assumption for social welfare implication
Prefer a_k to d_k

neither prisoner talks are preferred to the moderate sentences that each receive if both testify), then rational behavior leads to a Pareto inferior outcome: both testify, yet each would be better off if both had refused to talk.[5]

The analogy to collective action hinges on the assumption that no one person's participation has a decisive influence on the collective outcome. Now assume there to be *n* players, instead of two, deciding whether to participate in the joint endeavor. For example, imagine a game in which one hundred people are confronted with the following choice: contribute nothing to a common pool versus contribute $10 to a joint investment that yields dividends of $1 for each of the one hundred people, whether or not they contribute. (Assume that these players cannot make binding agreements, physical threats, or other side-payments.) The relation among the payoffs described in the previous paragraph holds here: regardless of what others choose to do, each person is better off not contributing to the collective cause. If others participate, rationality dictates that one should shirk the costs of participation; if

5. As Hardin (1971) points out, an interesting property of the Prisoner's Dilemma is that mutual cooperation constitutes a Condorcet winner. This outcome wins at least as many votes (from the players) as any of the other three alternative outcomes that might be paired against it.

others do not act, one would be foolish to take the costs of collective action upon oneself. The net result is that collective action on behalf of a valued cause fizzles, even though each potential participant would prefer a cooperative outcome.

Note that not all failures of group action are attributable to social dilemma–induced shirking. That millions of people pay no membership dues to the Ku Klux Klan stems not from free-riding but from the fact that this organization and its aims are widely despised. Similarly, such organizations as Earth First!, the Animal Liberation Front, the Eagle Forum, and Operation Rescue, which have goals that potentially appeal to a constituency of sympathizers, may lose adherents for reasons other than free-riding, whether because their tactics are too extreme, leaders too venal, or institutional practices too disorganized. A true social dilemma, in other words, arises not from distaste for the interest group or its methods, but from strategic behavior predicated on the realization that one can consume the collective good produced by the group regardless of one's own contribution.

When a social dilemma exists, conventional rational choice models—which make no allowance for strategic error and stipulate no special utility from "doing the right thing"—predict that no player will adopt a cooperative strategy. Such equilibrium predictions may be altered, however, by the introduction of side-payments that make defection no longer a dominant strategy. Were a third party to monitor and punish defection, for example, the payoffs associated with the game might no longer con- form to the pattern characteristic of a social dilemma. Conversely, side-payments may take the form of positive inducements, as when interest groups promise maga- zine subscriptions in return for membership dues. Similarly, were social pressure exerted on an individual so that he or she felt that cooperation were necessary to sustain a valued reputation, the payoff from defection might no longer be attractive. Feelings of guilt or altruistic sentiments might also transform an n-person Prisoner's Dilemma into some other game, possibly one with a different equilibrium. Taylor (1987, 22) dubs these alterations to the game "external solutions," insofar as they resolve a social dilemma by changing players' preferences or expected utilities.

Another way to overcome the free-riding problem is to structure the social dilemma in such a way as to make each individual's participation pivotal. Chong (1991), for example, characterizes civil rights boycotts of segregated public transportation as "all-or-nothing" forms of collective action, in which any defection leads to the collapse of the collective effort (see also Crenson 1987). Many rational choice ac- counts of collective action focus on these sorts of quasi-dilemmas in which defection is not a dominant strategy, because under special conditions one actor's cooperation may prove decisive to the provision of the public good (Marwell and Ames 1980; Hampton 1987; Sandler 1992). Free-riding may nonetheless occur in such quasi- dilemmas, but we will not devote much attention to these special cases because their step-level character seems ill suited to campaign contributions to presidential candidates, broad-based interest group membership, attendance at public meetings, civil rights rallies, and other forms of collective action that have attracted the bulk of scholarly attention.[6]

Three factors that should *not* resolve a true social dilemma, according to rational choice accounts, are interpersonal communication, changes in expected collective benefits, and expectations of a finite number of repetitions of the game in the future. Individuals may expose the social dilemma before them, denounce selfish behavior, and exhort others to cooperate. But unless the communication involves side-payments (threats or promised benefits) or brings about other changes in the payoff matrix confronting each actor (as would occur if altruism were engendered by conversation), the rational actor still confronts an overwhelming incentive to defect. Merely coming to grips with the problem of a social dilemma through group discussion is not enough; indeed, absent binding commitments, communication may be regarded with suspicion, since promises are presumably intended to deceive others into cooperating while one defects.

Supplementary collective inducements for cooperation are also predicted to be ineffective. For example, changes in the seriousness of a public problem such as air pollution should have no effect on one's likelihood of contributing money to an environmentalist lobby. This novel and counterintuitive insight stems from the fact that because one enjoys the collective benefits of whatever the lobbying effort accomplishes, regardless of whether one contributes, it pays to free-ride both when the air quality is bad and when it is horrible. A related point is that selective disincentives for defection will prove ineffectual if they are administered in a decentralized way. If, for example, social norms are the mechanism for inducing cooperation, and if violation of these norms is to be punished by individuals who must expend resources in order to scold defectors, then punishing defection itself creates a collective action problem.

Finally, although cooperation is an equilibrium outcome when players value future payoffs and expect to play a social dilemma game repeatedly for an indefinite number of "iterations"—indeed, the so-called folk theorem tells us that virtually any outcome is an equilibrium under such conditions (Fudenberg and Maskin 1986)—iteration does not sustain cooperative behavior as long as participants expect to play a fixed number of times. If, for example, a two-person dilemma were to be played ten times, it might seem advantageous for both players to forgo short-term gains and establish a pattern of cooperative play. The dominant strategy in the tenth period of the game,

---

6. Taking part in such collective activities as these *could*, under sufficiently imaginative conditions, prove decisive to the provision of a public good, and in a strict sense these collective action problems may be called quasi-dilemmas. If, however, one classifies collective action along a continuum ranging from true dilemmas to quasi-dilemmas in which any one person's contribution will prove decisive, it becomes apparent that the kinds of collective action that concern us are very close to the former pole. This, it should be noted, is Olson's view as well (1965).

however, is for each player to defect. Knowing this, each player assumes mutual defection in the tenth period and reasons that the dominant strategy in the ninth period is also defection. This process of "backward induction" eventually leads players to conclude that defection is a dominant strategy in every round of the game. In sum, rational choice theories caution that collective action problems cannot be resolved by communication, consciousness-raising, reliance on collectively supplied side-payments, or iterated play over a fixed number of interactions. We now consider the extent to which these insights comport with empirical observation.

Evidence Concerning Collective Action The classic rational choice argument concerning interest group participation, advanced in Olson's *Logic of Collective Action* (1965), contends that in the absence of coercion or selective incentives to participate, members of large groups will shirk the burden of providing a collective good. Any one person's participation is likely to constitute a negligible contribution to a collective effort. Furthermore, each "would prefer that the others pay the entire cost, and ordinarily would get any benefit provided whether he had borne part of the cost or not" (21). What motivates people to join or support collective causes, according to Olson, is the range of selective incentives that come with participation. In structure, this hypothesis about interest group participation is similar to the one Downs advances concerning voter turnout, except that it is broader in scope, applying "logically" to "all types of lobbies," whether "social, political, religious, or philanthropic" in their objectives (Olson 1965, 159).[7] Not surprisingly, many of the pathologies to be found in the accompanying empirical work are akin to those discussed in the previous chapter.

A peculiar implication of arguing that selective benefits are the key precipitants of collective action is that participation in interest groups becomes incidental to the collective good being pursued. A Christian fundamentalist walking through a park in which two demonstrations are going on simultaneously—a pro-choice rally to her left and pro-life rally to her right—might easily join the former if the refreshments provided were sufficiently enticing, because participation in either movement is unlikely to influence desired policy outcomes, and because she has no incentive to sacrifice the opportunity cost of a good snack for a pro-life policy outcome she would be entitled to enjoy whether or not she aided the pro-life cause.[8]

7. Elsewhere in *The Logic of Collective Action* Olson retreats from this position, arguing that the theory does not apply to "lost causes" consisting of people with a "low degree of rationality" (1965, 161). Olson does not elaborate on how we might identify such people; and since all successful movements that do not offer selective benefits sufficient to offset the costs of participation are on Olson's account destined to collapse, it is not clear how one might go about distinguishing intrinsically lost causes from those that are merely doomed to fail in the long run.

8. In this vein, Olson (1965, 133–34) notes: "An organization . . . may be able to retain its membership and political power, in certain cases, even if its leadership manages to use some of the political or economic power of the organization for objectives other than those desired by

That the rational choice account seems to give rise to counterintuitive scenarios suggests that some version of rational choice theory, if sustained empirically, has the potential to reshape the way we ordinarily think about interest group behavior. Many of the empirical studies addressing Olson's theory, however, are of limited diagnostic value because their authors fail to consider carefully whether the formal requirements of a social dilemma are met in the setting they examine. It may be plausible to argue that "the average person will not be willing to make a significant sacrifice for the party he favors, since a victory for his party provides a collective good" (Olson 1965, 164), but free-riding is by no means the only explanation for inactivity of this kind. For example, it has often been noted by those who study public opinion that a large segment of the American public finds politics distasteful and its attendant policy disputes uninteresting (Campbell et al. 1960; Neumann 1986). Nonparticipation for such people is not so much a matter of shirking as it is indifference, disinterest, or a matter of principle. By the same token, it has been argued that Americans tend not to consider political solutions for problems that affect them (Brody and Sniderman 1977; Hochschild 1981), often mistrust lobbying organizations (Lipset and Schneider 1983), and are reluctant to endorse (let alone participate in) collective protest and other manifestations of pressure politics (Olsen 1968). These kinds of alternative hypotheses are often ignored by Olson and others, like Hardin, who advertise the predictive success of theories that emphasize shirking.

We do not dispute the plausibility of Olson's claim as it applies to collective action in certain economic settings. Broad-based cartels of consumers or successful labor unions that offer no selective incentives are understandably rare, and the free-rider explanation seems persuasive there. But when the focus shifts to political participation, alternative explanations demand more serious consideration, something they seldom receive in Olson's work.[9] In 1965, Olson cited (somewhat ironically, given later developments) such "unorganized groups" as migrant farm workers, taxpayers, and consumers as the "strongest" evidence for his thesis (165–66). Certainly, many factors other than free-riding, such as active opposition from growers, might better explain the difficulties migrant farm workers have encountered in the course of organizing for political and economic purposes (Jenkins and Perrow 1977, 251–52; Tootle and Green 1989). As for taxpayers and consumers, it is not clear from Olson's brief description what sorts of political organizing he had in mind, but it seems clear

---

the membership, since the members of the organization will have an incentive to continue belonging even if they disagree with the organization's policy. This may help explain why many lobbying organizations take positions that must be uncongenial to their membership."

9. Part of the reason alternative explanations do not figure prominently in Olson's work is that not much attention is paid to discrepant cases. As Barry (1978, 29) has noted, Olson "tends to pick the cases which support his thesis rather than start by sampling the universe of organisations of a certain type within certain spatio-temporal boundaries."

that even when given opportunities to advance their putative interests by expressing preferences on ballot measures, these groups prove to be far from like-minded about what their interests are and how they should be pursued (DeCanio 1979; Smith and Bloom 1986). It is not obvious, in other words, how much these unorganized groups tell us about the prevalence of free-riding as opposed to apathy, ambivalence, or antipathy toward politics.

The diffuse and unsystematic way in which potential participants are compared with actual participants allows Olson—and his critics—to project their theoretical presuppositions onto the data. In 1979, Tillock and Morrison offered their case study of Zero Population Growth, a group that attracts members without the use of appreciable selective incentives, as evidence against Olson's thesis. In reply, Olson (1979, 149) interpreted this finding to be "dramatic" confirmation of his thesis, because although surveys imply that "belief in curtailment of population claims tens of millions of adherents," this organization claims a "minuscule" membership of twelve thousand. In some sense, perhaps, virtually everyone belongs to a latent group sharing an interest in a stable world population. That is not the same—vague references to survey data notwithstanding—as asserting that millions are sufficiently committed to this policy to expend significant resources to reduce the birthrate in the absence of a free-rider problem. Nor does it imply that those concerned about this problem believe that political steps can or ought to be taken to reduce the birthrate. And it is a far cry from asserting that people think that Zero Population Growth in particular is likely to be effective in bringing about a decline in birthrates. Once one winnows from the denominator of Olson's ratio the unconcerned, the tentative, and the skeptical, it is simply not clear how much deliberate free-riding goes on.[10]

Although the ratio of actual to potential participants is a crude standard by which to gauge Olson's theory, it seems to be what distinguishes the failure to explain voter turnout from the alleged success in accounting for collective action. To make matters more confusing, one might question whether the participation ratio is the appropriate criterion. As in the case of voter turnout, even a very low *rate* of collective action may nonetheless involve an anomalously large *number* of participants since the point prediction stemming from Olson's account anticipates a participation rate of zero. Mitchell (1979), however, finds that among the million members of environmental

---

10. This ambiguity surfaces in one of the best research efforts in this area, Walsh and Warland's 1983 study of interest group participation in the wake of the Three Mile Island nuclear accident. Walsh and Warland characterize 87 percent of those opposed to the Three Mile Island power plant as "objective free-riders" on the grounds that they opposed TMI but contributed neither time nor money to the local antinuclear organization. Their survey data (774), however, indicate that 26 percent of these supposed free-riders had never heard of the organization; another 8 percent said they had not been invited to participate; 4 percent denied the seriousness of the nuclear problem; and 9 percent were opposed to joining any groups.

organizations, about 100,000 join for reasons that cannot be linked in any plausible way to selective incentives. Comparable if not larger numbers describe individual financial contributions to national election campaigns (Sorauf 1988, 44–47) or protesters who travel long distances to demonstrate in Washington (Walsh and Warland 1983).

Defenders of rational choice accounts finesse the magnitude of these numbers in various ways. Sometimes it is argued that there may exist an irreducible core of irrational activists willing to make sacrifices for a collective purpose (Olson 1965; Hardin 1979; Oberschall 1980; Chong 1991, 160–62). At other times, the issue is skirted and attention directed to an alternative standard, the ratio of potential sympathy to behaviorally expressed sympathy.[11] Hardin (1982, 11), for example, argues,

> What about the apparent contradiction to this logic represented by the Sierra Club and other environmental organizations? The answer . . . is that environmentalists contribute woefully little to their cause given the enormous value to them of success and given the repeated survey results that show the strong commitment of a large percentage of Americans to that cause. Environmentalists annually spend less on their apparently great cause than 25,000 two-pack-a-day smokers spend on cigarettes. The amount spent is a trivium, and one might find it inconceivable except that it makes clear sense on a narrowly rational analysis. One could go on to note even more embarrassing statistics showing how little Americans have spent on such honored causes as civil rights, the contemporary women's movement, gun control (as opposed to anticontrol), and so forth.

Given the skepticism that economists often harbor about verbal, as opposed to behavioral, expressions of preference, this is a peculiar line of defense. How do we know, for example, that environmentalism or civil rights are really "honored causes" in the minds of ordinary citizens? Where private goods are concerned, economists typically instruct us to examine what people actually trade for the advancement of these honored causes. This approach is not feasible for nonmarket goods. Conventional survey measures of opinion (to which Olson and Hardin allude) do not purport to gauge respondents' "reservation prices," that is, the price at which they are indifferent between two states of the world: the status quo, with and without the public good in question. Thus, it is hard to say from surveys just how much people value a given public good, particularly because opinion on matters of race or the environment is notoriously sensitive to variations in question wording and survey context. In recent years, contingent valuation surveys (Mitchell and Carson 1989), which by

---

11. This variant is sometimes termed the "weak" free-rider hypothesis (Marwell and Ames 1979).

design ask respondents to state their reservation prices, have emerged as a method of valuing nonmarket goods. In principle, these surveys are better suited to gauge the extent of free-riding, but in practice they are beset by a host of problems, not least of which is external validity, since respondents are not asked to hand over any money in return for the imagined provision of some public good.[12] As an empirical matter, then, it is far from an established fact that people are holding back resources for causes they value in the hopes that others will pay.

As applied to social movements or interest groups, the comparison between actual behavior and the fund of potential willingness to contribute becomes more ambiguous. Whether a lobbying effort will succeed in altering policy is uncertain, as is the link between policy and outcome. Thus the value an individual assigns to a public good must be discounted by the probability of its realization through some specified course of action. An enthusiastic supporter of environmental protection may be willing to pay as much as $500 to save seabirds from oil spills along the Alaskan coast by fiat, but only a nickel to an organization that purports to champion this cause in Washington, D.C.

To claim, as Hardin and others do, that public goods are underprovided alerts us to a glaring deficiency in the free-riding literature: the lack of a control group in which the corresponding value is provided directly through individual action, thereby eliminating the temptation to free-ride. Those who have described the putative consequences of the collective action problem have seldom designed their research in ways that would identify the causal mechanism at issue, the desire and opportunity to get something for nothing. With reference to the environmental and civil rights concerns Hardin describes, it is arguable that action is relatively rare even when free-riding problems do not exist (for example, warning visitors about telling racist jokes in one's home, applying more costly nontoxic pesticides to the lawn on which one's children play). With respect to political action more generally, it is significant that the rate at which Americans contact government officials in an effort to remedy personal problems is no higher than typical rates of interest group participation (Verba and Nie 1972).

Comparative Statics The importance of control groups is not lost on Olson, who in the empirical chapters of *Logic* analyzes two sets of comparisons: large groups versus small groups and groups that offer selective incentives versus those that do not. The methodological problems with the former comparison have been discussed at length

12. For a review of misgivings about contingent valuation see Mitchell and Carson 1989, 128; Fischhoff 1991; Kahneman and Ritov 1994. Based on the myriad of framing effects that have been found to alter subjects' willingness to pay for public goods, Kahneman and his colleagues have questioned whether it is reasonable to suppose that people possess context-independent values for environmental goods.

elsewhere (Hardin 1982; Isaac, Walker, and Thomas 1984; Taylor 1987; Marwell and Oliver 1993), and since our interest is in mass participation we shall pause only to remark, as others have, that many factors change concomitantly with size besides the stake in the collective outcome and the likelihood of being a pivotal actor. More interesting for present purposes is the latter research project, which analyzes whether the ebb and flow of selective benefits produces changes in aggregate membership.[13]

Case studies of aggregate membership trends in interest groups representing agriculture, business, and labor (Olson 1965, 141, 152) are suggestive in that they seem to show that interest group participation responds to selective incentives, but they do not put the theory to a very demanding test. The null hypothesis that selective incentives have no pull is surely implausible. Few would dispute that, all things being equal, insurance discounts (provided by the Farm Bureau), hunting lodge discounts (National Rifle Association), or free vegetarian meals (Hare Krishnas) enhance the attractiveness of group membership in the eyes of potential participants. A further limitation of this test is that selective incentives are likely to attract members to a group *even when no social dilemma exists*. More people doubtless show up at book club meetings or computer users' groups when caviar and champagne are offered as refreshments, even though deciding whether to participate in such groups does not represent a social dilemma.

It is not so much the prediction that selective benefits matter as the claim that collective incentives do not that provides a compelling test of the theory. Here, studies of aggregate membership patterns run counter to Olson's predictions. Hansen's study of decades of membership figures for the National Association of Home Builders, American Farm Bureau Federation, and League of Women Voters showed that membership rolls increased with collective benefits, and that such "political benefits matter most when groups are threatened" (1985, 93). Imig (1992) finds a similar pattern in his study of the tactics employed by poverty advocacy groups to garner funds after the withdrawal of government subsidies; the most successful tactic was to develop a reputation as a whistleblower and critic of the administration.

Olson's predictions fare no better when the analysis focuses on the decision processes of individuals rather than aggregate trends. Marsh's 1976 interviews with potential and actual members of the Confederation of British Industry showed selective incentives to be but one of several factors influencing the decision to become dues-paying members of the group, particularly for larger firms. Frequently, decision

13. This kind of comparative statics analysis is doubtless a step up from testing the theory by reference to the absolute quantity of collective action observed. Still, the limitations of this type of analysis should be borne in mind. As we argued in Chapter 4 with regard to voter turnout, the fact that incentives matter at the margin would not necessarily imply that the ratio of benefits to costs was greater than unity for each actor. Price-elastic behavior need not be rational behavior.

makers voiced the "irrational" view that they joined the CBI because of its role as a counterbalance to the trade union movement (264). Much the same may be said of Hedges' study of financial contributors to the 1972 presidential campaign (1984), which found that a sense of civic obligation and desire to influence government policy to be among the most widely cited reasons for political involvement. Findings from other studies (summarized in Knoke 1990) are similarly inconsistent with Olson's conjecture that selective incentives matter while collective benefits do not.

It might be said in defense of rational choice theory that individual-level studies of this kind are often beset with what we termed in Chapter 3 pedestrian methodological defects. One may be rightly skeptical of surveys that ask people to recount the reasons behind such actions as joining an organization, particularly when the survey takes place long after the fact. As Olson (1979) notes, no less troubling are surveys that assess the motivations for joining interest groups by sampling only *members* (for example, Mitchell 1979; Tillock and Morrison 1979; Moe 1980; Godwin and Mitchell 1984; Hedges 1984). But this critique cannot be said to vitiate every individual-level study. Walsh and Warland (1983) find that the importance of the collective cause in the minds of potential participants, as gauged by such factors as ideology, affected the decision to act politically in the wake of a nuclear accident. In addition, several studies that do not advertise themselves as tests of the Olson thesis nonetheless speak to the role of collective incentives. Green and Cowden's study of participation in the antibusing movement among whites in Boston and Louisville during the mid-1970s, for example, found that parents of schoolchildren affected by court-ordered busing were significantly more likely to participate than were nonparents, parents living in unaffected areas of the city, or nearby suburban residents (1992). Moreover, respondents who were more passionately opposed to busing prior to the court order were more likely to turn up in antibusing organizations. These findings, in combination with other studies (reviewed in Knoke 1988; Green and Cowden 1992) that also find higher rates of participation among those with more at stake in the collective outcome, cast doubt on the main counterintuitive claim advanced by Olson, namely, that collective incentives fail to generate collective action.

Slippery Predictions and Post Hoc Embellishments It is possible, of course, to preserve a variant of rational choice theory by bending and stretching the conception of rational action to encompass such findings. Muller and Opp (1986, 478; 1987), for example, advertise their survey research–based study of rebellious collective action in New York City and Hamburg as vindicating a version of rational choice theory. In a manner reminiscent of Riker and Ordeshook's post hoc account of voter turnout (1968), Muller and Opp assert that their survey respondents vastly overestimate the effectiveness of their own participation and act rationally on their (unfounded) beliefs about the efficacy of their own participation.[14] Mitchell (1979) advances a similar argument about how people overestimate the importance of their own contribution to an environmental interest group, though he is quicker to attribute this seemingly unfounded belief to the effects of deceptive propaganda. Moe (1980, 205–7), drawing upon his survey of members from five Minnesota farmer and trade associations, gives the clearest statement of the misperceptions thesis:

> Data on the perceptual and value characteristics of members suggest that there also exists a rational basis for politically motivated membership. To begin with, most members believe that their individual contributions *do* make a difference for their group's political success or failure. . . . Between 60 and 70 percent of the members perceive their contributions as having an effect on political outcomes. Many individuals, even if acting purely on the basis of economic self-interest, may therefore find that they have an incentive to join at least partially for political reasons. The uniformity across groups is intriguing because it suggests that perceptions of efficacy may be widespread among group members generally, throughout the group system, and that the average member does not view his contributions as a drop in the bucket.

Leaving aside the fact that none of these studies establishes that an interaction exists between perceived efficacy and the utility a person derives from the collective good, as an expected utility model would suggest (see Chapter 4), it seems not to occur to Moe, Mitchell, or Muller and Opp that *stating* that each person's actions matter might be part of the ideology of political activism. One wonders whether the same impression about the perceived efficacy of individual action would have emerged had the surveys employed more subtle measurement techniques, such as asking the participant merely to describe (in an open-ended format) the changes in the organization and its policy output that would likely result if he or she were to drop out of the group.

Like Downs (1957), Olson (1965, 61) resisted the use of misperception and non-economic incentives to explain why people engage in collective action, contending

---

14. Muller and Opp's empirical results present other anomalies as well. How does the rational choice model explain why an individual is more likely to participate when he or she places a large value on the attainment of the group objective? And why the positive association between perceptions of the group's effectiveness and propensity to participate? Muller and Opp's answer (1987) is that individuals adopt the vantage point of the group and do what is rational from the group's standpoint—a conjecture that flies in the face of the collective action problem described by Olson, in which individuals are deeply committed to the group's goals but opt not to sacrifice their own resources when they may just as well free-ride. Despite their insistence that theirs is a rational choice model, Muller and Opp seem to adopt a nonstandard usage of the term (see Klosko 1987).

that such explanatory devices are both unnecessary and, when adduced in a post hoc \
manner, unscientific. Indeed, it must be said of Olson that, whatever one's misgivings about his theory or the data he offers to support it, he advocates a style of rational
choice theorizing that advances nontrivial and testable propositions. Subsequent
authors, however, have shown less restraint and, like theorists of voter turnout, have
tended to expand what counts as a selective incentive in order to evade problematic
evidence. Accounts of anomalous instances of large scale, uncoerced collective
action have pointed to the entertainment value of protest (Tullock 1971), the utility of
maintaining one's reputation among one's peers (Frank 1988; Chong 1991), or the
expressive benefits of acting on one's convictions or affirming one's moral identity
(Benn 1979).[15] Especially noteworthy in this regard is Moe's contention (1980, 117–
18) that the pursuit of collective goals in itself yields selective benefits:

> Because purposive incentives may be closely tied up with group goals, it is easy
> to make the mistake of assuming that they must derive from the provision of the
> collective good, and hence that they involve the same obstacles to contributing
> that characterize collective goods generally. It is important to be clear about why
> this is incorrect. Individuals can obtain purposive benefits in two ways: when
> collective goods are achieved and when purposive benefits take the form of
> selective incentives. . . . An individual may, for instance, derive a sense of sat-
> isfaction *from the very act of contributing,* when he sees this as an act of support   Moe
> for goals in which he believes. If group policies reflect his ideological, religious,
> or moral principles, he may feel a responsibility to "do his part" in support of
> those policies, and indeed he may consider the free-rider option morally repre-
> hensible. It is not the actual provision of the collective good that represents the
> source of purposive benefits in this case, but the support and pursuit of worth-
> while collective goods.

Interpretations of this sort blur the distinction between rational choice explanation   Amen
and other explanations; indeed, the notions of class consciousness and feelings of
solidarity that animate Fireman and Gamson's critique (1988) of Olson might comfortably fit within Moe's expanded rational choice model. By clothing the null hypothesis in the garb of selective incentives, revisionist models have robbed Olson's
theory of the predictions that make it provocative and testable.

The function of these embellishments on the Olson model is to change the payoffs
associated with political participation so that logic of an n-person Prisoner's Dilemma
no longer holds. Chong (1991), for example, suggests that once a handful of irrational

15. With reference to the civil rights movement, Chong (1991) suggests that when participants in collective protest have an eye toward establishing a reputation among their peers, the
costs of going to jail may actually represent benefits.

activists get a social movement off the ground, collective action is transformed from a Prisoner's Dilemma into an Assurance game, whereby participation becomes more rewarding than abstention.[16] Oberschall (1980) is even less restrained in his account of an NAACP rally in Nashville, appropriating almost every form of post hoc embroidery available: irrational activists, exaggerated sense of personal efficacy, exaggerated sense of the efficacy of the rally, and low participation costs.

What would the various expanded rational choice accounts predict about the behavior of Cheung's laborers? That in the absence of a taskmaster, the decision to pull hinges on the workers' sense of moral responsibility, taste for exercise, or concern for group standing? Whether any of these motives is sufficient to make pulling rational for any particular laborer is difficult to determine empirically. At the aggregate level, the eclectic model is no more testable, because it furnishes a vague prediction about the rate of contribution to the collective endeavor. And as for comparative statics analysis, to integrate Moe's claim that "pursuit of worthwhile collective goods" may furnish selective incentives means that what was once the null hypothesis—the magnitude of collective benefits at stake will influence an individual's likelihood of participating—becomes an outcome predicted by a revised rational choice account.

Revisionist versions of Olson's theory, then, are either post hoc accounts of unanticipated behavior (such as Tullock 1971; Chong 1991), slippery propositions in which the explanatory work done by rationality is difficult to discern (Muller and Opp 1987), or catchall theories that rule out little of what might conceivably be observed (Moe 1980). Although it may be said that the key empirical propositions advanced by Olson are not supported by existing investigations of social movements, the empirical achievements of subsequent rational choice embellishments are no easier to identify. In sum, Mueller's observation in reference to the rational choice literature on revolutionary collective action seems to apply across the board: rational choice theorizing in the wake of Olson has failed to "generate a rich harvest of testable implications" (1989, 175).

EXPERIMENTAL EVIDENCE

One might argue that the research methods by which collective action has typically been studied—survey research and aggregate time-series analysis—are too blunt to dissect the causal mechanisms of mass action. With so many unobserved factors guiding individual decisions to participate in real-world settings as complex as

16. Another way to grapple with the phenomenon of activism is to make activists out to be (optimistic) entrepreneurs or maximizers of some other sort of utility, such as wealth, status, or influence. See Frohlich, Oppenheimer, and Young 1971; Marwell and Oliver 1992; but also see Laver 1980.

a school desegregation crisis, it is possible that these techniques miss the hidden selective incentives that, if observed, would vindicate Olson's account. For that reason, we consider whether laboratory environments, in which these extraneous factors are deliberately minimized, cast a different light on the explanatory value of rational choice theories.

To be sure, laboratory games in which subjects decide between allocating cash to a collective purpose or saving it for themselves are not above methodological criticism. Commentators have called such experiments "contrived" (Walsh and Warland 1983, 765) or have questioned whether subjects (typically college students), who must weigh the decision to cooperate against the temptation of a cash sum seldom exceeding $25, in fact understand the n-person game in which they find themselves (Hardin 1982, 30). Another commonly expressed reservation is that the subjects may be unusually cooperative in lab settings because of a desire to look good in the eyes of the experimenter or of other players (Isaac et al. 1984; Weiss 1991).[17] For these reasons, one should not dwell on the absolute level of cooperation observed in the lab, since this statistic is unlikely to be informative about behavior in real-world settings. A more cautious and justifiable way to interpret laboratory findings is to focus on the differences in behavior across different treatment conditions of each experiment, for here the biases of the laboratory setting are apt to be held constant.[18]

In contrast with the underdeveloped empirical literature on interest group membership and nonelectoral participation, experimental studies of social dilemmas abound. Moreover, unlike observational studies, which tend to speak to theoretical propositions in an oblique or incomplete way, many of the lab experiments are designed to address a sharply focused theoretical question. These experiments may be divided into two categories: those that seek to falsify rational choice propositions by testing whether variables that are predicted to be ineffectual, such as interpersonal communication in a one-shot social dilemma, in fact influence willingness to contribute to a collective cause; and tests that ascertain whether variables expected to affect participation in fact do so.

Effects Inconsistent with Rational Choice Theory From the standpoint of game theory, nonthreatening communication between players who are unable to make binding agreements should have no influence on cooperative behavior in social dilemma situations. Regardless of whether others promise to cooperate, defection is a domi-

17. It should be noted that in most experiments involving just a single play of the game in question, players are not known to one another beforehand; moreover, players are instructed that their moves will be kept secret and that they will be paid in secret (see Dawes et al. 1986, 1175).

18. We take up these issues of internal and external validity again in Chapter 6 when we discuss legislative bargaining experiments.

nant strategy, and hence players who seek to maximize financial gain should always defect. In the game described earlier, in which each of one hundred players could provide everyone with a $1 dividend in return for a $10 contribution, the dominant strategy is to contribute nothing; claiming to do otherwise could be justifiably interpreted as deception. What in fact happens, however, is that experiments in which subjects are permitted to communicate generate much higher levels of cooperation than treatments in which communication is not permitted (Linder 1982). Dawes, McTavish, and Shaklee (1977), for example, found that about 70 percent of the participants in eight-person, one-shot dilemmas defected when no communication was allowed, as opposed to 28 percent when communication was permitted.

It may be argued that "rational altruism" accounts for the communication effect, insofar as communication engenders friendship and a concomitant taste for helping one's acquaintances (Elster 1986b).[19] What makes the communication effect especially interesting, however, is that it only manifests itself when the collective benefits are to go to the group within which the discussion occurs (Schwartz-Shea and Simmons 1990).[20] In an interesting series of experiments, Dawes et al. (1988) divided fourteen subjects into two groups of seven. Each subject was given a $6 note, which he or she could keep or contribute to the group. Contributing the note produced a dividend of $12 to be distributed, depending on the treatment condition, to six of the players in the other group or to the six others in one's own group. When no discussion was allowed, one-third of the subjects contributed to the collective fund, regardless of which group was earmarked to receive it. Allowing discussion produced no change in contributing among those whose donations benefited players outside the group. When contributions remained in the group, however, the rate of cooperation jumped to 69 percent. Lest one think that what is going on reflects merely the process of becoming acquainted with others, growing to like them, and donating to newly acquired friends, Dawes et al. (1977) showed that group conversation unrelated to the allocation problem at hand produces no increase in cooperation.

That individuals who are allowed to communicate cooperate with others in their group, despite the incentive to defect, represents one sort of anomaly. Another anomaly is that even though a social dilemma game features a dominant strategy, and thus any one person's actions should not be affected by the choices made by others, players are indeed sensitive to the behavior of others and to the condition of the

19. Palfrey and Rosenthal (1988, 326) characterize altruism of this sort as an increasing function of the total benefits others derive as a result of one's contribution, as opposed to a set amount of utility derived from the act of contributing itself.

20. Communication effects aside, this rational altruism hypothesis has not fared well in a number of experiments. Van de Kragt et al. (1988), for example, find that neither the number of beneficiaries of an individual's contribution nor the aggregate size of the benefits affects the level of contributions. See also Goetze and Galderisi 1989.

collective good. When confederates planted among the subjects model cooperation or defection, these "norms" carry over into subsequent rounds of iterated (but finite) Prisoner's Dilemmas involving only subject participants (Bettenhausen and Murningham 1991). Schroeder et al. (1983), Samuelson et al. (1986), and Fleishman (1988) find that subjects adjust their behavior in a commons dilemma to the behavior of others, exploiting more when others are reported to have done so. An exception to this pattern occurs when subjects operate within a defined group, in which case group identity tends to produce more cooperation as the commons becomes depleted (Brewer and Kramer, 1986; see also Kramer and Brewer 1984, 1986 for other experimental variants). In a social dilemma game involving contributions to a collective cause (rather than withdrawals from a collective fund), the pattern is reversed, with subjects compensating for the (reported) noncooperation of others by contributing more (Fleishman 1988), a phenomenon observed in nonexperimental studies of neighborhood activism (Oliver 1984). In sum, games that are similar in mathematical form, and thus expected to produce similar outcomes, produce levels of cooperation that vary considerably with the social context in which they take place.[21]

Effects Predicted by Rational Choice Theory What about factors that game theory does predict will be influential? Two interrelated arguments involve side-payments and learning. That the net benefits of contributing matter is in some sense tautological, since changes in the payoffs to each player may transform a dilemma into a nondilemma. Thus, to find somewhat less cooperation in true social dilemmas than in quasi-dilemma games where one has the opportunity to make a contribution that proves critical to the provision of a public good (Palfrey and Rosenthal 1988) is not particularly compelling.[22] The same may be said of experiments (Connolly, Thorn,

21. A brief list of other experiments that reveal effects that are not predicted *ex ante* by rational choice models includes McDaniel and Sistrunk's finding that more people cooperate when told that 50 percent of the other players are not cooperating, as opposed to being told that 50 percent are cooperating (1991); Komorita and Barth's finding that rewarding each player for the cooperative play of others leads to greater cooperation than does punishing each for others' defection (1985); and Ostrom et al.'s discovery that players expend more resources to enforce cooperative behavior by others than expected utility models would anticipate (1992) and Yamagishi's related finding that when players confront a social dilemma but have the opportunity to sacrifice resources in order to punish defectors, they are more likely to cooperate, even though the punishment system itself constitutes a social dilemma (1988).

22. Arguing that the rewards of altruism can make cooperative behavior rational for certain players, Palfrey and Rosenthal (1988) assume the degree of altruism to be an unknown part of each player's utility function. Under these conditions of uncertainty, one player may anticipate enough cooperative play on the part of others to make his or her own cooperation critical. Synthesizing the results of several experiments with different numbers of players and different critical participation thresholds, they find that the higher the expected benefits of cooperation, the more likely one is to adopt this strategy. For contrary findings see below.

and Heminger 1992, experiment one) which suggest that cooperation declines when it is more costly. Because few would dispute that cooperative behavior is to some degree price elastic, this empirical success is not particularly striking.

More engaging are rational choice accounts that introduce side-payments in subtle ways. Sometimes it is suggested, for example, that expectations of future interaction with the same set of players leads rational actors to adopt more cooperative strategies, whether because players wish to protect their reputations within an enduring social group or because players fear reprisals from others for their defection (Axelrod 1984). The former hypothesis, which hinges on incentives other than the monetary payoffs controlled by the experimenter, does not apply to games that subjects play via computer terminals in anonymous isolation from one another. The latter hypothesis, derived from one (of many) equilibrium solutions to iterated two-person Prisoner's Dilemma games, is of dubious application to the n-person context, particularly when players have no information about the defection or cooperation of specific players.[23] Moreover, the folk theorem result suggesting that cooperative outcomes may be Nash equilibria iterated games would not apply to experiments in which subjects are told in advance how many rounds of play will take place (Isaac et al. 1984; Selten and Stroecker 1986; Andreoni 1988).

Although one sometimes encounters the view that iterated play enhances cooperation, more often game theorists reason that cooperation will die out as players come to understand the strategic situation before them and learn the advantages of defection. There does seem to be some basis for this hypothesis, judging from the experiments reported in Isaac, McCue, and Plott (1985), Kim and Walker (1984), and Selten and Stroecker (1986). Other studies, however, reveal behavior patterns unanticipated by the Olson hypothesis that cooperation eventually collapses under the weight of the free-rider problem. Isaac et al. (1984, 129) find that cooperation erodes only when the rate of return to group investment is low, as in Isaac et al. (1985) or Kim and Walker (1984). When the group dividend is high, cooperation does not decline with repetition of a social dilemma game. Even more intriguing is Andreoni's finding that although cooperation declines when social dilemma games are iterated, "restarting" the game leads to an abrupt jump in contributions to the collective good (1988). Similarly, interrupting a repeated social dilemma with a period of communication produces an immediate increase in cooperation (Ostrom and Walker 1991). Iterated play, in other words, seems not to impart a lesson about the inherent advantages of defection.

---

23. Punishing defection effectively in a social dilemma may presuppose that players precommit themselves to an "Armageddon" strategy in which all cooperate unless any one person defects, in which case all defect from that point on. Leaving aside theoretical concerns about whether such strategies could work on paper, it is hard to envision such behavior in real-world contexts.

Rather, players strive to cooperate but apparently become disenchanted by the uncooperative behavior of others (Lowenstein, Bazerman, and Thompson 1989).

Before closing the discussion of how rational choice theory informs the understanding of cooperative play, a word should be said about experiments dealing with quasi-dilemmas, in which one individual's cooperation has the potential to "make-or-break" the provision of a public good. In this situation, cooperation could be rational (in the sense that expected benefits from cooperation might exceed the payoff from defection) if each player believed his or her contribution was likely to put the public effort over the top (Rapoport 1985). To test this thesis, Dawes et al. (1986) placed subjects in a step-level dilemma game in which five of seven players had to contribute $5 apiece in order for all players to receive a $10 bonus. Communication among players was not allowed. In addition to playing the game, each player completed a survey that asked him or her to state the probability that his or her contribution will be insufficient, critical, or redundant. Although twenty-five of the twenty-six defectors perceived the expected value of defection to be higher than that of cooperation, this perception was also true for seven of nine cooperators (1182). Perceived criticalness may marginally enhance cooperation (but see Marwell and Ames 1980; Kerr 1989; Messick and Rutte 1992), but it is apparently not a precondition for contributing behavior.

PLACING APPLICATIONS ON FIRMER FOOTING

The experimental evidence concerning social dilemmas is by no means unassailable. It is debatable whether the special features of the laboratory simulate the choice that people encounter when faced with real-world solicitations for money or time from political interest groups. In defense of social dilemma experiments, one might argue that contributing small sums of money is precisely the choice that continually confronts millions of unfortunate souls whose telephone numbers and addresses wind up in the hands of interest groups, public officials, or political parties. On the other hand, the fact that experimental gatherings of potential contributors are brought together by an outside party, available options are highly regimented, the collective cause lacks ideological content, and face-to-face negotiations tend to take place in demographically homogeneous groups renders uncertain the external validity of laboratory studies.

Rational choice scholars may resist the conclusions of experimental studies on precisely these grounds, but the burden of empirical investigation now shifts to them, particularly those who maintain that rational choice theory should be universal in application. As Ordeshook (1986, 434) has argued, "An adequate theory should be viable in every environment," and thus "we must take seriously negative as well as positive results" obtained under laboratory conditions. It is one thing to speculate about how patterns of strategic behavior change with the setting in which a social dilemma game is played, quite another to undertake alternative experiments that refute previous results or suggest why a theory that fares poorly in the lab might nonetheless work in the real world.

One methodological approach that might improve the external validity of laboratory research while simultaneously retaining the advantages of experimentation is field experimentation. A recent example of this type of research design may be found in Kaplowitz and Fisher's study of response to mail solicitations for contributions on behalf of a statewide nuclear freeze referendum (1985). A sample of petition signers and circulators received one of four solicitations that varied randomly in content, some emphasizing either or both the nonexcludability of this public good and the effectiveness or ineffectiveness of a single contribution to the collective outcome. Although the results of this particular experiment turned out to be ambiguous, the unobtrusiveness and flexibility of this research design merit consideration for future research on contributions, membership, and activism.

In the years since Harold Gosnell's classic 1927 field experiment on canvassing and voter turnout, students of interest groups and social movements have shown little interest in randomized research design. Those who have sought to test rational choice propositions have in fact shown little concern for more rudimentary design requirements, such as the presence of a control group. One essay after the next identifies the *potential* ingredients for a social dilemma in a given situation, be it neighborhood participation in antipoverty programs (O'Brien 1974), community organizing on behalf of toxic waste cleanup efforts (*Harvard Law Review* 1991), or the assassination of unwanted dictators (Olson 1991). Such accounts are then used to explain why collective action collapses in the instances described, without reference to other sufficient explanations.

The most extraordinary example of reasoning from a single sufficient explanation—extraordinary because it seems to turn up in every rational choice literature in political science—is the "rational ignorance" hypothesis. Hailed as one of the great achievements of rational choice theory (Tullock 1962, 337; 1967, 1975, 1979) and as Downs's "most influential contribution" (Noll 1989, 51), this hypothesis holds that "the information-seeker continues to invest resources in procuring data until the marginal return from information equals the marginal cost" (Downs 1957, 215).[24] For a wide array of circumstances in which a citizen's likelihood of influenc-

24. Note that this claim is the opposite of what is sometimes taken to be the nature of rational decision making when rationality is judged solely according to the efficiency with which ends are pursued (without regard for the potentially idiosyncratic or ill-informed beliefs of the actors). Verba and Nie (1972) and Converse (1975), for example, associate rationality with high, rather than low, levels of information.

ing the nature or provision of public goods is small, the marginal costs of procuring information will generally outweigh the benefits. To some, this hypothesis is so self-evident that it is elevated to the status of a premise (Weingast and Marshall 1988, 136). Rational ignorance has been used to account for a diverse array of phenomena, including the failure to punish recalcitrant elected officials (Olson 1990), voters' dim awareness of U.S. House challengers (Aldrich 1993, 262), public ignorance about the principles of economics (McKenzie 1976), and the alleged malleability of public opinion.[25] Noll (1989, 52), for example, asserts:

> Politicians can take advantage of salient issues by being the source of free information to voters on an important issue of the moment. An example from the early and middle 1970s was stagflation; the free information was inefficiency in regulated industries. Indeed a fairly common complaint was that "excessive regulation" was undermining business performance. Rationally ignorant voters, concerned about macroeconomic performance, could be expected to respond to this information by favoring economic deregulation, even though a fully informed analysis might conclude that economic regulation had only a trivial effect on national economic performance.

Sometimes rational choice theorists wrestle with the question of why rational citizens *would* bother to gather pertinent information, positing such factors as the intrinsic enjoyment "fans" receive from learning about sports figures and their favorite teams (Ordeshook 1986, 187; Fiorina 1990). No study of which we are aware, however, attempts to establish empirically that the collective action problem is the mechanism that produces political ignorance.[26]

Instead, the empirical basis for the contention that rationality begets ignorance rests solely on the observation that ignorance about politics is widespread. Very well, compared to what? Widespread ignorance is a common lament even in areas that do not involve collective action problems. Widespread "innumeracy," as it is called, robs its victims of money should they fall prey to medical pseudoscience, gambling fallacies, or stock-market scams (Paulos 1988). "Cultural illiteracy" runs rampant,

25. Lauded inexplicably by Tullock (1979), McKenzie's essay claims support for the theory of rational ignorance on the grounds that students compelled to learn economics later forget the material presented in the course.

26. Popkin (1991) gravitates in the direction of a test when he asserts that more people know their cholesterol level than the names of their elected representatives (24) and that "the proportion of adults who read the labels on food products in any given week is greater than the number who know their congressional representative's name!" (239). If being able to recognize rather than recall the name of one's representative is taken as the standard of knowledge, the first claim may be incorrect. One suspects also that the weekly rate of political news consumption compares favorably with that of food label reading.

despite the many inexpensive opportunities to enrich one's life by learning terms like *a capella, adultery,* and *all that glitters is not gold* (Hirsch 1987, 152–53). Similarly grim appraisals of public knowledge have been advanced regarding topics ranging from hypertension to household safety to negotiating the legal or bureaucratic hurdles necessary to extract government entitlement benefits. When public information pertaining to collective goods is contrasted with information touching on personal concerns, the connection between ignorance and the instrumental value of knowledge is by no means obvious.[27]

The literature concerning rational ignorance is indicative of the casual empiricism that seems to have convinced rational choice scholars that their perspective on collective action offers genuine insight. At the time of this writing, the main source of support for the conventional rational choice account of collective action is the datum that inspired Olson's theory, the rate at which people donate, attend, investigate, or work on behalf of political causes. Probing beneath the absolute level of collective activity for more exacting empirical tests reveals that the empirical basis for the standard rational choice claims derived from the work of Olson is quite thin, either because the relevant tests have not been conducted or because what little evidence exists tends to expose problems with rational choice theories, particularly the provocative implication that collective benefits do not inspire mass action. Were it not for this absolute level of political participation—which, when positive, remains an anomaly for variants of the theory that make no special allowance for altruism— rational choice insights concerning collective action would be no more highly regarded than corresponding accounts of voter turnout. For in neither case has the incentive to free-ride been established as the causal mechanism inhibiting mass behavior.

As for rational choice accounts that augment Olson's theory by expanding the range of values counted as selective incentives, our criticism is not that these theories are inconsistent with the data but the opposite: that these accounts are tautologies or that they merely account in a post hoc fashion for empirical regularities detected by earlier generations of scholars not working within a rational choice framework. Factors that are found to influence participation in collective causes are simply redescribed as incentives, rendering indistinct the predictions of Olson's theory. The ironic consequence of watering down Olson's empirical predictions is that nonpar-

27. One might criticize as well the related proposition that "voters use information shortcuts and cost-saving devices in thinking about parties, candidates, and issues" (Popkin 1993, 34). For one, the null hypothesis that, ceteris paribus, voters seek costly information is not credible. Second, it is not clear why rational voters would willingly incur any cost "to overcome the limitations of their knowledge" (18–19), given that the quality of the election outcome is a public good.

ticipation, once acclaimed as the successful prediction of his theory, is no longer a clear implication of the revisionist account.

Our recommendations for future research on collective action are twofold. First, the task of sampling observations requires much more scrutiny. This literature is dominated by case studies of existing social movements, often focusing on the preferences and beliefs of only those who participate. This sampling technique tends to lead to biased inference (Achen 1986). A better approach would be to study the choice of whether to participate by sampling decision environments that vary with respect to such *independent variables* as collective benefits, selective incentives, and prevailing social norms. Designing and conducting this sort of research is likely to be arduous. On the other hand, it is difficult to imagine how progress can be made without a sharp break from the convenience samples and armchair retrospection that has prevailed in this area to date.

The other recommendation echoes a point raised in Chapter 4, namely, the importance of keeping rational choice explanations analytically distinct from other accounts. Olson's theory of collective action clearly has the potential to explain certain forms of behavior; it is a mistake to broaden the theory to encompass apparent anomalies rather than to devise an empirically testable account of the conditions under which Olson's logic does apply. Many lines of potential demarcation (or gradation) readily come to mind, especially concerning the social context in which participation arises as an actively considered option. With whom and under what circumstances is the decision maker asked to participate?[28] To what extent does the situation encourage decision makers to take cues from the behavior of others? Does the situation make salient the opportunity costs facing the decision maker? Certainly, one could go much farther than this, taking up interpersonal differences in strategic thinking or orientations toward cooperative political activity, and at some point one must consider whether the marginal gains in theoretical texture outweigh the concomitant loss in parsimony. But bearing this limitation in mind, this adjustment in research focus has the potential to inform not only the study of groups and social movements, but also the understanding of when and where strategic thinking is likely to figure prominently in mass politics.

28. One might, for example, expect an interaction between the collective benefits people receive and how they evaluate selective incentives offered by the group. If this were not so, it would not be clear why private entrepreneurs could not undercut the prices of selective benefits (e.g., insurance protection) that interest groups inflate in order to provide revenues for group activities (Hardin 1982, 33–34).

CHAPTER SIX

LEGISLATIVE BEHAVIOR
AND THE PARADOX OF
VOTING

Much of the weakness of rational choice theorizing about voter turnout or collective action stems from the fact that it is difficult to say what the concept of rationality brings to the explanation of the behavior in question. Turnout, which would be irrational if voters sought merely to influence the election outcome, becomes rational when they seek to salve their duty-bound consciences. Cooperation in social dilemma games, which would be irrational if voters were maximizing monetary payoffs and employing dominant strategies, becomes rational when players seek to avoid social disapprobation. Ultimately, rational choice theorizing about these forms of political participation boils down to an assortment of "thick" stipulations about the kinds of gratification people derive from their actions.

By contrast, most spatial models of legislative voting are fundamentally "thin" theories whose principal theoretical propositions flow from the geometric arrangement of voters' preferences vis-à-vis one another, rather than from the particular types of goals legislators seek. Animating much of this literature is a fascination with the potential for disequilibrium in legislative politics. When policies are evaluated over two or more dimensions simultaneously (for example, guns versus butter), it is almost always possible to entice a majority into replacing the status quo with some alternative proposal, which in turn becomes vulnerable to a new majority coalition, and so on. For almost any configuration of legislators' preferences, majority rule is unstable in the sense that policy outcomes may be upset by a new majority coalition. By extension, it is theoretically possible to construct a series of votes from any given policy that will lead to the adoption of any other policy and back again, a phenomenon known as "cycling" (Arrow 1951; Plott 1967; McKelvey 1976; Bell 1978; Schofield 1978, 1983; Cohen 1979; Rubenstein 1979). This is the paradox of voting, which Mueller (1989) in his synopsis of the literature suggests may be *the* intellectual problem in the study of public choice.

We begin this chapter with an illustration and summary of some important features of the paradox of voting in legislatures. This section, which sketches some of the ways that cooperative game theory has been used to model legislative behavior, is intended to introduce readers unfamiliar with spatial models to some terminology and certain key analytic results. In the second section we review the nonexperimental literature on cycling and instability, in which the pathologies of adducing confirming instances, projecting evidence from the theory, and ignoring competing explanations are evident. In the third section, we examine laboratory experiments, which, unlike the corresponding literature on collective action, have primarily been undertaken by defenders of rational choice theory. Here the quality of empirical testing is higher, though serious methodological problems remain. Among the most important is the ambiguous character of tests in which analytic propositions—theorems—are evaluated empirically. We close the chapter by suggesting some of the challenges these methodological problems present for noncooperative game theory, an approach that is rapidly displacing its cooperative predecessor.

INSTABILITY, CYCLING, AND AGENDA-MANIPULATION

Imagine yourself a political scientist sitting on an academic committee whose function is to set professors' salaries. The committee consists of five members and legislates by simple majority rule.[1] The chair of the committee, however, has some special powers under the rules. Only the chair can propose policy changes, which a majority of the committee members may then enact. Moreover, the chair may choose to adjourn the committee meeting at any time, in which case the most recently enacted proposal becomes the policy of the committee. If no policy has been enacted, the decision of the committee reverts to the policy that was previously in force.

To lend the example some texture, suppose that this committee is asked by the provost of the university to make a pair of decisions. The first involves setting the salary for tenured full professors in political science, which presently stands at a meager $70,000. The members of the committee include an astronomer (Professor A), a dramatist (Professor D), and an economist (Professor E), none of whom is particularly enthusiastic about improving the lot of political scientists. Professor A and Professor D both regard the most appropriate political science salary to be $55,000, even lower than the status quo. The economist, the most sympathetic of the three, prefers the status quo. You (Professor B), on the other hand, regard a salary of $95,000 as preferable to all other policy options.

That leaves the chair (Professor C), who, it turns out, is even more enthusiastic

1. For the sake of illustration, assume that abstentions are not permitted, so at least three votes are needed to create a majority.

about raising salaries than you are. For years the chair and the provost have been feuding over academic pay, the latter trying to hold down costs and the former seeking to boost salaries in an effort to attract higher quality faculty to the university. Now, for the sake of illustration, let us assume that this issue is to be decided without regard for other issues, side-payments, threats from the provost, and the like. Moreover, as depicted in figure 6.1, let us assume that each committee member not only has a most-preferred policy or "ideal point" but also finds proposals less and less attractive as they diverge from this ideal point.[2] Specifically, assume that proposals that are equidistant in terms of dollars from one's ideal point are equally preferred. (Readers who find such an assumption at odds with their experiences on academic committees are asked to suspend disbelief for the purposes of this example.) Thus, Professors A and D prefer a proposal of $60,000 to $65,000 and are indifferent between $40,000 and the status quo, $70,000.[3] Finally, let us assume that each committee member always votes for the policy option that he or she most prefers, a behavioral assumption termed "sincere voting."[4]

The chair opens the meeting and proposes that political science salaries be raised from $70,000 to $80,000. The motion is defeated by nays from Professors A, D, and E. The chair invites you and Professor E into the corner of the meeting room for a chat. There you and the chair try to enlist Professor E's support for a compromise proposal of $75,000. No deal. Professor E informs you that he cannot be made any happier than he currently is under the status quo and that, furthermore, *any* attempt to raise salaries will automatically incur opposition from Professors A and D. As things stand, further negotiations seem futile. Professor E's strength comes from his position as the so-called "median voter" when the five committee members are arrayed along a single policy dimension (that is, how much to raise or lower political scientists' salaries).[5] Regardless of whether the chair proposes to raise or lower salaries, Professor E can always sustain his preferred policy by forming a majority coalition

2. Note that this assumption ensures what is called "single-peakedness," or the assumption that a utility function has one maximum and that proposals arrayed along a policy dimension steadily diminish in value as one moves to the right or the left away from the most preferred policy.

3. We have, in other words, assumed that circular indifference contours describe the preferences of the committee members. This assumption, which makes for a more tractable illustration, remains in force throughout the example as we consider preferences over two dimensions: political scientists' and economists' salaries.

4. We discuss the implications and defensibility of this assumption below.

5. In an electorate of N voters, N being odd, the median voter is the Kth voter in the electorate counting from the left of a unidimensional policy continuum, where

$$K = \frac{N + 1}{2}.$$

Note: Salaries in thousands of dollars.

Figure 6.1. Voter Preferences for Political Scientist Salaries

with the other two committee members who stand to lose from the policy change (Black 1958).[6]

In an effort to create internal divisions within the coalition of Professors A, D, and E, the chair tables the issue of political science salaries and raises the other charge of the committee, to set salaries for associate professors of economics. This move worries you, because it also exposes a difference of opinion between you and the chair: you would like to lower economists' salaries from their current level of $80,000 to $55,000, while the chair would like to raise them to $100,000. Indeed, the other three committee members fall between you and the chair on this matter. The two-dimensional representation of the committee's preferences, with political science salaries on the horizontal axis and economists' salaries on the vertical, shows that Professors A, D, and E represent a plausible coalition (fig. 6.2).

Again, Professor E, whose ideal point occupies the median position in the committee ($80,000), proves an immovable obstacle to change when the chair proposes to raise the salaries of economists. This is rather good news for you, since you side with Professor E when it comes to holding the line on economists' academic income. It looks as though the status quo will continue to prevail in the foreseeable future when the chair decides to try a new tactic, proposing a package that includes $10,000 pay hikes for *both* economists and political scientists. Naturally Professor E doesn't like the proposal and defeats the motion with help from A and D. It is at that point that Professor E alerts the chair to the fact that the status quo point constitutes a "core," or majority rule equilibrium, insofar as no majority coalition of sincere voters has an incentive to back an alternative proposal that is paired against Professor E's ideal point.[7] Further proposals by the chair are futile, and so the meeting adjourns.

6. Notice, incidentally, that the model supposes that there are no transaction costs for dumping one set of coalition partners for another. Nor do players receive special benefits or incur costs from forming alliances with certain coalition partners.

7. For a discussion of the core and cognate terms, see Ordeshook 1986. Zagare (1984, 76) offers this terse characterization of the set of proposals that comprise the core: "No individual or group has both the opportunity and the incentive to overturn a social arrangement if the imputation arrived at is in the core." Strictly speaking, the core is a set and "exists" even when it is empty. We will follow the more colloquial usage of the term and say that a core does not exist

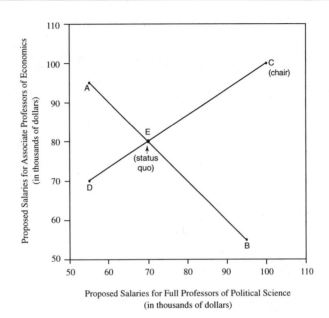

Figure 6.2. Preference Configuration for Faculty Salary Committee

Shortly thereafter, Professor E retires from the university and hence the academic salary committee. The vacancy on the committee affords the provost an opportunity to tighten her grip on salaries, and she appoints another economist (Professor E′) who is even more frugal when it comes to the pay of political scientists. You fear the worst when the committee meets again, because Professor E′, like his predecessor, bears the mantle of median voter along each of the two salary dimensions (see fig. 6.3). Thus, if the chair offers proposals that involve a single issue at a time—changes to political scientists' salaries or economists' salaries but not both—the ideal point of Professor E′ will represent the median-in-all-directions, otherwise known as the stable point.

Unbeknownst to you, however, the chair has brushed up on spatial voting theory since being rebuffed by Professor E. Rather than take up the two salary issues one at a time and end up at the ideal point of E′ (Kramer 1972),[8] the chair proposes a

---

to describe core sets that are empty. Here, since the proposal power of the chair limits the opportunity for change, the core consists of outcomes along the line segment connecting the ideal points of E and C.

8. Note that because the indifference curves are assumed to be circular (so that a dollar change in salary yields the same change in utility regardless of whether the salaries of political scientists or economists are in question), the stable point would be the outcome even under sophisticated voting.

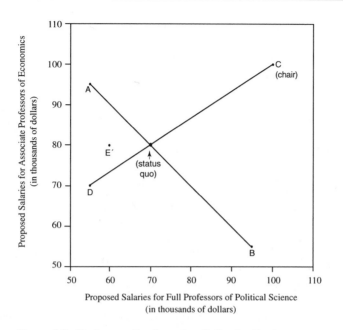

Figure 6.3. Preference Configuration Following Replacement
of Voter E with Voter E'

surprising policy change that nonetheless pleases Professors A, D, and E': a cut in
political science salaries coupled with a somewhat lesser increase in pay for economists (see fig. 6.4).[9] As this proposal passes, much to your dismay, it would appear
that the chair has caved in to the new balance of preferences, bringing to fruition the
provost's plan to cut salaries. Unexpectedly, the chair throws you a bone by proposing
a further salary boost for both departments (from point 1 to 2), which you enact with
votes from Professor A and the chair. The good news continues, as the chair now
moves to cut economists' salaries while increasing those of their political science
counterparts (from point 2 to 3), a motion passed with support from you, D, and the
chair. Your excitement quickly subsides, though, when this proposal is supplanted by
the steepest increase yet in salaries for economists coupled with a reduction for your
own colleagues, point 4, which gains the support of Professors A, E', and the chair.
The tables turn sharply in your favor when, with help from the chair and Professor D,
proposal five passes. As figure 6.4 shows, the battle between the two coalitions {B, C,
D} and {A, C, E'} produces policy swings that become increasingly radical, so that by
proposal eight economists are making more than $115,000; when proposal nine
passes, political scientists are finally making six figures! Proposal ten, however,

9. Note that while all *voting* is assumed to be sincere, we allow the agenda-setter to propose
policy changes that run counter to his or her interests.

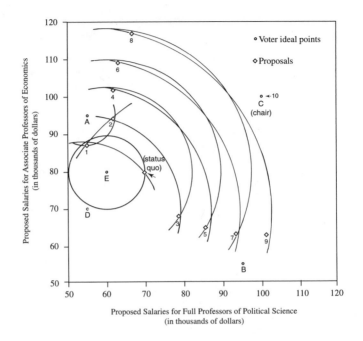

Figure 6.4. Agenda Manipulation and Faculty Salaries

reveals what the chair is up to: pitted against proposal nine, the chair's own ideal point wins the support of voters A and E'. In spite of the provost's efforts to stack the committee, the policy enacted proves to be anything but frugal. When the meeting adjourns, you find yourself worse off than before the meeting, for despite the substantial increase in pay for political scientists, economists received large pay raises as well.

Reviewing the proceedings of the committee reveals how the chair was able to bring about this wholesale shift in policy. Table 6.1 converts the circuitous trajectory of proposals presented in figure 6.4 into a more intelligible set of ordered rankings. The status quo and the ten policy proposals are ranked according to the preference schedules of the five committee members. The higher the proposal on the list, the more valued it is to a committee member. Inspection of the preference orderings reveals that among the eleven policy options there exists no Condorcet winner or option that beats all others in pairwise competition.[10] Hence, proposal one defeats the status quo with a coalition of {A, D, E'}. In the ensuing vote, {A, B, C} replace this policy with proposal two, which in turn loses to proposal three, which is backed by a

10. Before E' replaced E, the status quo was a Condorcet winner.

Table 6.1. Preference Schedule for Voters on Faculty Salary Proposals

Professor A	Professor B	Professor C	Professor D	Professor E'
2	9	10	1	1
1	7	Status quo	Status quo	Status quo
4	5	9	3	2
Status quo	3	8	2	4
6	Status quo	7	5	3
8	10	6	4	6
3	2	5	7	5
5	1	4	6	8
10	4	3	9	7
7	6	2	8	10
9	8	1	10	9

coalition of {B, C, D}. From that point on a coalition of {A, C, E'} alternates with {B, C, D} to enact policies four through ten.

What makes this outcome especially noteworthy is that proposal ten would have lost if paired against any of the other proposals except nine. Indeed, every member of the committee except the chair was better off under the initial status quo than under the eventual outcome. Why, then, would they fall for the sequence of moves culminating in proposal ten? Surely this sort of "myopic" or "unsophisticated" behavior seems, in retrospect, inimical to committee members' interests and in that sense irrational.[11] Recall, however, how the sequence of events looked from Professor B's vantage point. Professor B lacked a clear sense of where the sequence of proposals would stop and, indeed, after the first two votes, was repeatedly presented with irresistible incentives to vote against the prevailing status quo. It may be that a prescient Professor A might have figured out the chair's plan and resisted the move from point 1 to point 2. On the other hand, the chair had hardly seemed rational when he offered proposal one rather than adjourning the meeting and retaining the preexisting status quo; this line of reasoning might have impelled Professor A to play along with proposal two (which is worse for C than the preexisting status quo) in the hopes

11. Ordeshook (1992) suggests that rational choice theories may be agnostic concerning the question of whether to expect sincere or sophisticated voting. See Denzau, Riker, and Shepsle's discussion of how legislators acting within a representative institution may vote sincerely because it may be difficult to explain sophisticated roll call votes to their constituents (1985). See also Krehbiel and Rivers' analysis of the information required for sophisticated voting strategies (1990).

that something even better would be proposed by the quirky chair.[12] Furthermore, Professor A might have thought, "Why should I sacrifice the potential gains of moving from point 1 to point 2 just to keep Professors D and E' happy, especially since I have no clear sense of what subsequent proposals, if any, will be placed on the agenda?" The long-run costs to Professors A, D, and E' for failing to stand pat with proposal one seem clear in hindsight, but the prospect of short-term gain to any defector presents a threat to the coalition.[13]

This example illustrates several points in relation to spatial voting models in which an odd number of legislators operate under simple majority rule and side-payments are not allowed. First, it illustrates the power of the median voter when choices involve only one dimension and voters have single-peaked preferences. As long as voters cannot make side-payments, the median voter's ideal point will be in the core; if proposed, it cannot be defeated by any other proposal in paired voting. Single-dimension models, however, fail to describe many (perhaps most) political settings. Questions of redistribution, for example, may involve as many dimensions as there are financial winners and losers (Ordeshook 1992). When issues involve multiple dimensions but sincere voting takes place only on one issue at a time, the median voter's ideal point on each dimension, or parliamentary stable point, prevails. This result, which presupposes restrictions on logrolling and strategic behavior on the part of legislators trying to maximize utility over many dimensions, will play an important role in theories of "structure-induced" equilibrium, which will be discussed later.

But very unrealistic constraints

A majority rule equilibrium may exist when more than one issue is considered simultaneously, as in figure 6.2. A non-empty core, however, requires that a very special kind of symmetry exist among legislators' ideal points (Plott 1967) when the voting body consists of a large or odd number of voting members (Enelow and Hinich 1983). Notice that in figure 6.2, Professor E was located precisely at the intersection of the line segments connecting the ideal points of Professors C and D and Professors A and B. Although this configuration gives rise to an equilibrium, such special alignments are both rare and fragile. McKelvey (1976) has shown that in theory the *entire policy space* becomes part of a cycle set given "the slightest deviation from the

12. For a similar problem of strategic thinking under seemingly irrational play by one's opponent, see Ordeshook's exegesis of Rosenthal's centipede game (1992).

13. In experimental committees (see below) Herzberg and Wilson (1988), Wilson and Pearson (1987), and Cohen, Levine, and Plott (1978) find that even in settings where the advantages of strategic voting are more transparent than the example given here, sincere voting nonetheless prevails. Eckel and Holt (1989), for example, found that over a sequence of committee decisions their subjects had to play through the same voting agenda at least three times before venturing to cast a strategic ballot. Herzberg and Wilson's review of the quasi-experimental literature (1988) suggests that strategic voting may be rare as well in actual legislatures, confined to situations in which the agenda is relatively simple and known in advance, a thesis elaborated by Krehbiel and Rivers (1990).

conditions for a Condorcet point (for example, a slight movement of *one* voter's ideal point)." When Professor E left the committee, not only was it possible to get from the preexisting status quo in figure 6.4 to the chair's ideal point, but any destination would have been feasible. By the same token, a committee could "cycle" from any such outcome back to its starting point.

To say that a configuration of preferences lacks a core implies that a majority coalition can always be formed to supplant the status quo. Because the existence of a core or Condorcet winner requires a special configuration of preferences, it is commonly said that majority rule is "generically unstable" (Schofield 1983). Moreover, since an unstable committee can be led from one point to any other, it follows that a skillful agenda manipulator, such as Professor C, could in principle generate any potential outcome. Naturally the expectation that the other committee members will vote sincerely makes it easier for the chair to manipulate the outcome, but even sophisticated voting (insincere voting designed to protect one's interests against the adverse affects of subsequent votes) may not altogether prevent successful agenda-manipulation (Banks 1984). Even if not manipulated, majority rule outcomes are by this account arbitrary, reflecting the particular circumstances by which one majority coalition happened to overthrow another.

What makes this perspective on committee behavior intriguing is not only its depiction of the inherent indeterminacy and manipulability of simple majority rule, and hence the important challenge it presents for democratic theory (Riker 1982).[14] No less intriguing is the fact that predictions can be made that run counter to one's intuition about political power. In the preceding example, the provost was better off before she disrupted the majority rule equilibrium by appointing a new member more sympathetic to her views, even though none of the other members of the committee changed their preferences or the strategic calculations underlying their votes. Clearly, this perspective on legislative behavior brings something new and potentially important to the analysis of committee decisions. Now the question becomes an empirical one: as we move from theory and illustration to empirical applications, to what extent does this way of analyzing committees aid our understanding of legislative behavior?

FROM CYCLES ON PAPER TO CYCLES IN THE WORLD

The notion that majority rule is inherently unstable has spawned two very different research agendas. The first, led by William Riker, seeks to demonstrate the ubiquity and severity of majority rule instability. Like Dobra (1983, 242) and others who characterize the symptoms of cycling as "endless voting and manipula-

14. Miller (1983, 738) summarizes the rational choice theorists' interpretations of these generic instability results, the most common of which are that majority rule is arbitrary or internally contradictory.

tion," Riker (1982, 188) infers from the analytic results of McKelvey (1976) and Schofield (1978) that "wide swings in political choices are possible and expected" and that the outcome produced by continually shifting majorities depends merely on "how clever and skillful people stop the process to their advantage" (1986, 146). To Riker (1982, 190–91), instability is much more than a theoretical possibility.

> An equilibrium of tastes and values is in theory so rare as to be nonexistent. And I believe it is equally rare in practice. But individuals in society are not ambulatory bundles of tastes. They also respect and are constrained by institutions that are intended to induce regularity in society. And it is the triumph of constraints over individual values that generates the stability we observe. But tastes and values cannot be denied, and they account for the instability we observe. . . .
>
> No one doubts that there is occasional stability in the real world. Sometimes this stability is more apparent than real, for there are cycles of similar alternatives and disequilibrium moves from one outcome to another by increments so minute that political life seems stable even though it is not. But sometimes stability is real, and it is imposed by institutions not the product of preferences and values. If we consider only values, then disequilibrium seems inherent in majority rule. *Anything* can happen—incremental change or revolution.

The generic instability of majority rule, in other words, is a proposition consistent with any pattern of empirical observation about policy making: no change, incremental change, and radical change.[15] It is unclear, therefore, what potential observations would test the predictions of this model, insofar as it predicts that "anything can happen." Stable policies or coalitions would seem to disconfirm the hypothesis that majority rule begets instability, but Riker cautions us not to be misled by this kind of evidence. The absence of observed policy change may be a result of poor measurement, as in the case of "minute" change. Or it may be dismissed as momentary stability imposed by institutional constraints or clever agenda manipulators. In the long run, Riker contends, the latent instability of the reigning majority position will be exploited by political actors who stand to gain from building a new winning coalition, and significant policy change will occur. Indeed, if institutional constraints

15. Ordeshook (1986, 352) is a shade less equivocal, arguing that while the absence of a core does not render outcomes wholly unpredictable, "fundamental instabilities exist." Other textbook treatments of the subject, such as Zagare (1984, 78), go further still: "The existence or nonexistence of a core is arguably the most important characteristic of an n-person game. Games that have a core . . . are likely to evolve in a predictable and determinate way once (and if) an imputation in the core is reached. On the other hand, games without a core . . . are likely to be characterized by perpetual flux, as unsatisfied coalition after unsatisfied coalition attempts to overturn the existing order."

stand between an incipient majority and its aims, the institutional practices themselves may be suspended or overturned (Riker 1980).

Establishing the premise that legislative preferences are typically cyclical in nature has been an important focus of applied rational choice scholarship. Riker (1965, 1982, 1986) and Blydenburgh (1971) led the way in identifying historical instances in which cyclical preferences and the opportunity for manipulation existed. Their findings, though rarely cited outside rational choice circles, have turned up in numerous texts on game theory and spatial modeling and are therefore well known among rational choice theorists. Seldom, however, have the details of these historical case studies come under scrutiny. To assert the prevalence of cyclical preferences, as Riker does, by reference to certain "spectacular" examples immediately calls to mind methodological concerns about sampling procedures and extrapolation from small numbers of cases. These misgivings, however, are in some ways eclipsed by other questionable features of these historical narratives—in particular, their inattentiveness to competing explanations and their tendency to project confirming evidence from the theory.[16]

Consider one of Riker's favorite illustrations of how clever parliamentary tactics may capitalize on the existence of cyclical preferences. On several occasions (1965, 1982, 1986), Riker and those inspired by his account (Ordeshook 1986; Strom 1990) have drawn attention to the history of legislative activity that culminated in the Seventeenth Amendment to the U.S. Constitution, which mandates direct election of senators. Riker argues that although this issue initially involved discrete alternatives along one dimension (for or against amending the Constitution) for which the required two-thirds majority existed, a clever conservative tactician killed the legislation in 1902 by inserting an amendment in Senate committee that would have authorized federal oversight of statewide elections. When brought to the floor nine years later, the amendment passed with support of Republicans but alienated Southerners, who, though sympathetic to direct election, were compelled by their hostility to federal intervention to provide the necessary votes to scuttle the proposal as amended. This sequence of events is read by Riker to indicate a cycle: the amended proposal (call it *a*) was majority-preferred to the unamended proposal (*b*), which was majority-

16. The very nature of inferring cyclical preferences may open the door to this kind of projection. As Weisberg and Niemi (1972, 205) have noted, "In most situations it is impossible to tell whether the paradox has actually occurred. . . . Legislative voting generally does not provide complete information about the choices available. For example, when a legislature votes to adopt an amendment to a bill and then the amended bill is defeated, the legislature does not go back to determine whether the unamended bill would have passed. The result of the vote which was not taken has been inferred in a few historical instances (Riker 1958, 1965), but rarely is there sufficient information to reconstruct that vote with confidence."

preferred to the status quo (*c*), yet the status quo prevailed over the amended proposal. This ploy, according to Riker, delayed passage of the Seventeenth Amendment for a decade.

Whether in a deliberate effort to make the strongest possible case for his thesis or in an unwittingly biased survey of the historical record, Riker omits several discordant facts from his reconstruction of events. From 1902 on, the committee on Privileges and Elections consistently refused to report to the floor *any* version of the direct elections proposal. Motions to discharge the matter from the committee were defeated by a floor vote in 1902, and efforts to assign the resolution to the more sympathetic Judiciary committee also went down to defeat, in 1908. This pattern of events suggests that delay is more plausibly attributed to footdragging by an unsympathetic committee and floor majority than to agenda manipulation by a cabal of northeastern Republicans.

As for whether a voting cycle existed when a vote was finally taken in February 1911, Riker's story is tangled in contradictions. Critical to Riker's account of how the federal control amendment passed is the premise (1986, 15) that "no Republican would wish or dare to vote for a motion unfriendly to blacks—and a motion to delete the DePew [*sic*] amendment would, of course, be regarded as unfriendly." Yet at the same time Riker also assumes (1986, 16) that all senators who voted for the proposal as amended (*a* versus *c*) would have voted for the unamended states' rights version (*b* versus *c*). Judging from declarations made on the Senate floor by Republicans who could not brook a states' rights provision, the latter assumption is probably incorrect (Haynes 1938, 111), particularly if, as observers suggested at the time, some GOP senators voted yes on the final bill because they knew it would not have sufficient votes to pass (Easterling 1975, 500). In sum, support for the final proposal fell short by five votes (Haynes 1938, 112).[17] Judging from the floor debates and roll call votes in 1902, 1908, and 1911, it seems unlikely that the states' rights variant of the direct election proposal would have attracted enough Southerners to offset the loss of Northern support.

Whether or not one accepts Riker's narrative of this or other putative cycles, one may well be in sympathy with the general thrust of Riker's argument, namely, that

17. Riker (1965, 1982, 1986) believed support to be three votes short of passage in part because his vote tallies from February 1911 are each incorrect. Some other facts reported by Riker are a bit garbled, including the claim that the coalition of Southern opposition was led by John Sharp Williams of Mississippi, who was not a member of the Senate at the time (1986, 16). Also in error is Riker's epilogue: "In June 1911, the Democrats had a clear majority and defeated the Sutherland amendment, so the constitutional amendment passed. Thus the cycle was broken, but it had lasted more than ten years" (1982, 287). Actually, the Democrats did not become the majority party in the Senate until the session beginning in March 1913. The Sutherland amendment was not considered in June, and its successor, the Bristow amendment, did in fact win passage.

parliamentary "contrivance" at times forestalls or defeats the will of the majority. This thesis, while frequently an upshot of spatial models, is of course not an innovation of rational choice theories. Before the advent of rational choice models of legislative politics, astute observers of Congress (for example, Gross 1953, 218–22, 356) had called attention to the tactics of "crippling" or "defensive" amendments, as well as to various other backroom maneuvers or means of parliamentary obstruction. What seems to separate this traditional literature from rational choice interpretations is subtle but nonetheless important. In comparison with traditional narratives, Riker's accounts—like so many rational choice models that dwell on the strategic incentives that actors face rather than their varying cognitive capacities to recognize and seize upon the opportunities before them—place enormous emphasis on strategic coups and assign little weight to shortsightedness and blunder. For those skeptical of rational choice theorizing, the issue is not whether politicians are clever but whether events are reconstructed with descriptive balance. With regard to the Seventeenth Amendment, one may object that Riker, in the course of stressing the stratagems that rational actors developed to achieve their aims, downplays or ignores the pivotal role played by miscalculation or strategic myopia. It is, after all, not Depew (or Lodge or Hale) who proposed the amendment specifying federal control over elections in February 1911, but Sutherland, a sincere supporter. Later in this chapter, when we examine the experimental literature on legislative behavior, we will return to the theoretical complications that arise for spatial models when strategic talent is distributed unequally among legislators.

Our misgivings about the empirical basis for the paradox of voting concern not only the construction of historical narratives but the selection of cases to narrate. A fundamental inference problem hangs over the sampling technique of adducing snappy illustrations of cycling in Congressional history. It would not be clear even to a rather sympathetic reader, for example, on what grounds Riker (1982, 195) could claim the Seventeenth Amendment to be no "isolated example of manipulation, but a typical instance of electoral and democratic politics." Even if one accepts Riker's idiosyncratic narratives, he and others gathered at most a small handful of historical cases. And far from being selected at random, these were adduced as confirming instances of the paradox of voting; disconfirming instances, such as the strategically ill-conceived Smith Amendment to the 1964 Civil Rights Act (Mezey 1992), receive no mention. Indicative of this lack of concern for sampling is Riker and Weingast's survey of thirty-eight years of Congressional history (1988). Three instances of cycles or agenda-manipulation turn up and, in combination with one cited from earlier work, furnish "evidence that the majority rule constraint does not drive legislative choice toward some unique policy." From what population were these cases drawn? Were they sampled in ways that would make them broadly representative of Congressional decisions?

Overshadowed by the issue of how frequently cycles occur is the more significant causal question of whether the existence or nonexistence of a majority rule equilibrium generates observable differences in political outcomes. Approaching the issue this way suggests a quasi-experimental research design, in that it treats the existence or nonexistence of a core as the independent variable and the degree of policy stability as the dependent variable.[18] For example, one might ask whether, holding preferences constant, an exogenous change in institutional arrangements (such as increasing the size of the majority required to pass a motion) thought to induce a core leads to greater policy stability.[19] If it should turn out that similar degrees of instability obtained regardless of a theoretically predicted change in institutional arrangements or preference configurations—a null hypothesis to which we shall return in the next section—we would be led to question the empirical payoff from the vast literature focusing on the existence and compass of legislative equilibria.[20]

Our survey of the empirical literature in this area turned up very little in the way of comparative analysis of institutions and policy stability. Extant work tends to be cursory and unsystematic. Riker (1992), for example, has argued that in Britain, which now has an effectively unicameral system governed by something close to majority rule, massive changes in economic policy—nationalizations and denationalizations of major sectors of the economy—have occurred twice since 1945, whereas in the United States, with its functioning bicameralism, changes of this order have been enacted but not reversed. He explains this alleged difference by arguing

18. We hesitate to call this comparative research design a comparative statics analysis, since one would not assess how the location of equilibrium changes under different circumstances, but rather how the existence or nonexistence of equilibrium affects outcomes.

19. In formulating this hypothesis, one must be careful to avoid tautology. If a unique retentive equilibrium exists, then by definition no coalition has both incentive and opportunity to depart from it. Further, if rationality is taken to be a behavioral postulate, not an empirical conjecture, then by construction such an equilibrium guarantees no policy movement; any movement away from the equilibrium would indicate that one's assessment of the factors thought to give rise to an equilibrium was in error. To translate this hypothesis into a meaningful test, the conjecture must focus on the effects of changing institutional arrangements rather than on the existence or nonexistence of an equilibrium. The effects of the latter may be inferred analytically; the former involves empirical conjectures about the correspondence between institutional rules and individual incentives.

20. We focus here on the institutional variables that might affect the location or existence of the core. As we pointed out in our introductory example, the configuration of preferences is itself an independent variable insofar as it determines the existence and location of the core. Rational choice theorists have been reluctant to rely on preference configuration when making empirical predictions because the conditions necessary to induce a core are regarded as very stringent. Riker, for example, warns that disequilibria of tastes are endemic, arising even when preferences seem to be unidimensional (1982, 1993).

that unicameral parliaments are comparatively more susceptible to cycles. Yet he simply ignores major legislative reversals that have occurred in the United States since World War II (such as those embodied in successive amendments to the Wagner Act or the passage and subsequent reversal of catastrophic health insurance legislation in 1988 and 1989) and major pieces of social legislation that have not been repealed in Britain (such as the creation of the National Health Service). He offers no account of which criteria were employed to determine the sample of legislation, nor of how apparently anomalous observations (of the occurrence or nonoccurrence of repeals in his two cases) square with his cross-institutional comparison.

This kind of casual empiricism does not begin to address the complex problems of inference that arise in comparative research. For even if one were to select a pair of institutions that were more closely matched in terms of party system and political culture (for instance, a historical comparison of unicameralism in nonpartisan Nebraska versus bicameralism in nonpartisan Minnesota), policy instability might result from any number of sources beyond those generic to simple majority rule. A long but no doubt incomplete list of such factors includes changes in legislators' underlying preferences within a legislative session, changes in membership (hence preferences) between sessions, side-payments or logrolling opportunities, and changing beliefs about the effects of a proposed policy. Rational choice theory may be credited with positing a mechanism for policy change that does not stem from changes in tastes or beliefs, but suggesting this hypothesis is a far cry from showing that the generic instability of majority rule generates observed policy change, net of other factors.

In sum, the generic instability of majority rule is a topic that reflects the imbalance between theory and empirical research. The hypothesis that legislative preferences tend to be cyclical and subsidiary propositions about agenda manipulation and policy instability represent potentially interesting claims, but what these insights amount to as an empirical assertion remains unclear. Few would take exception to a modest variant of this hypothesis, one stating that instability and manipulation are *possibilities* under simple majority rule. It is the more ambitious and interesting conjecture—that variation in the structure of institutions affects the degree of observed stability and agenda-based power—which calls for close investigation of the link between various institutional structures and their policy outputs. The latter has not gotten off the ground as an empirical research endeavor. To be sure, rational choice theorists have advanced the analytic study of institutional structure, producing, for example, penetrating expositions of procedures such as Congressional amendment rules (compare Ordeshook and Schwartz 1987). The full value of these kinds of detailed accounts of the formal properties of institutions, however, can be realized only when augmented by empirical studies investigating the causal influence of institutional structures on legislative behavior.

[handwritten marginal note: "modest acceptance of possibility vs. 'pervasive'"]

POST HOC ACCOUNTS OF STABILITY

As noted earlier, there are two strands of empirical research on instability of legislative outcomes. Riker's seeks to establish that instability is more than a
theoretical possibility, that it is in fact pervasive.[21] The other research agenda contends that instability is scarcely more than a theoretical possibility, that it is in fact
rare. The underlying premise of the latter perspective is expressed by Tullock (1981,
189): "Without the most improbable conditions endless cycling would be expected.
This is particularly true when logrolling is present as it normally is. If we look at the
real world, however, we observe not only is there no endless cycling, but acts are
passed with reasonable dispatch and then remain unchanged for very long periods of
time. Thus, theory and reality seem to be not only out of contact, but actually in sharp
conflict."

For Tullock this conflict indicates not that spatial models of legislative behavior
rely on a flawed set of assumptions about the inclinations and strategic capacities of
legislators, but that new theoretical accounts should be promulgated to explain stability by reference to hitherto unappreciated facets of the strategic setting. Thus there is
an interesting division of labor among rational choice scholars. While Riker adduces
confirming instances of instability, others, such as Tullock, start with the premise that
instability is rare and produce post hoc accounts of stability.

Before discussing the many ways that rational choice theorists have proposed to
explain stability, we pause to note that Tullock's synopsis of legislative behavior "in
the real world" is based on no identifiable survey of policies, periods, or legislatures.
It is not clear what Tullock has in mind by the key terms "unchanged" or "very long
periods of time," nor is it clear how this sweeping characterization of democratic
policy making copes with the changes in defense budgets, health policy, immigration
laws, or regulatory legislation that have occurred since World War II. Especially
troublesome in this regard are transient policies, such as Nixon's wage and price
controls, that emerge and disappear out of sync with shifts in popular sentiment (Page
and Shapiro 1983, 180). As for the claim that acts are passed "with reasonable
dispatch," one may say that this generalization doubtless applies to some types of
legislation but can hardly be said to apply to such issues as campaign finance reform,
which languish for decades. Even when legislatures are assigned a specific task and
given a deadline (for example, statehouse elections of U.S. Senators prior to 1913),
the result is at times deadlock and inaction.

Rather than argue for a more variegated image of legislative output and an empirical research agenda designed to explore why some legislative arrangements are more

---

21. Ordeshook (1992, 276), for example, asserts that the fact that redistributive games tend
not to have cores "helps explain a great many things," one being the tendency for overly large
coalitions to form because risk-averse legislators fear being on the wrong end of a voting cycle.

stable than others, Tullock launched a research agenda aimed at identifying features of the legislative setting that are sufficient to induce equilibrium. His explanation (1967, 1981) focuses in particular on the stability-inducing effects of logrolling and coalition formation, but a host of other sufficient explanations have been advanced in response to Tullock's question, "Why so much stability?" Equilibrium has been said to be a product of information costs and legislative specialization arising from a system of permanent committees (Hoenack 1983), from regulation of floor behavior by party leadership (Kiewiet and McCubbins 1991), or from transaction costs incurred by coalition organizers (Cox and McCubbins 1993). Stability has been linked to a variety of special preference configurations—be they widely shared preferences (Kramer 1973), semi-singlepeaked preferences (Niemi 1983), or quasi-concave preference distributions—in conjunction with de facto supermajority requirements (Caplin and Nalebuff 1988). Other sources of stability have been traced to certain institutional arrangements, such as unidimensional committee jurisdictions and restrictions on amendments (Shepsle 1979; Shepsle and Weingast 1981), backward-looking versus forward-looking amendment procedures (Shepsle and Weingast 1984; Wilson 1986), or bicameralism and the executive veto (Hammond and Miller 1987). Such phenomena as sophisticated voting (Enelow and Koehler 1980; Shepsle and Weingast 1984; but see Ordeshook and Schwartz 1987), the presence of uncertainty (Shepsle 1972a), budget constraints (McCubbins and Schwartz 1984), and expectations of future consideration of similar issues (Bernholz 1978; Coleman 1986) have also been regarded as sufficient conditions for stability. To this list we may add anticycling theories specific to legislative bodies with many representatives, such as the computational difficulty (Bartholdi, Tovey, and Trick 1987) and political infeasibility (Tullock 1981) of manipulating an outcome to any appreciable degree by capitalizing on the potential for cycling. Bringing up the rear is the argument that cycling is avoided because of the "metapreferences" of legislators, who frequently operate in a normative environment that discourages "rocking the boat" (Grofman and Uhlaner 1985). Each of these claims offers an account of how there could be an equilibrium (or a set of tightly packed equilibria) in actual legislatures despite the theoretical possibility for cycling under simple majority rule.

From the standpoint of theory development, these analytic inquiries into the conditions under which various aspects of the legislative setting give rise to equilibria represent a series of advances. And to the extent that the aim has been to explain behavior in state and national legislatures, those models that incorporate such institutions as committees have improved the realism with which spatial models depict the legislative process. In spite of their increasing sophistication, however, even the more elaborate spatial models are still quite far from being realistic, and they remain only tenuously connected to empirical inquiry. The common practice seems to be to motivate the introduction of a new set of formal assumptions by reference to illustrations, without an accompanying empirical investigation that considers the causal influence of the specific mechanisms hypothesized to induce stability.

Even essays that seek explicitly to apply cooperative game theory to American national institutions attest to the diffuse linkage between theory development and empirical evaluation. In two essays, "The Core of the Constitution" (Hammond and Miller 1987) and "Committees and the Core of the Constitution" (Miller and Hammond 1990), Thomas Hammond and Gary Miller argue that bicameralism, the executive veto, and the internal organization of the legislature may combine to induce a core and hence policy stability. Invoking the assumptions that proposals are confined to a two-dimensional policy space, that legislators have circular indifference curves, and that committees have unidimensional jurisdictions as well as "gatekeeping" power over all proposals to the floor along that dimension, the authors conclude that "the more that the members of a committee are unrepresentative of their chamber as a whole, the larger any resulting cores will be. Similarly, the more distinct the executive is from the House and Senate, and the more distinct the House and Senate are from each other, the larger any resulting cores will be" (1990, 224). A larger core means that a broader sweep of policies are invulnerable to majority disruption. It also implies that the status quo, if in the core, is less susceptible to change as a function of change in the ideological composition of the legislature.

These hypotheses are suggestive, but they hinge critically on characteristics of the core. The authors do not set out to ascertain the size or existence of the core, nor do they tell us how we might go about doing so. They do not examine empirically the degree of preference overlap between representatives and senators or the divergence between executive and legislative preferences, nor do they attempt to link divided or unified party control to policy output (see Mayhew 1991). They make no attempt to convince the reader of the empirical basis for their model of committees, which makes no allowance for the various ways that floor majorities and the majority party leadership can circumvent or overrule recalcitrant committees (see below). Nonetheless, they suggest that their model may explain why "it might take a shift of extraordinary magnitude in actors' preferences—on the order of the changes in Congress in the early FDR years or those that the 1964 congressional elections created—to shift the core so that the old status quo falls outside it" (1990, 226). In effect, the authors turn Riker's description of the ever-changeable political landscape on its head, reformulating Tullock's question "Why so much stability?" to read "Why do things ever change at all?" (226).

The widely discussed notion of structure-induced equilibrium (Shepsle 1979, 1986; Shepsle and Weingast 1981) provides another illustration of a literature groping for realism without being rooted in empirical inquiry. Reacting against the "spartan quality of social choice theory and the inadequacy of embellishments to it found in spatial models of elections" (Shepsle 1986, 167), Shepsle and Weingast (1981) present a model that has as its central feature a system of committees, each entrusted with a monopoly over a unidimensional jurisdiction. Within a committee the median voter's ideal point prevails, and when a committee reports its proposals to the floor, the model presupposes that amendments are either forbidden or subject to a germaneness requirement that allows change on only one dimension at time.[22]

Over the years, this model has won acclaim among rational choice theorists, who applaud the extent to which its assumptions "approximate" Congress (McCubbins and Schwartz 1985, 56) or, at any rate, are "not inconsistent with" the structure of the House of Representatives (Aldrich 1989, 225; see also Weingast and Marshall 1988). The basis for this praise is not clear. Even committees entrusted with a narrow band of policy concern, such as Energy and Natural Resources, do not in a technical sense have a unidimensional jurisdiction; even less so, Foreign Relations or Appropriations. Nor can congressional committees plausibly be described as having monopolies over their policy jurisdictions. Granted, when it comes to floor activity, "germaneness is the prevailing formal practice for amendment control in nearly every legislative body" (Shepsle 1986, 158), but leaving aside the prominent exception of the Senate, the fact remains that admissible amendments (or substitutes) can and do involve more than one policy dimension. Further complicating matters are the provisions enabling the floor to discharge a bill from an intransigent committee or to refer it to a more sympathetic committee.[23]

The manifest unrealism of this depiction of the committee structure represents something of a safety net. If the model is disconfirmed by evidence, its failures may be blamed on its "stylized" assumptions; in the meantime, it may be applauded for predicting the policy stability that is observed. Rather than elaborate the model so as to account for the manifest complexity of Congressional procedures or test the model as it stands by instrumental criteria (applying it to phenomena other than those it was crafted to predict), the tendency among rational choice scholars has been to ruminate over the formal mechanics of the structure-induced equilibrium model, considering the complications that arise because of sophisticated voting (Denzau and Mackay 1981) or "thick regions of indifference" in actors' utility functions (Dion 1992).[24]

22. It is further assumed that legislators have separable preferences (circular indifference curves), which is to say that they have no incentive to trade off proposed changes along one dimension for desired changes in another. For an insightful exegesis and critique of the structure-induced equilibrium model see Krehbiel 1988.

23. Shepsle's (1986, 143) grudging admission that his model "overstates matters inasmuch as most legislatures preserve the authority of extraordinary majorities to 'pry the gates open,' e.g., the discharge petition" leaves students of Congress to puzzle over what *in principle* is "extraordinary" about a 50 percent majority of the membership.

24. Dion (1992) in particular stresses the ways that certain procedures and informal norms, such as de facto majority requirements, patterns of policy specialization, and expectations of reciprocity, shore up the claims of earlier structure-induced equilibrium models.

Perhaps these ruminations will someday culminate in the formulation of testable propositions and an empirical research program. For the present, just what the structure-induced equilibrium model has contributed to the empirical study of Congress is not clear.

What kind of empirical investigation do we have in mind? Any hypothesis test must at a minimum involve a control group and some variation in the mechanism thought to alter the propensity for policy change. The structure-induced equilibrium argument would suggest that variation in the structure of committee jurisdictions and floor amendment procedures should coincide with differing degrees of policy stability.[25] The connection between the dimensionality of preferences toward a policy proposal and the existence of a core (Schofield et al. 1988) suggests that multidimensional policy proposals, such as distributive legislation, should be more prone to cycling than issues that have a more unidimensional character. The supergame argument set forth by Coleman (1986) suggests that, all other things being equal, policies emerging from temporary or lame duck legislatures should be more unstable than those from legislatures in which there is an expectation of future interaction. Granted, comparing one legislature with another or examining the effects of changes in institutional structure plunges one into the sea of practical problems that make applied political science so arduous. It will be necessary to define stability in operational terms; to distinguish between policy changes caused by disequilibrium and those caused by preference change; and to identify natural experiments in which institutional arrangements change, thereby altering the strategic environment. Until this sort of work is undertaken, however, the explanatory value of analytic propositions derived from spatial models remains an open question.

Not only is there little comparative analysis of the kind just described, scant attention is paid to hypothesis testing of any kind. What little there is (Dobra and Tullock 1981; Dobra 1983; Chamberlin, Cohen, and Coombs 1984) amounts to scarcely more than an exercise of tallying the number of "cycles" that appear to emerge from a hodgepodge of elections and committee decisions—mostly academic committees—and comparing that to the number of noncycles. Dobra, for example, finds evidence of cycling in four of thirty-two decisions, despite the absence of a core, and takes this 87 percent rate to mean that anticycling theories are right. This rate, however, seems equally consistent with the passages quoted earlier from Riker (compare Bowen 1972; Niemi and Weisberg 1972). In any case, with no meaningful

25. Shepsle (1986) offers two further comparative statics predictions. The first is that the committee will become less inclined to report a bill as its median position diverges from that of the floor. The second is that a committee's stance will not be affected by changes in membership unless there is a change in the location of the pivotal committee member.

control group, inferences about the causal role of majority rule equilibrium cannot be drawn one way or the other.[26]

Even worse, discussions of equilibrium-inducing properties of legislative bodies such as Congress frequently descend into a kind of functionalism in which institutions and practices are explained by reference to the fact that they produce a core. Political issues tend to arise in two-dimensional form because higher dimensions increase the risk of instability (McCubbins and Schwartz 1985, 57); the longer terms and greater collegiality of the Senate obviate the need for an equilibrium-inducing germaneness rule (Dion 1992, 476); past institutional experiences of cycling lead to closed rules when the House takes up the federal budget (Blydenburgh 1971). Ignoring the questionable empirical foundations of such arguments, the irony is that stability of the sort anticipated by equilibrium analyses is arguably dysfunctional for democratic institutions. As Miller (1983) has pointed out, systemic stability may hinge on some degree of policy disequilibrium, insofar as losing coalitions retain an incentive to continue their participation in legislative politics in the hopes of one day forging a winning coalition.

There are at least two ways that the methodological quality of rational choice applications could be improved. First, theorists should eschew the tendency to contrive post hoc accounts of a stylized fact about the degree of legislative (in)stability. No single stylized fact concerning policy stability is likely to hold true over time or legislative settings. Coming to grips with the variability in rates of policy change directs attention to more productive research questions, which concern why instability manifests itself under some circumstances and not others. A further advantage of uncoupling rational choice theories from stylized facts is that it reduces the incentive for theorists to sift from a diverse array of possible assumptions those that have as their implication a legislative equilibrium. It is no accident that the realism Shepsle (1979) imported into the study of legislatures consists of committees with unidimensional and exclusive jurisdictions; the choice of this unlikely set of premises is driven by the desire to obtain the conclusion that committees induce equilibrium.

Second, those who advance a model of the legislative process should at the same time advance testable propositions and describe the sorts of legislative institutions to

---

26. Dobra considers the role of group size in relation to the number of choice dimensions, but this hypothesis, which received attention early in the development of this literature, now seems ancillary to the major theoretical approaches to instability and its solution. Note that the operationalization offered by Dobra leads to certain surefire predictions. If voting ends, does that falsify a prediction of "endless" cycling? Dobra implies as much when he asserts that compromise is a solution to the cycling problem in the decisions he studies. Indicative of the peculiar character of Dobra's sampling technique is the fact that his collection of cases contains no observations of deadlock or inaction in academia.

which the model applies. As models of Congress go, Shepsle and Weingast's, for example, may be a step up from spatial models that presuppose no institutional structure whatsoever (but see McKelvey and Ordeshook 1984a), yet it is unclear how the distinction between simple majority rule and the institutional arrangements posited by Shepsle and Weingast translates into a research agenda that students of Congress could pursue. If the stylized institutions posited by Shepsle and Weingast have never existed in Congress, is the theory nonetheless capable of explaining its legislative outcomes? If so, is it subject to meaningful refutation given that it can always be defended as a "stylized" rendering of Congressional institutions? If rational choice models are to inform the understanding of American legislative politics, their empirical status ought to be less mysterious than is currently the case.

EXPERIMENTAL EVIDENCE

In the previous section we found the empirical research purporting to test the implications of majority rule disequilibrium to be wanting. In fairness, however, it may be that the dearth of well-executed research on legislatures stems from a recognition of the inherent limitations of nonexperimental research (Cook and Campbell 1979; Achen 1986) or the practical problems that arise when researchers try to measure legislators' preferences or to identify natural experiments in which institutional change occurs more or less exogenously. These and other methodological concerns have led many scholars working with rational choice models to turn to laboratory experimentation as a means of testing their propositions empirically. Indeed, some have argued that experimentation may be the only feasible way of testing rational choice theories in this domain (compare Plott 1979; Palfrey 1991).

Experiments offer at least three advantages over quasi-experimental inference. First, the laboratory environment enables researchers to gain control over the ordinal preferences of actors through a system of induced monetary incentives (Smith 1976). Second, the experimental setting allows the investigator to regulate the information available to decision makers. Third, the lab affords the opportunity to study exogenous changes in the institutional structure within which decision making occurs. In sum, the experimental method enables scholars to simplify the complexities of the legislative environment in such a way as to focus attention on particular forces at work, such as amendment procedures, agenda control, or required majority size.

The clarity with which the laboratory addresses theoretical claims comes at a cost, however. As critics are quick to point out (Chamberlin 1979; compare defensive remarks by Fiorina and Plott 1978, 592–93; Plott and Smith 1979), real legislative settings differ in many ways from impromptu convocations of experimental subjects. The laboratory settings in which legislative deliberation occurs lack founding principles, conventions, preexisting patterns of factional division, or expectations of future interaction. By design they are devoid of objectives other than the production of monetary rewards for their participants. It is not surprising, then, that the arid institutional environment of the experimental committee strikes students of legislative politics as lacking many of the more interesting facets of parliamentary institutions.

This line of criticism, however, is not altogether fair to the experimental literature. The stated aims of experimental research in this area are not so much to simulate the operation of particular institutions as to test theoretical propositions about behavior in games that are similar in *structure* to interactions in actual legislative settings. Indeed, most researchers in this area have been quick to concede the dubious "realism" of their experiments (McKelvey and Ordeshook 1980, 156, and McKelvey and Ordeshook 1990b, 311–12; see, however, Fiorina and Plott 1978, 576). To be sure, experimental studies would shed more light on the workings of actual political institutions if they tried to incorporate the complexities of actual legislative institutions into their work. Still, as was true of the social dilemma experiments reviewed in the previous chapter, the external validity of these experiments is not so obviously deficient as to enable one to dismiss this literature out of hand.

Although we harbor certain misgivings about the external validity of various experiments on legislative behavior, we do not wish to make this point the central focus of our critique. The experimental literature on legislative voting contains some of the most imaginative and thought-provoking empirical work to emerge from rational choice theory, and a dismissive critique fails to do justice to the potential contributions of this line of research. Rather, our methodological concerns about the legislative experiments inspired by rational choice propositions have to do with the fundamentally ambiguous relation between theory and experimental results. As we show in our survey of experiments on the paradox of voting, many experimental studies lack a well-defined null hypothesis or clear statistical standards for evaluating evidence. In cases where the standards are reasonably clear, disconfirming evidence frequently arises, but sometimes without any apparent effect on the experimenter's faith in the validity of the theoretical approach. In a manner reminiscent of rational choice responses to anomalous quasi-experimental evidence, scholars such as Plott and Smith (1979) have expressed the conviction that what appear to be grave setbacks are in fact minor annoyances and that a wide array of factors that seem to throw rational choice predictions off track, such as universalistic norms (see Weingast 1979; Miller and Oppenheimer 1982), can be incorporated into rational choice accounts of behavior. Others resist the temptation to blur the distinction between rational choice hypotheses and alternative hypotheses by absorbing the latter into the former, expressing the hope that yet undiscovered solution theories will render the anomalies unproblematic (McKelvey and Ordeshook 1981; Herzberg and Wilson 1991). Still others, as Salant and Goodstein (1990) note, strain to conclude that disconfirming data are not in fact disconfirming (Berl et al. 1976; Fiorina and Plott

1978). In each instance, it is unclear what datum, if observed, would lead those who subscribe to the theoretical notions they test to relinquish their convictions.

To their credit, experimental researchers in this area generally describe their results in sufficient detail to enable readers to draw their own inferences. On our reading, it would appear that the specific rational choice hypotheses put forth fare rather poorly, even though spatial models of committee behavior are sometimes regarded as exemplars of successful rational choice applications (Lalman et al. 1993) and experimental evidence touted as imparting "confidence that the large body of theoretical research into spatial models of committees and elections is not without sound empirical content" (McKelvey and Ordeshook 1990a, 140). Laboratory studies, for example, repeatedly demonstrate how mathematical characterizations of voting games founder on the inability of actors to pursue optimal strategies. One experiment after another shows that when faced with legislative tasks in which the path to self-interest is less than obvious, subjects make suboptimal choices, thus throwing off predictions based solely on an analysis of the system of payoffs.[27] In addition, even in the controlled environment of the laboratory rational choice predictions routinely run afoul of such unanticipated factors as the asymmetrical game-playing capacities of the actors, deference to norms of fairness, or indifference among closely valued alternatives. Thus, although rational choice theories purport to explain and predict the effects of exogenous changes in the institutional environment, the experimental evidence indicates that these effects are highly contingent on the actors' strategic talents. These problems of theoretical prediction, we contend, would be even more acute were the lab a closer approximation of actual legislative settings, in which computational tasks and social-psychological forces are, if anything, more pressing.

In sum, our critique of experimental legislative research inspired by rational choice is threefold. Although it is less methodologically slippery than quasi-experimental research, there is still ample opportunity for investigators to circumvent discordant facts, thanks to the vagueness with which null hypotheses are framed. Second, experimental investigations have not gone very far in probing the social-psychological factors that might affect the rate at which rational choice succeeds in predicting the outcome. Third, even in the rather sterile political environment in which experimental voting occurs, anomalies frequently arise, particularly when

27. Granted, one can always fall back to the position that rational choice models depict the behavior of actors conditional on how they understand the strategic options before them, but then these theories become at once less interesting and less susceptible to empirical evaluation. Besides, as far as the experimental literature is concerned, strategic perceptions are ostensibly the random variable producing variation in experimental outcomes. Thus, to say that rational choice encompasses both the predictions based on an objective analysis of a game form as well as the subjective interpretations of the actors is tantamount to saying that rational choice anticipates all possible experimental outcomes.

subjects are given room to display their varying strategic capacities. The last two points in combination mean that extant rational choice models tend to fail whenever they set forth a prediction that strays from what intuition might suggest. Thus, although we are less critical of experimental than quasi-experimental research, the bottom line remains the same: the empirical successes of applied research inspired by rational choice models of legislative politics have been limited.

OVERVIEW OF EXPERIMENTAL METHOD

Various studies since the mid-1970s have examined a genre of voting games with nontransferable utility that allegedly "captures the essence of the basic majority rule committee process" (Fiorina and Plott 1978, 576).[28] One research agenda, inspired by the paradox of voting, examines how a configuration of legislators' preferences affects the outcome. In such games the institutional rules are held constant, and players' preferences are manipulated experimentally. The other primary research agenda examines how various institutional structures, such as the imposition of a closed rule or the adoption of a fixed agenda, affect legislative outcomes. In this instance, the configuration of preferences among the legislators is held constant while the institutional structure is manipulated.

Before summarizing these two lines of experimental research, let us first give a brief characterization of how experimental committee games work. Subjects, who are by and large recruited from graduate and undergraduate courses, confront a schedule of monetary payoffs that will result from various legislative outcomes. Usually, these payoffs are small sums of money or lotteries for cash. Now and then, subjects are offered appreciable payoffs (that is, more than $25), but in no case, for obvious practical reasons, do the rewards approach levels that are sizable by actual political standards.[29]

The legislative game itself involves voting on proposals represented by points on a two-dimensional grid or by the success or failure of one or more bills. Games typically end when a majority decision is reached, although some games allow the legislature to reconsider its decision after a majority-approved outcome has been reached.[30] Rules pertaining to interplayer communication vary. Sometimes players

28. That is, players are not allowed to make side-payments, be they financial trades or physical threats. For a review of games in which transfers are allowed see Michener and Yuen 1982.

29. Following the lead of recent work in experimental economics, this literature may well move to China, where, given the level of disposable income, $25 really means something. Grades, incidentally, seem to have the same motivating power as monetary incentives, at least among the students Kormendi and Plott (1982) used as subjects.

30. For the most part, the games operate without any special time limit. The imposition of a

are allowed to negotiate directly, while in other cases participants are isolated from one another. A standard rule, however, is that players are forbidden from communicating the exact nature of their payoffs with others, so as to prevent side-payments. Frequently, although not invariably, subjects know the ideal points or preference orderings of the other players. Before the actual experiment begins, subjects complete a quiz to ensure that they understand the rules and objectives of the game.

Conspicuously absent from these experiments are social-psychological manipulations. Preference configurations, payoff magnitudes, group size, and institutional structure sometimes figure in the experimental design, but the role of social norms, ideological commitment, group attachment, and the like is ignored. Granted, in experiments in which discussion is allowed, subjects are free to invoke any normative or ideological appeal they care to use. But since the "bills" on which they are voting lack content apart from monetary reward, it is not clear how the usual terms of ideological discourse—historical precedent, natural right, founding principles, and so forth—could be invoked with any effectiveness.[31] Similarly, although the experiments allow for the formation of coalitions, the subjects enter the experiment as undifferentiated strangers with no group identifications, loyalties, or prejudices.[32] That these kinds of alternative hypotheses are given short shrift does not necessarily invalidate the experimental findings, but it does hamper efforts to assess the explanatory power of game theories in relation to other behavioral hypotheses or to test hypotheses that are unanticipated by, or at variance with, rational choice theories.

What we are left with, then, is a body of evidence that can tell us the extent to which the mathematical features of a game shape the outcome, holding constant a host of social influences that are known to affect behavior in group settings. The experimental manipulations center on subjects' preferences, their information about others'

---

time limit in one study (Wilson 1986, 405) seems to be regarded as a design flaw by other researchers in this area. Salant and Goodstein (1990), on the other hand, defend the practice of holding subjects for a fixed period of time (regardless of how long it takes them to complete their legislative task) on the grounds that releasing legislators who adjourn early creates an incentive for subjects to satisfice and get on with their lives. In their studies, however, fixing the time commitment of subjects does not have a discernible effect.

31. As Margolis (1982) points out, it is not even clear that participants can make a coherent argument based on what they know about the system of monetary payoffs. In order to prevent side-payments, players are almost never given exact cardinal information about others' payoffs. Thus, players are seldom in a position to know (bluffing aside) what policy would maximize the collective payoffs of all participants.

32. The social setting is even more denuded of interpersonal contact and influence in the more recent legislative voting experiments, in which subjects have no face-to-face contact with each another and "interact" solely through a computer terminal. Although this design offers greater control over the experimental environment, it undermines further the verisimilitude between the lab and actual legislatures.

preferences, their opportunities to communicate, and the rules of the institutions in which they bargain. The essential uncontrolled factor in these experiments is the strategic talent of the players, that is, their ability to discern a strategy that would maximize their expected gains. In essence, then, these experiments test predictions based on a formal analysis of the game structure against outcomes generated by ostensibly greedy but strategically fallible players.

EVALUATING EXPERIMENTAL EVIDENCE

The objective of game theoretic and kindred decision theoretic models is to predict the outcome of a legislative game based on a mathematical characterization of the game structure—its rules and the configuration of actors' preferences (McKelvey and Ordeshook 1982, 120–21). Equivalent formal characterizations should generate similar empirical outcomes; divergent characterizations, divergent outcomes. To the extent that this correspondence between characterization and outcome breaks down, the theoretical models are called into question.

Evaluating the empirical adequacy of game theory is complicated somewhat by the fact that there are many different game theoretic approaches to predicting the outcome of a given type of game, particularly games without a core. Because the various "solution concepts" are more mathematical abstraction than behavioral theory, one subagenda within the experimental literature is to evaluate the empirical adequacy of these different proposed solutions, an endeavor guided largely by an instrumental vision of theory. The process is not unlike that of a runoff election to select a nominee to represent the game theoretic party in a more general theoretical contest. For a time, the apparent theoretical nominee seemed to be the competitive solution proposed by McKelvey, Ordeshook, and Winer (1978), which predicts the core when it exists and bargains struck by particular minimal coalitions when it does not. By the instrumental standard of predictive accuracy (McKelvey et al. 1978, McKelvey and Ordeshook 1979 and 1980, Ordeshook 1986, chap. 9; see, however, Miller and Oppenheimer 1982), and perhaps even by the realist standard of verisimilitude with actual negotiation processes (McKelvey and Ordeshook 1980, 1984a; but see Fiorina and Plott 1978), the competitive solution seems to win out over its competitors as a model of legislative behavior in majority-rule games with nontransferable utility. Therefore, in our discussion of the empirical adequacy of game theoretic accounts of legislative behavior we will be thinking for the most part of the competitive solution. But, in recognition of the fact that alternative solution concepts have come into greater prominence in recent years, we will also discuss some other contenders.

A second and more profound difficulty in interpreting the pattern of experimental findings is that many of the studies, particularly those conducted early in the development of this literature, contain no independent variable; they are designed simply to illustrate game theoretic propositions. In such instances, it is unclear against which null hypotheses rational choice propositions are tested. Many of the experiments test hypotheses of the form: "under the conditions ostensibly created in our lab, our theorem predicts equilibrium outcome(s) θ" by assessing the proportion of trials in which θ occurs. On the surface this would appear to be sensible enough. It is important to bear in mind, however, that the formal results of rational choice theory are analytic truths, not empirical conjectures. Consider, for example, the widely cited literature on the success with which the core predicts legislative outcomes. The existence and location of a majority rule equilibrium is, of course, a mathematical fact that follows from the design of the experiment. When the core predicts successfully, we infer that it is *possible* to instantiate this mathematical result—just as it is possible to illustrate an arithmetic claim by counting apples. If preferences have been induced successfully (so that no extra-experimental preferences exist),[33] then the only way the core can fail to predict is if one or more of the players makes a mistake. But when the core succeeds, do we applaud the skill of the experimenter, who successfully induced preferences, or that of the subjects, who continued to negotiate until each was made as well-off as possible? If the core fails, on the other hand, we could question either the validity of the preference inductions or the strategic acumen of the actors, but not the truthfulness of the theorem used to generate the prediction. The empirical results, in the end, do not speak to the truth of the theoretical result. At most, they tell us whether the assumptions on which the result rests can be approximated in the lab.

But even here there are ambiguities associated with how inferences are to be drawn from the data. What do we conclude when θ obtains 60 percent of the time? Or 90 percent? Or 99 percent? The answer is unclear because there is no explicit control group in this experiment against which to compare the outcome. Hence, the only null hypothesis that admits rigorous testing is the conjecture that θ *always* obtains, which would be rejected with any success rate short of 100 percent. It seems obvious that this sort of deterministic covering law is not what scholars in this area have in mind. Instead, they seem to operate with a probabilistic view of their theoretical predictions but harbor a vague sense of what a successful rate of prediction might be. As we will see, this rate varies considerably from one scholar to the next.

Although this sort of empirical test is sometimes called an experiment, a more apt description would be a demonstration under laboratory conditions (Boring 1954; Campbell and Stanley 1963). A true experiment examines the effects of one or more

33. To the extent that players have preferences about the configuration of collective outcomes (nonegoistic motives, to borrow from the Fiorina and Plott [1978] terminology), the internal validity of the experiment is compromised (McKelvey and Ordeshook 1980). Another way to interpret this problem is to say that the theoretical derivation makes inaccurate assumptions about the decision rules used by the actors. Players may be maximizing not their own utility but that of the group as a whole.

controlled interventions on the rate at which θ obtains. A demonstration, on the other hand, shows that θ *can* obtain or furnishes evidence (in)consistent with the proposition that θ always obtains. To say that many rational choice experiments are in fact demonstrations is not to call them worthless but rather to point out that the data they generate are difficult to interpret.[34] For without an experimental control group the problems of quasi-experimental inference resurface: one cannot readily distinguish the effects of rational agency from other confounding factors.

It is not hard to understand how game theoretic studies might occasionally lapse into laboratory demonstration. Unlike models of group behavior that seek to account for variability in observed outcomes, rational choice models, as we noted above, attempt to find specific points of equilibrium to which legislative deliberations will converge.[35] Thus there is a natural desire on the part of rational choice scholars to know whether the predicted points of equilibrium actually obtain. The problem with this research objective is that it seems to descend into an exercise of tallying prediction rates and finding ways for each theoretical conjecture to be declared a success.

Studies of committee behavior when a majority rule equilibrium exists provide an informative illustration of this problem. What proportion of all trials must the core predict in order for it to be deemed adequate? Fiorina and Plott (1978, 583–84) report that three of twenty trials in which subjects were offered "high payoffs" resulted in a core outcome, but they still conclude that the core is a powerful predictor because fourteen of twenty trials were closer to it than any other sort of prediction the authors specify.[36] McKelvey and Ordeshook (1984a, 189) infer that "the core receives considerable support" from a pair of experiments in which the core obtains four times over nineteen trials. Herzberg and Wilson (1991) recommend the core as a "reasonable prediction" even though it obtained in two of four trials. Eavey and Miller (1984a, 721–22) regard the Condorcet winner as a powerful predictor, but in their own *one-dimensional* voting experiments, the median voter's ideal point prevails in just five of eight trials.

34. Some famous "crucial experiments" in physics have no explicit control group, but here the hypothesis being tested is indeed the proposition that θ always obtains. As mentioned earlier, hypotheses derived from rational choice models do not take this form.

35. Although some models of this sort are stochastic in nature (see Hoffman and Packel 1982), most provide point predictions.

36. The use of a comparative standard for hypothesis evaluation raises an important point about the relationship between research design and analysis. In essence, this method of analysis transforms the experiment into a quasi-experiment, because within a given experimental trial no manipulation takes place. Thus, the inference to be drawn is entirely contingent on the external validity of the experimental setting. A striking example of this style of analysis may be found in Laing and Olmstead (1978) and Laing and Slotznick (1987, 1991). Although these experiments, taken together, approximate an experiment on the effects of the size of a required majority on legislative outcomes, the authors dwell instead on the intra-treatment comparison between alternative predictions.

This interpretive ambiguity is in no way resolved by recourse to conventional statistical hypothesis testing. In the seminal experiments reported by Berl et al. (1976, 467), which involve voting on proposed points in a two-dimensional grid, the core obtains in just three of seventeen trials, and three of the trials result in outcomes that the authors judge to be "far" from the core (what constitutes "near" or "far" in an open grid of points is not specified *ex ante*). Yet, the authors conclude that their results *support* the core's empirical applicability, because—in a twist on the usual statistical logic of hypothesis testing—they are unable to reject the proposition that the *average* experimental outcome they observe was generated by the location of the core. The same statistical reasoning shows up in Endersby's investigation of structure-induced equilibrium resulting from issue-by-issue voting (1993). Endersby reports that "when communication is prohibited and voting is limited to one issue at a time, the average outcome in an experimental game is not significantly different from the theoretical prediction of a stable point at the issue-by-issue median" even though just four of twenty committees enact the predicted outcome (233). To see that this is an inappropriate way of gauging the predictive accuracy of the theory, imagine if none of the outcomes were at all close to the core yet the mean location of the experimental outcomes were at the equilibrium. Clearly such an outcome, however attractive by the standards of conventional hypothesis testing, would run counter to the predictions of the game theoretic model. What does it mean to say that an equilibrium generates nonequilibrium outcomes?

Apart from these interpretive ambiguities, it is apparent that no general conclusion can be reached about the success of the core, because its success rate fluctuates widely across different preference configurations and legislative tasks. In certain vote-trading experiments, for example, McKelvey and Ordeshook discover that the core has an overall success rate of 50 percent or less (1980, 1981, 1982), while in other cases, the success rate jumps to more than 90 percent (1982, 127). The same contrast may be found among experiments reported in Plott 1991, Fiorina and Plott 1978, and Hoffman and Plott 1983. In one study, Isaac and Plott (1978) obtain success rates ranging from 33 percent to 100 percent depending on the structure of the three-person game they examined. For these reasons we find ourselves less taken with the fact most frequently cited in references to this experimental literature: the success rate of the core (see Mueller 1989). A more compelling evaluation of the data would focus on the conditions under which the core predicts successfully.

UNDER WHAT CONDITIONS DOES THE CORE PREVAIL?

Given the spotty performance of the majority-rule equilibrium in legislative voting games, it is natural to consider factors that prevent committees from adopting policies in the core. One set of hypotheses examines the internal validity of experimental attempts to induce preferences over legislative outcomes. Strictly speaking, the ordering of payoffs, and not their magnitude, determines the core; but when payoffs are small, the experimentally induced ordering may be superseded by extra-experimental preferences of various sorts. This hypothesis has not undergone extensive testing, but there is some reason to believe that the intensity of players' motivation makes a difference. Fiorina and Plott (1978) argue that the size of the payoffs offered to players affects the success with which the core predicts laboratory outcomes. Salant and Goodstein (1990) attribute some of the core's failures to players' indifference between core and near-core payoffs, an interpretation corroborated by McKelvey and Ordeshook's suggestive but statistically inconclusive experimental evidence (1981).

This pattern of results, if reliable, may be interpreted in different ways.[37] Because we ordinarily suppose that real legislators receive substantial utility payoffs from policy outcomes, this evidence speaks well of the external validity of these spatial models. But without any a priori notion of what is a sufficiently large payoff for the actors involved, rational choice theories are at a loss to describe, based on the formal structure of a game, when their theoretical equilibria constitute a viable prediction. A similar situation arises when considerations of fairness impinge on the deliberations of small groups. McKelvey and Ordeshook find that fairness is an unusually potent factor in committees composed of three rather than five members and contend that "considerations of equity or fairness arise to distort the preferences the experimenter seeks to induce—thereby invalidating the application and test of the theory of the abstract game" (1980, 170; see also McKelvey 1991). Eavey and Miller argue that perceptions of the fairness of the outcome figure prominently even in games involving more than three participants (Eavey 1991; Eavey and Miller 1984b), though the evidence is mixed in other studies (Laing and Olmstead 1978; McKelvey, Ordeshook, and Winer 1978). Again, even if this murky pattern of results were to indicate clearly that fairness matters, the finding would be open to opposing interpretations. On the one hand, fairness may be regarded as an experimental annoyance preventing investigators from inducing the preferences assumed in their models (Plott 1979; McKelvey and Ordeshook 1980). On the other hand, one might view norms of fairness as antithetical to the utility-maximizing assumption underlying rational choice.[38] In light of the Miller and Oppenheimer experiments (1982) it might be said that norms of fairness can be superseded by large payoffs, but that only reopens the question

37. Eavey (1991, 1994) contests the claim that players' zones of indifference account for noncore outcomes. She presents evidence suggesting that experimental committees, when presented with a range of options that enable players to select a policy that promises something for everyone, regularly enact policies that fall outside Salant and Goodstein's "selection set."

38. Still another move is to construe norms as the endogenous product of rational calculation (Weingast 1979; Panning 1982; Sinclair 1986).

encountered in earlier chapters of whether rational choice theory specifies a priori when payoffs *are* sufficiently large.

Questions of motivation, group size, and extra-experimental rewards are interesting, but empirical evidence is at present inconclusive. There is, however, one variable that seems to have a decisive influence on the success rate of the core: cognitive complexity of the strategic task before the legislators. In an important and forthright critique of their own work McKelvey and Ordeshook (1981) draw the distinction between logrolling and selection of a single option from a fixed list of alternatives. In the former case, players are asked to dispose of several pending pieces of legislation in one session. In the latter, players select one option from a list of available alternatives. The two games can be arranged so as to offer equivalent payoff schemes; the various permutations of legislative end states that might emerge from the logrolling game comprise the list of ranked outcomes in the fixed alternative game. From the standpoint of the incentive structure, there is no distinction between these two cooperative games.[39] Thus, as McKelvey and Ordeshook (1981, 713) note, "from the point of view of cooperative game theory, there is no reason the two experimental designs should yield different outcomes." Yet logrolling games are much less likely to result in core outcomes than "finite alternative" games because of the frequency with which subjects make shortsighted vote-trades. Not only is this kind of strategic myopia damaging to game theoretic accounts that presuppose that individuals will pursue optimal strategies; it also calls into question the external validity of virtually all of the experiments in which the core fared well. It seems farfetched to think that legislators behave as though they were evaluating a fixed list of end states. Logrolling, on the other hand, is to all appearances the sine qua non of legislative politics.

The importance of strategic complexity is apparent not only from such experimental tests as the one described above, but also from anecdotal reports of individual differences in the gaming talents of laboratory legislators. Herzberg and Wilson (1991) describe a committee in which a subject cleverly dragged an outcome away from the core by creating a cycle and then filibustering. Isaac and Plott (1978, 304) report a radical departure from the core caused by a player who outfoxed her colleagues by blustering. Miller and Oppenheimer (1982) observe a player who obtained a disproportionately large payoff by misrepresenting her utility function in order to upset consensus on a fair outcome. Less spectacular but perhaps more telling is the case of a botched experimental trial in which an experienced player was inadvertently

---

39. The strategic mechanics of the two games may differ, however, insofar as logrolling games allow players to enter into binding agreements. Of course, given the prohibition against side-payments, it is not clear why subjects would have any incentive to enter into binding commitments that result in noncore outcomes. It remains to be seen whether noncooperative theories (see below) shed light on the distinction observed here.

pitted against novices and reaped a windfall by deceiving his hapless colleagues about rules of the game (McKelvey and Ordeshook 1980, 170). Other experimental anec- dotes depict poorly executed ultimata (Eavey and Miller 1984a, 724–25) and vocal leaders who are double-crossed for their hubris (Eckel and Holt 1989, 767). It would appear that even when players are doing their level best to maximize their payoffs, asymmetry in game-playing talent may produce outcomes at variance with rational choice predictions.[40]

It is rather ironic that gamesmanship should emerge as a threat to the predictive accuracy of game theory. What makes this pattern of results especially interesting is that several studies have found that the success rate of the core does not improve when the players become "experienced," having played in previous committee voting games.[41] As McKelvey and Ordeshook (1981, 713) note, experienced players as a group are no better than the inexperienced at achieving core outcomes, in part because having participated in a legislative session or two, experienced players expect voting cycles and therefore adjourn before finding the core! Even when payoffs are manipu- lated so that logrolling games discourage certain trades that lead away from the core (710), other myopic exchanges lead to eventual noncore outcomes. In sum, unlike the case of payoff magnitude, in which big stakes seem to encourage players to conform to theoretical expectations, the general level of player experience does not seem to make much difference. Moreover, one cannot evade this pattern of experimental results by appealing to the long political experience of real world legislators. Even if one should find a lower aggregate level of strategic myopia among elected officials, there remains the problem of variance among legislators' strategic talents.

It is interesting to speculate about the implications of this lacuna in the empirical

40. Game theorists themselves have at times suspected that the effects of variability in strategic reasoning could be more acute outside the lab. As McKelvey and Ordeshook com- mented early on in the development of this literature (1980, 178–79), "To date, the core and κ [the competitive solution] have been tested principally in the context of spatial games—games that present no incentive for disaggregating the eventual choice into its component parts or that preclude such disaggregation. . . . These contexts seem too devoid of strategic complexity to reveal the forces that might operate in real, nonexperimental institutions such as legislatures— forces that invite outcomes other than those predicted by some solution concept operating over mathematically abstract representations of these institutions."

41. There is an interesting tension between evidence and theoretical conviction on this point. Isaac and Plott (1978, 310) express the view that experienced subjects would have strengthened their results, echoing the assertion of Berl et al. (1976, 473) that "if subjects understood better the properties of their indifference contours, deviant points would vanish." Yet, none of the experiments that have controlled for player experience support this presupposition. It is rather interesting that Berl et al. would suggest that player sophistication might salvage mispredic- tions while at the same time trumpeting the fact that players may arrive at the core without understanding its properties (475).

applicability of rational choice theory. Most established political institutions are inhabited by public officials who vary markedly in terms of political experience and talent. Some representatives seem to know every jot and tittle of House procedure, whereas others count themselves fortunate to find their way to the House floor when a vote is called. To augment rational choice models so as to take into account the preferences of the actors, rules of the game, *and* the varying strategic capacities of the players makes an already complex analytic system much more so, and some explicitly resist moves in this direction in an effort to retain analytic tractability (Strom 1990).

As an empirical matter, incorporating interpersonal variability into strategic capacity adds yet another measurement problem to the heap of difficulties facing the applied researcher. From the standpoint of theory, the topic of strategic capacity calls attention to a broader set of issues concerning strategic innovation in complex institutional settings. In principle, a set of parliamentary rules defines the strategic options available to legislators in the House. In practice, however, some of these rules are active and binding while others lie dormant, ignored or forgotten (Strom 1990). Furthermore, the boundary between de jure and de facto rules is fluid, so that from time to time certain obscure provisions are taken out·of mothballs (for example, the Rules Committee's authority to discharge legislation from other committees [Matsunga and Chen 1976]). Attempts to transform the formal structure of an institution into a game in which players have access to a specified set of strategic options tend to ignore the open-ended quality of these options and legislators' asymmetrical capacities to take advantage of them. In effect, game-theoretical representations of legislatures face a conundrum: How does one model institutions in which legislators may ignore or discover existing rules or, when operating under provisions allowing for suspension of the rules, invent new ones?

GAMES WITHOUT CORES

Experimental efforts to identify the conditions under which majority rule produces core outcomes are interesting from a theoretical standpoint, but of course the core may not exist for an arbitrary configuration of preferences over multidimensional alternatives. Analytic results suggest that a core rarely exists in legislative bodies governed by simple majority rule, especially when substantial numbers of legislators are involved (Plott 1967; Schofield 1983). Consequently, game theorists have sought solution concepts that would produce predictions for games without cores. As mentioned earlier, the competitive solution (denoted κ), which predicts the formation of particular minimum winning coalitions that offer pivotal members maximal payoffs, has scored some empirical victories, predicting relatively few of the available end states yet accounting for a large majority of the eventual outcomes

(McKelvey and Ordeshook 1979, 1980). Even so, the competitive solution is not without its discordant results. Players sometimes choose non-κ outcomes when they are risk averse, when there are only slight differences between a particular non-κ outcome and its κ counterparts (McKelvey and Ordeshook 1983), or when concerns over fairness impel players to find a more "universalistic" outcome (Eavey 1991). In particular, players who are informed of each others' preference schedules eschew the competitive solution because, by virtue of knowing other players' payoffs, it is regarded as arbitrary, and a reasonably well-paying fair alternative is available (Miller and Oppenheimer 1982). Indeed, one of the earliest published reports of voting experiments with nontransferable utility found this "problem" of fair play to be rampant (Kalisch et al. 1954, 326–27; see also Laing and Olmstead 1978).

One attractive analytic property of several leading solution concepts (for example, the competitive solution, Copeland winner, uncovered set) is that they all predict the core when it exists. This means, however, that each solution concept is also hampered by the inadequacies of the core. If we believe that majority rule equilibria seldom exist, this deficiency is not a particularly damaging criticism from the standpoint of external validity. On the other hand, it does raise some troubling theoretical issues. It may be that the success of the competitive solution, like that of the core, is contingent on the way that alternatives are presented to players, and that the strategic complexity of logrolling or certain finite alternative games (see McKelvey and Ordeshook 1983) would severely undermine the predictive accuracy of κ.[42]

Since roughly the mid-1980s, interest in the competitive solution has waned, replaced by growing fascination with the uncovered set (Miller 1980; Shepsle and Weingast 1984; McKelvey 1986). An alternative Y is said to *cover* X if Y is majority preferred to X and all proposals Z that defeat Y also defeat X. The *uncovered set* is characterized as follows: "Consider an alternative W in the issue space X. . . . Generally there will be a set of alternatives that W does not cover. Collectively, these alternatives can be called the uncovered set of W or UC(W). Now, consider another alternative, Y, and the set of alternatives not covered by Y, or UC(Y). Proceeding in this way for all alternatives in the issue space, one could define the uncovered set for each alternative. Having done this, one could look at the intersection of all of these sets, which would define all the alternatives not covered by any other alternative in this issue space. This set is the uncovered set UC(X) for the whole issue space" (Strom 1990, 115).

42. McKelvey and Ordeshook (1980, 178) speculate that κ sometimes outperforms the core (even though the core is a subset of κ) when no core exists because κ outcomes arise more naturally in negotiations, but here the notion of a natural series of proposals is only dimly specified by current theorizing.

When sophisticated voters consider proposals under open rule and a forward-moving agenda process, outcomes are expected to lie within the uncovered set (Shepsle and Weingast 1984).[43] The location and size of the uncovered set depends on the shapes of legislators' indifference contours, the dimensionality of the issue space, and the distribution of the ideal points within that space. When legislators have circular indifference curves, the uncovered set tends to be located near the geometric center of the legislators' ideal points. The size of the uncovered set tends to grow as the distribution of legislators' ideal points becomes more asymmetrical, but the uncovered set is always confined to the Pareto set, which for circular indifference curves falls within the polygon connecting the outermost ideal points (Miller 1980; McKelvey 1986; Cox 1987). Thus, the uncovered set may be small and centrally located for certain issues and quite diffuse for others. As applied to redistributive questions, for example, which may involve as many dimensions as legislators, the uncovered set may expand to fill the entire policy space.

It is not clear how this solution concept has fared over the range of experiments conducted to date, if only because it is extremely difficult to identify the region encompassed by the uncovered set, even in simple cases where just five legislators with circular indifference curves evaluate policies in two dimensions (Tovey 1993; Eavey 1994). Since the distribution of legislators' ideal points, shapes of indifference contours, and dimensionality of the issue space are seldom known with precision, the predictions of the uncovered set are especially hard to pin down outside the laboratory. Cox and McCubbins (1993, 130) suggest that the uncovered set imposes "definite limits to the policy platforms that those seeking leadership positions will adopt—limits more restrictive than the full range of opinion in the party." They do not go on to say what those definite limits are or how they could be ascertained.[44] And, even if their claim were substantiated by a record of centrally located Speakers, there would remain the question of determining whether centrally located candidates are more attractive than others because of their ideological inclinations, or rather that those whose ambitions and personal style propel them into contention for Speaker tend not to have extreme ideological convictions. In sum, it is hard to say what reference to the uncovered set lends this empirical claim other than spurious formal precision.

43. Under an open rule, a covered proposal, by definition, would always be vulnerable to defeat. Hence, sophisticated legislators would not bother enacting a covered policy. Ordeshook (1986) and Ordeshook and Schwartz (1987) point out, however, that the amendment procedures of Congress, which are backward-moving and disjointed, do not lead to predicted outcomes in the uncovered set.

44. Kiewiet and McCubbins (1991, chap. 3) assess the centrality of the House and Senate floor leaders, but they presuppose a unidimensional liberal-conservative continuum. Restricting the policy space to a single dimension obviates the need for solution concepts like the uncovered set.

DOES THE EXISTENCE OF A CORE MATTER?

The overarching argument in the paradox of voting literature is that the existence or absence of a core affects the observed stability of legislative outcomes. Before summarizing the evidence bearing on this point, let us first consider what "instability" means in the context of these laboratory games. Whereas we ordinarily think of instability as applying to the same legislature's (and same actors') decisions over time, in the experimental setting instability is gauged by the extent to which different legislatures with identical preference configurations enact different policies.[45] One immediate problem, to which we alluded earlier, is that the concept of instability bears only a loose operational connection to the degree of variation in outcomes. When players must choose a policy within an unmarked two-dimensional grid, it is hard to say how much divergence among different committees' output may properly be labeled "instability." This operational task is no easier in the case of finite alternative games, in which outcomes are ranked ordinally for each player. It is not hard to imagine examples of policies in which outcomes that are close in ordinal ranking vis-à-vis other outcomes are nevertheless sufficiently distinct substantively to be labeled significant policy change.

The vagueness with which instability is conceptualized and assessed robs this literature of some of its theoretical impact. Nevertheless, it is possible to draw some impressionistic conclusions from the pattern of experimental results. The most provocative such finding is that coreless games do not produce markedly more unstable outcomes than do games with cores (Fiorina and Plott 1978; Laing and Olmstead 1978), and sometimes the distinction between the two game forms is hard to detect at all (Laing and Slotznick 1987, 1991). To be sure, the dispersion of outcomes is typically greater for noncore games, but the difference is not as striking as the McKelvey (1976) result and subsequent commentary (Riker 1980) might be taken to imply. This finding, as noted by Fiorina and Plott (1978), represents a sharp divergence from how rational choice theorists have characterized the empirical consequences of social choice within majoritarian rule. Indeed, this outcome continues to be regarded as "puzzling" and "problematic," though, as one textbook author reports, "the experimental results have not been accepted as sufficient to discredit the theory" (Strom 1990, 74–75).

If the existence of the core does not have an appreciable effect on the observed

---

45. One might speculate that, ceteris paribus, a single committee's decisions tend to display less variance over time than several ostensibly identical committees considered at one point in time, because legislators in the former setting may not wish to reverse their earlier policy stance or form a given coalition more than once (Mueller 1989; Ordeshook 1992). If this extra-theoretic reasoning is correct, the experimental outcomes reported in this literature will tend to be look more "unstable" than those from legislatures observed over time.

instability in experimental outcomes, then one of the central empirical claims motivating game theoretic analyses of legislative behavior—the influence of majority rule equilibrium on legislative stability—receives little support. There are various ways that rational choice theorists seem inclined to react to this pattern of results. Some question whether the experimental data are sufficiently sound and numerous to disturb this theoretical expectation (Strom 1990). Others regard the general question of instability as passé or empirically irrelevant (Krehbiel 1991). Still others attribute the empirical failings to the deficiencies of cooperative game theory, though conceding that attempts to model committee games in noncooperative terms has not led to an improvement in predictive accuracy (Salant and Goodstein 1990).

Cooperative game theorists who neither skirt nor dismiss the issue tend to envision ways to paint a bull's-eye around this finding, suggesting that a solution concept (perhaps one waiting to be discovered) predicts that, in the absence of a core, outcomes will nonetheless fall within some circumscribed range of proposals. Therefore, the absence of equilibrium need not, as Riker claimed, imply that "anything can happen." In this regard, the Copeland winner predicts a point; the competitive solution, when it exists, predicts a handful of points; the uncovered set or heart suggests that the outcome will lie within a centrally located region whose size depends on the symmetry of the legislators' ideal points. Put another way: although any outcome is possible under simple majority rule when no core exists, only a small set of proposals may be regarded as likely outcomes.

The problem with the last argument is that it fails to grapple with the weak contrast between configurations with and without a core. Even such solution concepts as the competitive solution, which suggest that chaos need not result from coreless preference configurations, nonetheless imply contrasting degrees of stability. Although the concept of the uncovered set offers a wider net with which to capture the dispersion of legislative outcomes, the problem of explaining policy stability or instability remains. Solution concepts like the uncovered set place some boundaries on the range of outcomes likely to be observed when forward-moving agendas and simple majority rule decide the fate of a low-dimensional policy question. Chaos of the "anything can happen" sort tends to be ruled out. But the uncovered set seems to be insufficiently restrictive to explain why experimental games with and without cores (including those with seemingly large uncovered sets) do not produce more sharply contrasting outcomes. Second, this defense overestimates the degree of empirical support for various solution concepts. At very least, this argument underestimates the sensitivity of these solution concepts to exogenous factors, such as game-playing skill. Third, if the existence of majority rule equilibrium is interpreted as a factor of little relevance to policy stability, then what does explain varying degrees of policy change?

THE EFFECTS OF STRUCTURAL FACTORS

Much rational choice theorizing draws its inspiration from the conviction that "procedures and other institutional aspects of committee processes should be important in determining the outcome" (Plott and Levine 1978, 146). Indeed, scholars working within this tradition have argued that the study of procedural effects is the central intellectual objective within the study of public choice (Plott 1979). Recent years have witnessed the proliferation of scholarship on the effects of agenda control, open versus closed voting rules, delegation of policy responsibility to legislative committees, and the like. As we noted earlier, this line of research has produced many significant analytic works and holds out the promise of offering empirical insights that bear directly on ways to understand and construct political institutions. To date, however, empirical support has been mixed.

Before we review the experimental evidence on the effects of changes in institutional structure, let us consider what kinds of findings would be inconsistent with the underlying thrust of this perspective on institutions. Since a game theoretic approach distills predictions about the effects of institutional change from alterations in the mathematical structure of a game setting, it would be damaging to find that seemingly important formal changes in institutional structure had little effect on the outcome or that seemingly irrelevant changes had substantial effects.[46] In addition to asking whether experimental anomalies arise, we might also ask whether these models offer *powerful* insights in circumstances where they seem to work as predicted. It is one thing to claim, for instance, that policies debated under open or closed amendment rules will result in different outcomes; such claims have long been made by informal observers of legislative politics. It is quite another to argue that the Rules Committee's decision to assign an open or closed rule is an important determinant of the eventual outcome in comparison to other factors that are exogenous to game theoretic accounts, such as the strategic skill with which legislators pursue their objectives.

There can be no doubt that certain basic propositions about the effects of institutional structure are supported by experimental results. Plott and Levine (1978) demonstrate that the way in which alternatives are paired in a series of binary choices can dramatically alter legislative outcomes.[47] Isaac and Plott (1978) show that whether

46. Granted, when the relation between institutional change and policy outcomes is mispredicted, game theorists can always retreat to the position that more complex models will succeed where simple ones fail. Time will tell.

47. In a similar vein, Ordeshook (1986, 427), summarizing several studies conducted in collaboration with McKelvey, suggests that when an agenda is open, the outcome is predicted by κ; at the opposite end of the continuum, where an agenda pits a series of proposals against one another in binary votes, the outcome is predicted by the issue-by-issue median.

one player is given exclusive power to recognize amendments by other players can have a marked influence on the legislative outcome. Wilson (1986) shows that forward voting procedures, whereby amendments are voted on immediately after being proposed and become the status quo if passed, produce substantially more policy change than do backward voting rules, which dispose of all amendments before pitting the fully amended bill against the status quo.[48]

On the other hand, more subtle manipulations have not produced predicted effects. In particular, whenever the predictions hinge in a nontrivial way on the strategic abilities of the actors, anomalies arise. In one telling experiment, Isaac and Plott (1978) conferred on one player not only the power to recognize amendments from other players, but also the opportunity to offer a single take-it-or-leave-it proposal to the others. In none of the experimental trials did the player who controlled the agenda capitalize on this special ultimatum power. In similar experiments involving finite alternative games, some agenda-setters cleverly took advantage of committee members' cyclical preferences while others inexplicably settled for markedly suboptimal bargains (Eavey and Miller 1984a).[49]

Perhaps the most noteworthy games of this sort—noteworthy because they mirror in many ways the hypothetical example offered at the beginning of the chapter—are the two-dimensional spatial games discussed by Kormendi and Plott (1982). In these games the status quo was a policy that all players found very unattractive, yet in none of the trials did the agenda-setters seize the opportunity to offer a take-it-or-leave-it proposal that coincided with their ideal points. The pattern of outcomes in fact suggests tremendous variability in the inclination or ability of agenda-setters to orchestrate an outcome to their liking.

Herzberg and Wilson's study of the effects of transaction costs produces equally dismal results (1991). Notwithstanding the fact that the exaction of a penalty for passing amendments was designed to induce an equilibrium, the presence or absence of transaction costs had no significant effect on the pattern of legislative outcomes. In fact, this equilibrium was never reached in any of the eleven experimental trials utilizing an open agenda. Even when players were forced to consider this equilibrium proposal as part of a pre-set agenda imposed by the experimenter, the predicted outcome obtained in just four of seventeen trials. Evidently, calculating an optimal strategy in light of these transaction costs was beyond the strategic capacities of the actors.

Not only do certain structural manipulations fail to produce predicted outcomes,

48. It is sometimes argued that models which assume a forward-moving agenda are flawed insofar as "legislatures generally use a backward moving agenda process" (Strom 1990, 117). Forward-moving agenda models nonetheless apply to an important class of legislative phenomena, policies considered under closed rule during successive legislative sessions.

49. Other examples of suboptimal play may be found in Laing and Slotznick 1987, 1991.

but theoretically irrelevant variables seem to have profound effects. When a nonvoting agenda-setter has a like-minded "ally" on the committee, he or she tends to obtain much more favorable outcomes than when the agenda-setter lacks a representative on the committee who shares a similar preferences schedule, even if the median voter's preferences are unchanged (Eavey and Miller 1984a, 728). Outcomes are affected by such nuances as whether legislators engage in premeeting negotiations and whether committee proceedings are governed informally or by Robert's Rules of Order (Hoffman and Plott 1983).

The upshot of these experiments is that although rational choice offers a method by which to predict the effects of exogenous institutional changes, the empirical adequacy of these predictions is contingent upon factors that lie beyond the bounds of the formal analysis of institutions and spatially based incentives. From an analytic standpoint, two equilibria may look alike. But when gauged empirically, they may prove to be very different in terms of the accuracy of their predictions. In general it would appear that a posited equilibrium's empirical success varies inversely with its reliance on strategic calculation and ruthless execution. Part of the problem is doubtless that some experimental subjects are simply "muddling through," for as Plott and Levine (1978) noted early on in the development of this literature, fully 30 percent of their legislators followed no consistent decision rule across a series of voting choices. A variety of studies, in particular those by Laing and Olmstead (1978), McKelvey and Ordeshook (1983), and Eckel and Holt (1989), have broadened this conclusion, revealing laboratory legislators to be neither uniformly myopic nor farsighted, selfish nor fair, Machiavellian nor retiring, but rather a varied lot. Heterogeneity of this kind throws sand into the gears of an analytic system that draws its predictions about the outcomes of group processes from a small set of axioms about human motives and conduct.

THOUGHTS ON THE INTERNAL AND EXTERNAL
VALIDITY OF EXPERIMENTS

Those who use experimental methods to test rational choice propositions typically justify their work in seemingly modest terms. On the one hand, as we noted earlier, investigators have hastened to acknowledge the limited external validity of their experiments, portraying the lab as a screening device by which to check the serviceability of empirical hypotheses (Fiorina and Plott 1978). McKelvey and Ordeshook (1984b, 92) remark that their "experiments show only that our model is feasible, not that it describes actual voting behavior," and they are elsewhere no less self-effacing (compare 1980, 156; 1990b, 311–12). In a similar fashion, Plott and Levine (1978, 156) suggest that laboratory demonstration is a necessary condition for external application, stating: "If by using our ideas about the influence of the agenda, we are unable to influence the decisions of groups in a simple laboratory setting, then we cannot in good faith claim that our theory works in the more complicated 'real world' case."

The obverse of this argument, however, is that the lab affords scholars the opportunity to discard unsupported propositions. In this vein, Fiorina and Plott draw broad inferences from their study of committee behavior (1978, 590), concluding flatly: "Numerous widely known models which have natural interpretations in [the laboratory] setting do not work. Applied scientists who wish to study situations that fall within our specifications should not look to these models for help." It seems strange to acknowledge the unrealism of the laboratory setting while at the same time reserving the right to denounce hypotheses as inapplicable to the outside world. Could one not argue that the very features that render these experiments externally invalid facilitate the influence of variables that were found to be inconsequential in the lab? To cite but one illustration of this problem, we return to the fact that the operative preferences in these games are induced solely through monetary payoffs. Perhaps norms of fairness or feelings of group loyalty, which are in some ways suppressed by the format of laboratory committees, might figure more prominently if negotiation concerned an ideologically charged issue toward which players have deeply held preferences.

One direction for future experimental research would be to measure subjects' preferences on substantively meaningful issues (for instance, the procedures by which grades are to be assigned to test results in a class), assign sets of players with putatively identical preference rankings to committees under different treatment conditions, and allow these subjects to debate substantive issues related to their (previously measured) ideological preferences. In addition to or in lieu of monetary incentives, a randomly selected committee could be rewarded by having its policy decision enforced.

It may be fruitful to rethink other basic features of legislative voting experiments as well. The method typically used to study the effects of differences in institutional structure is a between-subjects design, in which one group is assigned, say, a closed rule, and another is assigned an open rule. One problem with this approach is that it fails to capture the psychological effects of institutional *alterations* to the status quo. The few instances in which subjects encountered institutional changes over the course of an experiment suggest that there is an interplay between alterations in structure and how individuals play games. Isaac and Plott (1978, 304), for example, find that bestowing agenda-control upon one player and subsequently withdrawing it produced noncore outcomes. This was because the erstwhile agenda-controller in their experiments, who could have easily forced core outcomes, "was frequently mad or frustrated by his inability to control the actions of the other individuals and never revealed this preference." What state does not harbor a disgruntled class of people still smoldering over some timeless loss of privilege? What legislative gambit involving clever manipulation of procedure does not cause some opposing faction to cry foul? The point to be made is that memoryless formal models of institutional effects on legislative behavior may fare even worse when subjected to experimental tests that introduce "framing" or "endowment" effects (Tversky and Kahneman 1981; Kahneman and Tversky 1984).

To date, laboratory tests of rational choice models have focused on a fairly narrow band of factors potentially important to legislative decision making. There has been no attempt, for example, to assess the robustness of game theoretic predictions in the face of social-psychological manipulations involving conformity (Asch 1958), social identity (Tajfel 1978), mood (Salovey et al. 1991), or social roles (Biddle and Thomas 1966; Abelson 1976) that from the standpoint of game theory ought to be irrelevant to the outcome.[50] Judging from the bibliographies of the studies reviewed here, rational choice scholars are largely unacquainted with or unimpressed by the broader spectrum of social-psychological research. In this respect, experimental studies of legislative bargaining lag behind other literatures examining rational choice hypotheses, such as the research on social dilemmas reviewed in the previous chapter.

Consider, for example, the significance of group identification in actual legislatures, in which public officials are known to divide along lines of party, ideology, region, and race. An enormous amount of psychological research replicated in several countries suggests that people readily draw group boundaries and are quick to discriminate against outsiders and on behalf of in-group members—even when the basis of group identification is as trivial as aesthetic preference (Tajfel 1978). One might imagine a bargaining experiment in which subjects' social identities were induced prior to negotiation, with or without a correlation between social group division and preference configuration. To what extent would the predictive accuracy of game theoretic predictions concerning coalition formation and policy outcome be affected by this type of manipulation?

Or consider the role of institutional norms on legislative behavior. At present, bargaining experiments make no effort to use confederates in order to socialize players, even though the learning of institutional norms appears to be a predictor of experimental behavior (Bandura 1977) and actual legislative behavior (Matthews 1960). How would subjects behave in a given bargaining session if, in previously staged committee interactions involving confederates, they had each been exposed to "universalistic" as opposed to "cutthroat" behavior? Do game theoretic predictions

50. Even in the arid social environment of these lab experiments, where strangers interact briefly and then go their separate ways, there are signs that such factors manifest themselves. McKelvey and Ordeshook (1984) report a noncore outcome that occurred when a subject repeatedly acted against her self-interest in order to punish two subjects she found distasteful. Miller and Oppenheimer (1982) find that subjects who insisted on negotiating competitively were punished for violating a norm of universalism by being shut out of the winning coalition.

fare equally well in both normative environments? To what extent do legislators suppress their policy inclinations and go along to get along? Until experimental research addresses the kinds of effects that inform these lingering questions about external validity it will be difficult to say what the behavior of experimental committees tells us about the politics of legislative institutions and the social systems they embody.

SPATIAL THEORIES AND THEIR RELATION TO EVIDENCE

Spatial models of legislative behavior have tended to ignore or downplay such phenomena as persuasion or endogenous preference change, group or party solidarity, position taking, and various leadership-supplied side-payments. In addition, these models have generally presupposed a rather sparse institutional environment in which procedural rules are few and legislators incur no transaction costs when they make legislative proposals or organize coalitions. Nonetheless, it should be noted that these deficiencies are not inherent to spatial modeling. One could envision, for example, a model of legislative behavior in which legislators receive a utility bonus in return for adherence to their party caucus' preferred policy position (see Kiewiet and McCubbins 1991, chap. 6). By the same token, one could imagine a model that allows for a complex array of procedural arrangements concerning the manner in which bills are referred to committee or amended on the floor. Granted, the introduction of more than a handful of such embellishments at once might make it extremely difficult to derive analytic insights from the model. The point remains, however, that the conceptual framework of spatial modeling does not preclude the introduction of ever more elaborate depictions of legislative politics.[51]

The general trend in spatial modeling of legislative behavior has been in the direction of greater verisimilitude with such institutions as Congress. Committees, parties, transaction costs, and a host of procedural rules have become more common features of legislative models. Concurrent with this change in content has been a shift in the form of rational choice modeling. Rational choice theorists have gradually distanced themselves from cooperative game theory and its focus on the equilibrium strategies of maximizing coalitions, as opposed to maximizing individuals.[52]

51. As noted earlier, the problem of analytic tractability is compounded greatly when one attempts to construct formal models of institutions whose procedures include suspension of the rules. A game representation of such an institution would have as one available strategy the creation of a new game form.

52. As Ordeshook (1992, 303) has commented: "Once we reconceptualize players as coalitions and strategies as the payoff vectors coalitions can secure, the concept of a core seems a natural extension of the idea of a Nash equilibrium to a cooperative context. The remaining solution concepts such as the V-set and the competitive solution, on the other hand, have a

Most new work is grounded in noncooperative game theory, focusing on self-enforcing, Nash equilibria. These models have tended to highlight the role played by the sequence in which actors move, the information their moves reveal, their expectations of future interaction, and their ability to sanction one another.[53] It seems safe to say that the vast majority of political science graduate students who nowadays develop an expertise in rational choice theory are trained in the noncooperative game theoretic tradition.

The tension between cooperative and noncooperative theory is not new, and in some ways the preference for one over the other reflects different assessments of the analytic tractability of different theoretical approaches. In 1982, for example, McKelvey and Ordeshook observed: "Nash . . . originally suggested that a more appropriate way to model cooperative games was precisely to include all such possibilities for communication and cooperation . . . and then to analyze this extensive form as a noncooperative game, looking for Nash equilibria to this game. . . . Unfortunately, the obvious problem with this approach is specification of the extensive form when any reasonably rich possibilities for communication are available. It has been the hope of cooperative game theorists to circumvent these problems by not including cooperative moves in extensive form, but rather summarizing the possibilities for cooperation in the characteristic function" (1982, 127). Cooperative game theory, in other words, may be regarded as a theoretical shortcut, a collection of formal accounts that ignores many strategic subtleties and utilizes equilibrium concepts other than Nash equilibria. It was hoped that from a simplified analytic framework (albeit one with a more debatable foundation in individual rationality) might flow empirically sustainable predictions. In particular, it was hoped that these predictions could be applied successfully to a range of legislative situations that, from a noncooperative standpoint, would seem analytically distinct and perhaps intractably complex.

The advent of noncooperative game theory seems attributable less to the empirical deficiencies of its cooperative cousin than to a desire to ground rational choice theory

---

disturbing ad hoc quality to them, because the hypotheses that form their definitions are not derived from any readily identifiable postulates of rationality. Moreover, if the mechanisms for enforcement are germane to the kinds of agreements people reach, then, because these ideas sidestep this issue of enforcement, we cannot be certain that they apply universally."

53. Baron and Ferejohn (1989, 1200), after suggesting how noncooperative game theory may be applied to legislative decision making concerning a distributive issue, suggest that the weakness of cooperative models stems from their inattentiveness to strategic nuance: "Cooperative models of politics abstract from the process by which alternatives arise and assume that coalitions will freely form to defeat alternatives when a majority of members prefers another available alternative. Cooperative theories generate weak predictions because they ignore the implications of structure for undertaking coordinated activity (or coalition formation) in a legislative setting."

entirely on the maximizing behavior of strategic individuals. A good deal of effort has gone into supplying the noncooperative "microfoundations" for results derived from cooperative theory, but many cooperative results, in particular those that presuppose sincere voting, are thought to have little or no basis in noncooperative theory. In the eyes of some rational choice theorists, therefore, much of cooperative game theory (and by implication, much of this chapter) properly resides outside the boundaries of rational choice theory.

Division of opinion about what properly constitutes a rational choice theory as opposed to a social choice theory or a spatial theory places us in a peculiar position. The literature on the instability of majority rule is widely cited, and its themes continue to be taken up in recent works grounded in noncooperative approaches (Kiewiet and McCubbins 1991; Cox and McCubbins 1993). Failure to consider this literature in detail would have exposed us to the charge that we had overlooked one of the most important domains of application. On the other hand, having now critiqued the instability literature in some detail, it may be said that we have grappled with applications that are not truly grounded in rational choice theory. Note that the latter argument would remove from consideration the bulk of empirical work suggesting how rational choice theories enlighten our understanding of policy stability, leaving relatively little for us to review. In an effort to be comprehensive, we return to noncooperative theories of legislative behavior in Chapter 8 when we discuss three recent treatments of Congress and the committee system. For the present, we observe that although a number of noncooperative game theory models have touched on the themes of legislative stability and the effects of procedural rules on policy outcomes (Epple and Riordan 1987; Baron and Ferejohn 1989), concomitant empirical testing has not yet materialized.

As noncooperative game theories of legislative studies develop to the point where hypothesis testing becomes possible, this emergent empirical literature has the opportunity to overcome some of the methodological deficiencies of previous scholarship. Fundamental to the methodological concerns we have expressed in this chapter is the issue of what it means to test an analytic proposition with empirical evidence. As Page (1978, 18) notes, rational choice theorists seem to approach empirical applications of rational choice propositions in two very different ways: "Sometimes they choose and commit themselves to a set of assumptions, letting the theory stand or fall in terms of its predictive power. At other times they apparently regard some of their assumptions as boundary conditions or empirical parameters, intending the theory to apply only when those assumptions are met." The first mode of inquiry retains the distinction between analytic conjecture and empirical outcome, exposing the hypothesis to falsification. The second, however, creates a tautology insofar as it contends that *when the assumptions of the model hold,* the prediction holds. Naturally, if the model's assumptions are satisfied, the prediction follows as a matter of logical necessity. A failed prediction can only mean that the correspondence between the analytic proposition and the application has somewhere broken down. In order for rational choice theory to generate informative empirical inquiry, it must be the case that the theoretical terms in the model are distinct from the empirical circumstances to which the model is applied, yet a prediction is made anyway.

Applying a game theoretic model that makes no allowance for norms leads to potentially interesting predictions because the correspondence between the assumptions of the model and the empirical application is uncertain. But to say, on encountering discordant evidence, that utility derived from behaving fairly is experimental error renders the model at once less interesting and less vulnerable to empirical disconfirmation.

In practice, where spatial models of legislative politics fall along the continuum from testable to tautological has been hard to pin down. Quite often, what starts as a bold, testable proposition ends up as a timid tautology after an encounter with discordant data. Shepsle and Weingast (1987a), for example, initially contend that committees derive their power from the opportunity to enforce an ex post veto in conference committee: *"The ex post veto . . . is sufficient to make gatekeeping and proposal power effective, even though their effectiveness appears to most observers to be the product of nothing more than informal reciprocity arrangements"* (89). But when confronted with the fact that only a portion of legislation goes to conference and that the floor and Speaker have various ways of reining in recalcitrant conferees or circumventing the conference process entirely (Krehbiel 1987), Shepsle and Weingast retreat to the position that, although they have the U.S. Congress "in mind," theirs is a "stylized argument" and "an exercise in theory" (937).[54]

Note that our objection here is not with stylized accounts. We remain agnostic about whether one can develop empirically fruitful predictions from models of institutional processes that, for example, ignore legislators' opportunity to suspend the rules. Indeed, we are not in principle opposed to simplifications that treat legislatures and bureaucratic agencies as unitary actors (Banks 1989) or populate a legislature with just three members (Epple and Riordan 1987). Our concern centers on whether the resulting hypotheses are to be tested with data. To the extent that the distinction between a parsimonious conjecture and an analytic boundary condition remains murky, for practical purposes the answer is no. Any such model that runs into difficulty can be rescued by the claim that the data represent an invalid application of the model. In effect, when the data prove to be at variance with a prediction, the model impeaches the data, rather than the other way around.[55]

54. Shepsle and Weingast (1987b, 941) claim also that "the committee system of our model has, as its empirical referent, the House committee system of the 1950s and 1960s," something that was not indicated in their initial (1987a) essay.

55. Notice that this problem seldom arises when rational choice models are offered specifi-

It is customary for reviews of rational choice scholarship on legislative politics to close with a call for empirical work (Krehbiel 1988; Strom 1990; Rieselbach 1992). Ours is no exception, but in calling attention to the dearth of compelling empirical applications we hope also to encourage political scientists to reflect on the special problems that arise when deductive systems are evaluated empirically. For any given theory of the legislative process one might ask, What is the correspondence between the theoretical terms in an analytic expression and the world of politics? How might one go about measuring these terms? To what kinds of institutions is the model intended to apply? What evidence, if observed, would shake our confidence in the explanatory value of the model? Finally, if the model should prove inconsistent with the data, should the model be scrapped? If not, how might it be revised and yet preserve its ability to generate nonobvious, testable hypotheses?

---

cally to account for a particular domain of legislative phenomena (say, policy making in the U.S. Congress). Granted, a variety of practical constraints may make it difficult to test a given hypothesis in a convincing fashion, but once the model is addressed to a particular explanandum, the researcher cannot easily retreat to the position that his or her model explains *some* phenomenon even if it inadequately accounts for Congressional data. For this reason, we are more favorably disposed toward rational choice accounts that are inspired by and directed toward particular applications (e.g., Kiewiet and McCubbins 1991, Krehbiel 1991, and Cox and McCubbins 1993) than the myriad of rational choice works that take up the question of application as something of an afterthought.

CHAPTER SEVEN

SPATIAL THEORIES OF ELECTORAL COMPETITION

There is a sense in which the vast majority of political scientists who study American electoral politics subscribe to rational choice theory. Among the commonplaces of political science is the observation that politicians pursue strategies designed to enhance their chances of winning or retaining elective office. It comes as no surprise that U.S. senators who were up for reelection in 1990 were far less likely to vote for the "Read My Lips" tax increase of that year than were those who were insulated from electoral reprisal (Jacobson 1993) or that many elected officials spend a good deal of their time engaging in the otherwise unpleasant task of fundraising for their next campaign (Green and Krasno 1988). Few commentators have failed to note how presidents ranging from Franklin Roosevelt to Dwight Eisenhower have adapted their policy agendas and political tactics to accommodate public sentiment (Dallek 1979; Greenstein 1982) or how presidential candidates have adjusted their messages strategically to enhance their electoral appeal (Polsby and Wildavsky 1991). Many such insights concerning the "electoral connection" (Key 1965; Mayhew 1974) between public opinion and the behavior of politicians have been floating around for some time, quite independent of rational choice theorizing.

Similarly, most students of mass political behavior subscribe to some variant of the rational choice notion that, ceteris paribus, voters are more attracted to the candidate perceived to be closest to some ideal set of attributes, whether that closeness refers to ideological proximity, personal style, or reference group identity. Few scholars would quarrel with the view that Barry Goldwater, George McGovern, Walter Mondale, Jesse Jackson, Pat Robertson, or Michael Dukakis lost electoral support because of platforms or personal characteristics that were in some ways at variance with the electorate's tastes. The banner of rational choice surely flies above the discipline when it comes to the general proposition that elected officials who seem to be out of step with the mores of their constituents court electoral reprisal.

Just as one does not qualify as a Marxist simply by believing that deep-seated conflict exists between economic classes or as a Freudian by believing that human beings have unconscious motives, subscribing to the view that elected officials act strategically to enhance their popularity among voters qualifies one as a rational choice theorist only in the loosest sense. In contrast with the informal theorizing about the strategic behavior of politicians that has traditionally dominated the study of electoral politics, rational choice theorizing seeks to determine the existence and location of equilibria based on a set of axioms about the objectives of the actors, the information available to them, and the constraints on their strategic alternatives. Put another way, rational choice theorizing holds out the promise of distilling from the complexities of electoral competition the essential features of a game, which in turn may be used to predict how candidates will behave under the assumption that they play this game in ways that are in some sense optimal. The question, then, becomes whether the game metaphor and the theoretical results concerning equilibrium strategies that flow from it provide novel and empirically substantiated insights about electoral politics.

Without contesting the attractiveness of an analytic framework that emphasizes the strategic dimensions of electoral competition, we find little indication that rational choice theorizing has contributed to the empirical study of campaigns or candidate strategy. On the whole, the interplay between theory and evidence has been sporadic and diffuse. As one rational choice theorist observed in 1983, "Almost all of the literature has been devoted to the important and fundamental question of the existence or nonexistence of an equilibrium. As a result, the research on formal models has been almost devoid of empirical content" (Wittman 1983, 142). Little has changed in the interim. If anything, in the years following the publication of Page's *Choices and Echoes in Presidential Elections* (1978), Aldrich's *Before the Convention* (1980), and Enelow and Hinich's *Spatial Theory of Voting* (1984), among the few systematic empirical assessments of spatial theories of campaigns, the pace of nonexperimental research in this area has slowed. Typical of recent work is Peter Coughlin's *Probabilistic Voting Theory* (1992), which in the course of 252 pages makes just four passing references to actual political events and one reference to an election campaign. More than three decades since Downs brought spatial models into currency in political science, there is simply not much applied research on American elections for us to evaluate.

The dearth of empirical scholarship in no way reflects the level of interest in candidate competition among rational choice theorists. The list of published works in this area is long and expanding rapidly. Nor can the state of applied work be attributed to fluctuations in intellectual currents within rational choice theory. In contrast with rational choice theorizing about legislative behavior, which has undergone a shift from cooperative to noncooperative game theory, analysis of two-party competition has always been predominantly noncooperative in form. Yet the subject of candidate competition, which would seem well suited to showcase what rational choice can contribute to the empirical study of American politics, has generated little by way of applied research.

Why this imbalance between theory and evidence exists is not entirely clear to us, though we have the impression that for many rational choice theorists the investigation of electoral competition is primarily a modeling exercise. The driving question at times appears to be, "What happens to the implications of a given model when one alters a particular assumption?" To be sure, exploration of the contours of a model may be motivated by empirically based misgivings about its predictions. It would be unfair to say that empirical evidence is unimportant to those who are drawn to the analytic nuances of modeling candidate competition; such theorists clearly would prefer that their models predict outcomes that correspond to the real world. Still, testing is not a major concern, and empirical evidence weighs in primarily in the form of "stylized facts" that guide the selection of particular theoretical assumptions.

Accordingly, the literature on candidate competition develops more or less as follows. A theory is advanced, and confirming evidence is adduced in a rather casual manner in order to lend some credence to the model's predictions. Next, a stylized fact comes into currency that calls into question the validity of some earlier prediction, setting off a torrent of post hoc theorizing designed to count this anomaly as a phenomenon that follows from rational action. This process repeats itself for different stylized facts, though in somewhat different form as models are updated to incorporate the latest technical fashions in game theory. Indeed, sometimes the very stylized facts that were earlier discarded as unrealistic are rehabilitated.

One stylized fact that has held sway over rational choice theorists is the notion that electoral competition engenders centrist politics. "It has often been observed that the center of voter opinion exerts a powerful force over election outcomes," write Enelow and Hinich (1984a, 462). "We maintain that election theory must explain what we observe. The center of voter opinion is important in democratic elections," and the model Enelow and Hinich offer "provides part of the explanation."[1]

Although models that anticipate centrist politics are from time to time applauded as "arguably accurate" (Calvert 1985, 87), in recent years many rational choice theorists have been impressed by the extent to which candidates stake out positions that are not centrist. "Why is it that there seem to be persistent and predictable differences

---

1. They go on to say: "The repeated finding of multidimensional scaling analysis that the major party candidates in democratic elections tend to cluster around the center of voter opinion is supported by theory. It is possible to construct a general theoretical explanation for the center as an attractive force in democratic electoral politics. To do so is to perform what should be the obvious goal of election theory: to explain what actually happens" (477).

between political parties?" ask Chappell and Keech (1986, 881) in the opening line of their essay on electoral competition. Perhaps the best indicator of this drift in stylization is an essay by Enelow, Endersby, and Munger (1993, 127), who advertise that because their model typically predicts that the candidates will adopt distinct equilibrium platforms, it "accounts for what is widely observed in real elections: candidate divergence on the issues."[2]

The unsystematic fashion in which evidence inspires and confronts these theories becomes apparent when one reflects on the stylized facts that these models purport to explain. As noted, some rational choice models predict that, in equilibrium, competing candidates will converge to the same campaign platform. Other models predict that equilibrium is achieved when candidates stake out distinct platforms. Still others depict electoral competition as having no equilibrium, with candidates continually upsetting majority coalitions. Assuming these models could be translated into operational terms (so that one would know how to identify cases of convergent, divergent, or nonexistent equilibria), it seems unlikely that any single prediction could accommodate the wide range of historical outcomes. Presidential elections, for example, arguably include instances of divergence (Goldwater-Johnson, Reagan-Mondale), of convergence (Ford-Carter, Nixon-Kennedy), and of candidates groping for new issue dimensions by which to destabilize an opposing coalition (Bush-Dukakis, Hoover-Smith). Even within a given election campaign, as Page (1978) has documented with care, candidates sometimes diverge, converge, or flail about depending on the issue in question. Thus, to our general apprehensions about post hoc theorizing we add a specific concern about the stylized facts that animate this literature.

As in previous chapters, we begin with some expository remarks concerning the modeling efforts in this area. Our point of departure is a rudimentary model of two-candidate competition typically associated with Anthony Downs (1957), in which politicians attempt to garner votes by appealing to the policy tastes of voters. The next section traces the evolution of this model, noting how its predictions about strategic equilibrium change as certain key assumptions are modified. The observation that a great many variants of the spatial model generate overlapping predictions leads us next to consider the problems that arise when one attempts to discriminate empirically among competing models. In addition to voicing reservations about post hoc theorizing, we express concern about the large and growing number of unobservable terms used in spatial models of electoral competition. The practical barriers to measuring candidates' beliefs or motives, we argue, narrow the range of research designs that are likely to inform any assessment of spatial models. Although we indicate some

---

2. Naturally, one cannot argue with the objective of trying to explain what is observed. But the array of facts to be explained seldom ascends beyond a sketch of converge or divergence. For a more extensive list of stylized facts to be explained see Grofman 1993c, 180–81.

advantages to a research design patterned after "comparative statics" analyses, we remain skeptical about the plausibility of claims about equilibrium strategies in a strategic environment as complex and nuanced as candidate competition. We therefore think it imperative that empirical inquiry based on spatial models be designed so as to allow for the possibility that something other than optimal strategic play accounts for candidate behavior.

A RUDIMENTARY SPATIAL MODEL OF ELECTORAL COMPETITION

Consider an election in which two identical candidates square off, each seeking to win as many votes as possible.[3] The means by which candidates attract votes are their respective platforms, which may be located anywhere along a single ideological dimension. Thus, instead of supposing that candidates or parties seek election in order to enact preferred policies, this model of electoral competition suggests that parties adopt platforms in an effort to win office (Downs 1957, 28).

Candidate locations along a single evaluative dimension are assumed to be the sole basis on which voters evaluate the candidates. Furthermore, the utility a platform provides any voter is assumed to diminish steadily with the distance between the platform and the voter's ideal point, ensuring that voters have single-peaked preferences. Each voter maximizes utility, therefore, by casting a ballot for the candidate with the closest platform.[4] Candidates are assumed to know both who will vote and how they will vote given any pair of platforms that might be chosen.[5] The strategic task before the candidates, then, is to use this information to choose an optimal platform.

The analytic result that follows from this characterization of two-candidate competition parallels that of legislative bargaining along a single-issue dimension: both

3. The model we describe is often attributed to Anthony Downs (1957), but it differs in important ways from the full account he gives, which includes uncertainty, voter abstention, restrictions on candidate mobility, ambiguous platforms, and so forth. Also, Downs's account focuses on party behavior, whereas we speak of candidates, as the latter are more plausibly regarded as unitary actors (see Davis et al. 1970; Budge and Farlie 1977). Finally, throughout this chapter we consider only competition between two candidates on the grounds that spatial models of multicandidate competition, which figure prominently in Downs's discussion, are much more complex conceptually and seldom applied to American politics.

4. The strategic behavior of voters may come into play when there are more than two candidates (Shepsle and Cohen 1990) or in general equilibrium models in which voter turnout and candidate platforms are strategically interrelated (Ledyard 1984). We ignore these complications here.

5. We set aside the question of why voters in a large electorate would vote based on issue preferences given that their vote cannot plausibly be regarded as decisive. See Brennan and Buchanan 1984.

candidates adopt platforms identical to the ideal point of the median voter along the ideological continuum. The location of the median voter is a Nash equilibrium in the sense that neither candidate can unilaterally make himself or herself better off by departing from this strategy in favor of some alternative course of action.

To get an intuitive understanding of this result, suppose there were an election in which the only issue voters cared about was the size of the protective tariff that each candidate advocated. This one-dimensional race is depicted in figure 7.1. For ease of illustration, we will assume that the electorate consists of just three voters, $\{1, 2, 3\}$, whose own ideal points are arrayed along the size-of-tariff continuum. Their voting rule is straightforward: the candidate who advocates a position closest to each voter's favored stance receives his or her vote. Now suppose that the two candidates—call them L and R—can choose among eight possible platforms to set forth in this campaign. Platform A promises a very low tariff, while platform H proposes to raise it substantially.[6] Based on this stylized portrayal of strategic alternatives and voter tastes, we can translate the diagram into a schedule of ordered preferences for each voter, presented at the foot of figure 7.1. If both candidates choose their strategies simultaneously, it should be apparent that both should pick platform D, which corresponds to the ideal point of the "median voter," voter 2. Platform D defeats any other platform that might be chosen; for example, if one candidate adopts D but the other adopts C, then the former candidate wins the election with a coalition of voters 2 and 3. The median voter's ideal point is a Nash equilibrium, because when both candidates locate themselves at the median neither candidate can garner more votes by moving to some other location.[7] The result generalizes in a straightforward fashion to situations involving large numbers of voters.

Perhaps because of the normative implications of the median voter result for

6. Note that the distribution of voters defines what is an "extreme" position. We could have constructed the same example using three voters who were each, to varying degrees, committed to a highly protective tariff.

7. Ordeshook (1992, 104–5) summarizes the Median Voter Theorem, as applied to electoral competition, in the following terms: "In two-candidate elections that concern a single issue, if both candidates know the distribution of citizen preferences on the issue, if each candidate's strategy consists of a position on the issue, if citizens know the candidates' strategies, if all citizens have single-peaked preferences on the issue, and if no constraints are placed on the candidates' strategies with respect to the issue, then both candidates will converge to the electorate's median preference." Notice that if the nature of the equilibrium indeed drives a pair of candidates to take identical stances, then a so-called pure theory of electoral competition (Ledyard 1984), in which voters are enticed to the polls solely based on the ideological gains they would reap if their preferred candidate wins, predicts near zero turnout. That is to say, rational voters have two reasons to stay home: as noted before, they cannot hope to influence the outcome; and even if they could, they don't care who wins because the candidates adopt indistinguishable platforms.

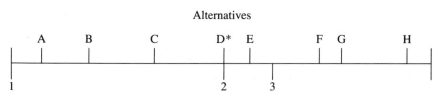

Alternatives

*Deterministic voting equilibrium (the median).

Voter preference schedule

	Voter 1	Voter 2	Voter 3
Most preferred	A	D	E
	B	E	D
	C	C	F
	D	F	G
	E	G	C
	F	B	H
	G	H	B
Least preferred	H	A	A

Figure 7.1. Illustration of the Median Voter Result

theories of representation, this analytic result is quite well known, even among scholars who otherwise have limited familiarity with rational choice scholarship. This stylized rendering of electoral competition, however, incorporates a variety of assumptions of dubious applicability to American elections. The model presupposes, for example, that campaign politics occurs along a single issue dimension; that candidates set forth a clear platform (Shepsle 1972b); that candidates are certain about how voters will react to their announced stances; that candidates are willing to sacrifice their own convictions in pursuit of office; that candidates are able to alter their historical ideological location for the purposes of the present campaign; that no other candidates can enter or credibly threaten to enter the race; that candidates make no side-payments to their financial backers or party activists (or to one another!); and so forth. Voters, for their part, are assumed to judge the two candidates solely on their one-issue platforms (Stokes 1963) and to ignore the fact that no enforcement mechanism exists to ensure that elected officials do what they promised as candidates (Ferejohn 1993). As we will see, many of these assumptions are essential to the existence and location of electoral equilibria.

Rational choice theorists vary in the stock they place in the median voter result. Some contend that the theorem suggests the "strong centralizing tendency of simple two-candidate plurality rule elections" (Ordeshook 1992, 105). Others go further and suggest that this centralizing tendency offers an empirically accurate account of two-party politics. Writing in 1929, Harold Hotelling observed (1929, 54–55):

> So general is this tendency [for competitors to adopt convergent strategies] that it appears in the most diverse fields of competitive activity, even quite apart from what is called economic life. In politics it is strikingly exemplified. The competition for voters between the Republican and Democratic parties does not lead to a clear drawing of issues, an adoption of two strongly contrasted positions between which the voter may choose. Instead, each party strives to make its platform as much like the other's as possible. Any radical departure would lose many votes, even though it might lead to stronger commendation of the party by some who would vote for it anyhow. Each candidate "pussyfoots," replies ambiguously to questions, refuses to take a definite stand in any controversy for fear of losing votes. Real differences, if they even exist, fade gradually with time though the issues may be as important as ever. The Democratic party, once opposed to protective tariffs, moves gradually to a position almost, but not quite, identical with that of the Republicans. It need have no fear of fanatical free-traders, since they will still prefer it to the Republican party, and its advocacy of a continued high tariff will bring it the money and votes of some intermediate groups.

As one might infer from both the tone and content of Hotelling's remarks, the median voter result has been put to use by innumerable authors seeking to complain about the craven, Tweedledum-and-Tweedledee character of American party competition.[8]

Although the spatial model that gives rise to the median voter result is the best-known spatial model of its kind in political science, not all rational choice theorists share Hotelling's high regard for its verisimilitude. Many of the assumptions of the basic model are unpalatable to those who seek to extract from spatial models a realistic depiction of electoral competition. Accordingly, many rational choice theorists have distanced themselves from this model, offering instead theories that loosen one or more of its key assumptions. Three of the more important areas of theoretical development include the expansion of the issue space to many dimensions, the move from deterministic to probabilistic models of voter behavior, and the allowance for candidate objectives other than electoral success. After discussing each in turn, we then survey some of the miscellaneous theories that have been developed by theorists'

---

8. On the other hand, the median voter result is viewed as heartening to those who see the objective of democratic institutions as transmitting the preferences of the typical voter, arguably the median voter (see, e.g., McKelvey and Ordeshook 1986).

attempting to account for the fact that candidates frequently adopt divergent policy platforms.

Multidimensionality Of longstanding concern to rational choice theorists is the assumption that candidates compete over a single issue dimension. Rather than assume tariffs to vary merely in magnitude, for example, one may characterize them as "particularistic" policies that in various ways favor or harm a host of different interests. Such arguments could be applied to virtually any issue that comprises an assortment of component issues. In effect, the unidimensional spatial model assumes that candidates have no opportunity to introduce cross-cutting issues during a campaign, which hardly seems plausible.

The consequences of expanding the model to allow for multiple policy dimensions are akin to the cycling problem discussed in the previous chapter. Unless very strong symmetry conditions apply to the array of voters' ideal points, no equilibrium will exist. Given an opposing candidate's platform, one always can find a platform that will garner a majority of votes. Conversely, for whatever platform one adopts, this opponent can always counter with a better one.

Consider a simple illustration in which the question of tariffs is broken down into two dimensions, tariffs for agricultural goods and tariffs for finished goods (fig. 7.2). The ideal points of three voters $\{1, 2, 3\}$ are arrayed in this two-dimensional space. In relation to the other voters, voter 1 may be described as preferring low tariffs on both sorts of goods; voter 3, by contrast, prefers relatively high tariffs on both. Voter 2 favors relatively high tariffs for agricultural products and quite low tariffs on finished goods. For purposes of illustration, we have arbitrarily assigned a metric to each dimension of the grid and assumed each voter to have circular indifference contours, implying that a ballot will be cast for the candidate whose platform comes closest to the voter's ideal point. This configuration of ideal points does not give rise to a Nash equilibrium. If candidate R locates at A, candidate L can obtain a majority by locating at B. In reply, candidate R can offer platform C and regain the majority. It turns out that any platform that one candidate might choose is vulnerable to defeat.

Disequilibrium of this kind need not imply, however, that the platforms of rational candidates may be expected to turn up anywhere in the multidimensional policy space. If candidates are revealing their platforms simultaneously, neither has an incentive to adopt a platform that is inferior to another available option in the following sense. Consider, for example, the disadvantage of locating a platform at C. Although this location is good enough to beat B, there exists another location slightly west of C, call it C', which not only defeats C, but defeats every platform that C defeats. Thus, there is no reason to select C, given the opportunity to choose C'.

Points like C, you may recall from Chapter 6, are said to be "covered," while the

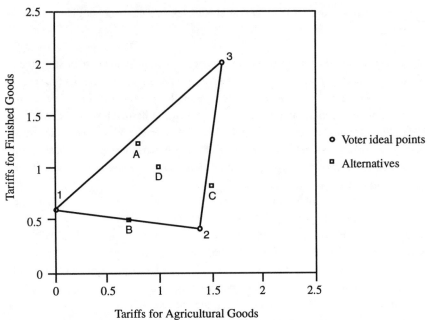

Squared distances from voter ideal points to platforms:

	Voter 1	Voter 2	Voter 3
Platform A	1.00	1.00	1.28
Platform B	.50	.50	3.06
Platform C	2.29	.17	1.45
Platform D	1.16	.52	1.36

Figure 7.2. Candidate Disequilibrium in Two Dimensions

"uncovered set" comprises those points that are not covered by any other alternative. One might argue that candidates for whom the sole objective is maximizing the chances of winning office would have no reason to select covered platforms, but to what degree does the uncovered set narrow the range of anticipated candidate locations? In our three-voter example, the uncovered set (the shaded region in figure 7.3) turns out to encompass a rather diffuse set of points. (The only daring predictions have to do with points such as C, which, like A, lie near the edge of the uncovered set. The uncovered set rules out the former but treats the latter as plausible.) For cases more complex than our hypothetical illustration, the shape and size of the uncovered set become ambiguous. In situations in which voters' ideal points are dispersed nearly symmetrically throughout the issue space, the uncovered set will tend to be a small,

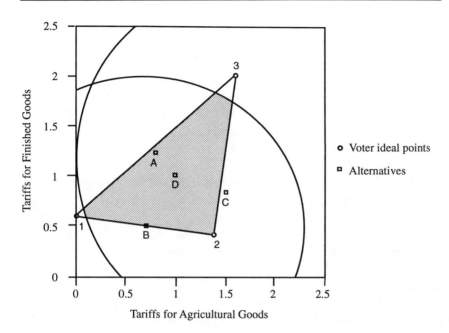

Figure 7.3. Illustration of the Uncovered Set

centrally located region (McKelvey 1986; Cox 1987). In general, however, the location of the uncovered set is difficult to determine empirically, particularly when applied to a large electorate evaluating candidates along many dimensions (Tovey 1993).[9] To the extent that the uncovered set is large, disequilibrium within the uncovered set may engender wide swings in platforms and unstable majority coalitions.

One way to narrow the predictions of the uncovered set is to imagine a pair of candidates competing against each other over a series of elections. Suppose candidates have full knowledge of voter preferences, and assume that they unveil their platforms simultaneously and just once during a campaign. One might imagine candidates in this situation playing a mixed strategy, or randomly selecting among points within the uncovered set.[10] Because determining the location of this set is "exceedingly difficult—so difficult in fact that it seems to push the as if principle beyond credulity" (McKelvey and Ordeshook 1976, 1181), candidates arguably learn through trial and error to adopt policies near the center of opinion, which is virtually

9. Indeed, it is no mean feat to ascertain the dimensions along which candidates compete in a given election, an even more basic empirical question.

10. Technically, the region discussed by McKelvey and Ordeshook is the "admissible set," which is defined similarly to the uncovered set.

assured to fall within the uncovered set. Over a series of elections, therefore, one may *"anticipate finding successful candidates at or near the electorate's median preference on each salient issue of the election even if the distribution of ideal points is not symmetric"* (McKelvey and Ordeshook 1976, 1182).[11]

Evaluating these analytic results empirically is seldom done in a systematic fashion. There is some speculation, dating back to Downs (1957), that even if the preferences of the electorate remain stable, multidimensional electoral competition hurts incumbents, who, when running for reelection, are forced to retain the policy positions of their administration. In the absence of an electoral equilibrium, the immobility of incumbents allows challengers to devise a platform that forges a new majority coalition. A related conjecture is that incumbent executives avoid distributive issues during an election year, since their multidimensional character threatens to undo the incumbent's majority coalition (Ordeshook 1992). But neither the multidimensional character of electoral competition per se nor the salience of distributive issues in particular has been linked empirically to the campaign tactics or electoral fortunes of incumbents.

As for dynamic competition, one wonders how rapidly candidates in fact converge to the center of opinion over time. Again, this issue has not received much empirical attention, apart from Campbell et al.'s remarks on the Stevenson-Eisenhower rematch (1960) and Page's discussion of how the policies advocated by McGovern and Goldwater evolved over time (1978). One would expect a trade-off between the number of voters won over by a move to the center and the number repelled by a candidate's apparent waffling. Unfortunately, studies that have addressed the phenomenon of sequential elections most directly—laboratory experiments in which candidates compete in a series of mock elections—have focused exclusively on the advantages of moving closer to the center of opinion. In experiments reported by Collier et al. (1987), McKelvey and Ordeshook (1982, 1984b), Plott (1991), and Williams (1991), candidates were rewarded financially for winning elections. Voters consisted of actual experimental subjects or mock players whose assigned payoffs decreased with the distance between their ideal points and the "platform" of the winning candidates. Each candidate subject selected a platform (from a grid or list of finite alternatives, depending on the experimental design), votes were tallied, and payoffs to candidates and voters disbursed. When candidates were informed about the distribution of voters' ideal points, the platforms selected were sometimes initially

11. Kramer (1977) relies more explicitly on sequential elections to narrow the predictions of the multidimensional spatial model. Under the assumption of vote maximization, full information, and an incumbent unable to alter his or her platform, the trajectory of policy platforms converges to the "minmax" set, which encompasses the platforms that minimize the maximum possible number of votes against a candidate. One peculiarity of this model is that the incumbent loses every election.

quite far from the expected convergent equilibrium, but with successive elections, the candidates tended to move toward the center. When candidates were given little initial information about the distribution of voter preferences and were forced to learn about the electorate through its voting patterns, convergence to the center occurred more gradually (sometimes taking a dozen elections to accomplish), but central outcomes still prevailed.[12]

These findings are suggestive but remain tenuously linked to state or national elections, where rematches seldom occur more than once under similar conditions, candidates need not announce their positions simultaneously, competition may occur over a great many policy dimensions, and candidate images may be hurt by changes of position. Moreover, these experiments impute just one motive to candidates: the desire to win election. This aim is simply one of many that has been attributed to candidates by rational choice theorists. As the basic spatial model expands to encompass other motivations, the strategic imperative to "go where the voters are" is pitted against other imperatives—"go where your heart is," "go where the campaign funds are," "go where you hope to lead voters," or "stay where you're stuck."

UNCERTAINTY

One of the main developments in spatial modeling of electoral competition since the 1970s is the shift from deterministic to probabilistic models. In deterministic models, each voter automatically casts a ballot for the ideologically more proximate candidate no matter how small the difference between the two competing platforms. Probabilistic models, on the other hand, allow for the possibility that voters have reasons to vote for a candidate with a relatively unattractive platform, especially when the differences between the platforms are slight. As Enelow, Endersby, and Munger (1993, 125) note, the distinguishing feature of probabilistic models "is the presence of a random element either in the voter's decision calculus or in the candidate's ability to predict the vote. In either case, probabilistic models allow all candidates in an election campaign a nonzero chance of winning and assume that each candidate's vote share varies continuously with a change in strategy. In contrast, deterministic models assume that for any given choice of candidate strategies one candidate wins with probability one and all other candidates with probability zero."

Three substantive arguments have been advanced on behalf of the assumption of

12. It is interesting that it often requires many plays before subjects converge to an equilibrium point. Even in the simple finite alternative game with full information presented in McKelvey and Ordeshook (1982), the equilibrium strategy was adopted just 38 percent of the time in the first election and only 67 percent of the time after four elections. One wonders how convergence might have fared in the limited information experiments had voter preferences or issue salience changed from one election to the next.

probabilistic voting. An early model (Hinich, Ledyard, and Ordeshook 1972) asserted that candidate positions may alter the probability of voter turnout, either because the candidate platforms are so close to each other that voters are indifferent about the outcome or because voters are unenthusiastic about the platform offered by the more ideologically proximate candidate.[13] Although turnout varies with candidate positions, voter turnout is treated as stochastic, that is, influenced by nonspatial factors over which the candidates have no knowledge or control. Another construction of probabilistic voting (Enelow and Hinich 1982, 1984a, 1984b) attributes to voters nonpolicy preferences concerning candidate attributes (for example, ethnicity, experience). Candidates are uncertain how voters evaluate them on nonpolicy grounds and, moreover, are powerless to alter these evaluations. To the extent that voters perceive and value these characteristics differently, the nonspatial utility difference between two platforms is from the candidates' viewpoint a random variable. Voters maximize their utility, but there is more to their utility functions than ideological affinity. Another version of the probabilistic voting model less directly tied to utility maximization (Coughlin 1984) holds that turnout and vote choice may be buffeted by voter uncertainty about the utility difference between the candidates, as well as by a host of environmental forces that are unknown to the candidates. Regardless of how the probabilistic component of the vote is justified, the implication is the same: some aspects of voter choice lie outside what may be affected by candidate strategy. Candidates can win votes by moving closer to voters' ideal points, but a proportion of these voters will nonetheless end up supporting the other candidate.

To see how probabilistic voting may affect how candidates formulate their platforms, consider a variant of the one-dimensional case listed in figure 7.1. When voting was deterministic, both candidates converged to the platform most preferred by the median voter. Under probabilistic voting, the median may no longer be an optimal location. Suppose, for example, that each of the three voters in figure 7.4 is a utility maximizer but that utilities are derived from both spatial and nonspatial candidate characteristics. For a given pair of candidate platforms (x,y), one may express the utility function of a voter whose ideal point is θ as follows:

$$U_i(x,y) = (\theta - y)^2 - (\theta - x)^2 + \mu_i$$

where μ_i is a standard normal variate representing all nonpolicy sources of utility.[14]

13. In their study of the 1988 election, Erikson and Romero (1990, 1120–21) conclude that indifference and alienation have relatively small effects on voter turnout. Other studies of voter turnout for presidential contests have drawn similar conclusions.

14. The normal density with mean zero and unit variance is chosen simply for convenience; other parameters or densities could be substituted. Our illustration also adopts the conventional assumption that utility diminishes with the square of policy distance rather than with the absolute value of this distance. Although the distinction between quadratic and absolute loss

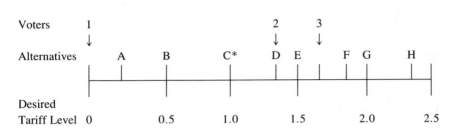

*Probabilistic voting equilibrium (the mean).

Probability of voting for candidate positioned at C, given opponent is positioned at an alternative platform or $\Pr[Ui(x,y) > 0]$:

Opponent	A	B	C	D	E	F	G	H
Voter 1	.169	.227	.500	.831	.894	.995	.999	.999
Voter 2	.900	.742	.500	.436	.440	.536	.579	.800
Voter 3	.945	.802	.500	.374	.363	.394	.421	.610

Expected vote for candidate at platform C:	2.014	1.771	1.500	1.641	1.697	1.925	1.999	2.409

Figure 7.4. Illustration of Probabilistic Voting Equilibrium

As before, suppose for simplicity that the two candidates may choose among eight campaign platforms, as in figure 7.4. At the bottom of the figure are the probabilities with which each voter will cast a ballot for a candidate located at C when the opposing candidate is located at various positions. It can be seen that the platform offering the highest expected vote for this opponent is location C, which turns out to be the average of the three voters' ideal points. In other words, when the candidates locate their platforms at C, neither candidate can expect to win more votes by switching to another platform. Thus, while deterministic voting drives candidates toward the median voter, probabilistic voting equilibria (when they exist) may be found at the mean voter's ideal point.[15]

---

functions seems innocuous, it can determine both the existence and location of the equilibrium (Enelow and Hinich 1989). Substantively, the quadratic loss specification implies that an extreme conservative is more sensitive to small ideological differences between a pair of liberal candidates, relative to equivalent differences between two conservative candidates. This seems unlikely, but we do not know of work that addresses this question. We therefore echo the concerns of Page (1977), who noted the lack of empirical study devoted to such fundamental concerns as the shapes of voters' utility functions.

15. This result is contingent, however, on the shape of voters' utility functions and the salience of issues in relation to nonpolicy considerations. In cases where the salience of policy considerations varies across voters, equilibria may exist at the mean weighted by salience.

As we move from one evaluative dimension to many, probabilistic voting may have the effect of generating an equilibrium that would not otherwise exist under deterministic voting. Recall our earlier example of three voters evaluating a pair of candidates according to their stances along two issue dimensions; the closer the platform to the voter's ideal point, the more utility it conveys. This time, however, we introduce a stochastic component into each voter's decision calculus, so that for $M = 2$ issues:

$$U_i(x,y) = \sum_{j=1}^{M} b_{ij}[(\theta_{ij} - y_j)^2 - (\theta_{ij} - x_j)^2] + \mu_i$$

b_{ij} indicates the salience weights each voter assigns a given policy issue j. For simplicity, let's consider the case in which the b_{ij} are merely vectors of ones, so that both issues are equally salient. As shown in figure 7.5, policy D now yields a higher expected vote percentage than any of the other alternatives (be they {A, B, C} or any other point) against which it might compete. It is a Nash equilibrium in the sense that no candidate can obtain a higher expected vote by switching to another platform if his or her opponent adopts policy D. In general, probabilistic voting does not guarantee the existence of equilibrium (Enelow and Hinich 1989; Coughlin 1992). As Erikson and Romero (1990, 1107) note, however, "For probabilistic models the likelihood of a global equilibrium is proportional to size of the random disturbance term in comparison to the degree of issue voting. . . . Since voters supposedly engage in little issue voting, we should be encouraged about the possibility of global equilibria among actual electorates in the real world."[16]

Is there evidence suggesting that nonpolicy considerations indeed give rise to an equilibrium? Two analyses of survey data (Erikson and Romero 1990; Enelow et al. 1993) answer this question in the affirmative. Erikson and Romero examine how vote preference for Bush versus Dukakis reflected an assortment of eight policy preference measures as well as two nonpolicy factors: party identification and a summary measure of open-ended evaluations of the candidates.[17] Using the parameter estimates from this probit model, Erikson and Romero then simulate how the vote total would

16. Issue-based evaluation of candidates has made something of a comeback in recent years in rational choice scholarship. A theoretical and experimental literature has emerged suggesting ways that voters could use cues drawn from polls, endorsements, and other low-information devices to discern the ideological stances of the candidates (McKelvey and Ordeshook 1990b). Nonetheless, it remains to be demonstrated that such techniques are in fact employed by voters as they evaluate candidates. For an application to referendum voting see Lupia 1994.

17. The latter measure is based on questions asking respondents whether there is anything they like or dislike about either candidate, which leaves open the question of whether these evaluations are policy- or nonpolicy-based.

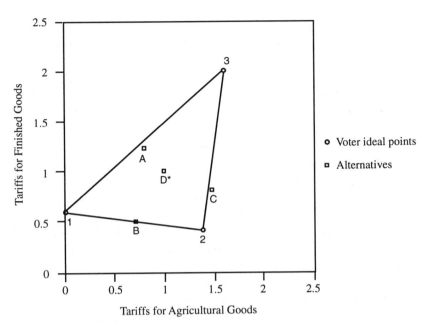

* Probabilistic voting equilibrium.

Probability of voting for candidate positioned at D, given opponent is positioned at A, B, or C:

	Opponent A	Opponent B	Opponent C
Voter 1	.44	.25	.87
Voter 2	.68	.49	.36
Voter 3	.47	.96	.54
Expected vote for Candidate D	1.59	1.70	1.77

Figure 7.5. Candidate Equilibrium with Probabilistic Voting

have changed had the candidates adopted different issue positions. After examining various potential candidate stances, the authors conclude that a platform that is more or less at the center of opinion on each issue constitutes an equilibrium, insofar as it promises a maximum vote share.

Leaving aside any misgivings one might harbor about how the terms of the vote equation are specified or measured, these statistical demonstrations raise as many questions as they answer.[18] This study and related vote models (Enelow and Hinich

18. Quantitative studies that examine the effects of perceived distance between the voters and the candidate may underestimate the degree to which policy distance grows out of concern about the candidate's persona (Page 1978; Markus 1982; Miller, Wattenberg, and Malanchuk

1982, 1984a, 1984b; Enelow et al. 1986, 1993) beg the question of whether non-policy determinants of the vote are subject to influence by campaign strategy. Image-building and the interplay between image and policy stances are prominent themes in traditional scholarship on presidential politics, yet they receive little attention in rational choice theorizing about candidate strategy. One explanation for this contrast may have to do with an effort on the part of rational choice theorists to distance themselves from social psychological perspectives on vote choice, which emphasize longstanding group attachments (Campbell et al. 1960) and what has been called "symbolic politics" (Sears et al. 1980). Issue voting, perhaps because it seems to involve conscious calculation, has often been regarded as the antithesis to the social psychological approach (Converse 1975; Enelow and Hinich 1984b).

The desire to defend issue voting can only be part of the explanation, however, because rational choice models have gradually incorporated nonpolicy determinants of the vote. The reluctance to place nonpolicy-oriented strategy on an equal footing with policy-based appeals may also be attributed to certain inherent limitations of the spatial model as applied to such phenomena as presidential character. Early in the development of spatial models it was speculated that candidate image could be treated as just another issue dimension (Davis et al. 1970, 445). But it seems clear that even if one were to posit a finite number of traits—like integrity, intelligence, charisma, or compassion—candidate appeal is not merely a matter of exhibiting as much of each personal trait as the the public finds attractive. Building a coherent image, one whose "stylistic elements mesh with one another" (Fenno 1978, 125), seems to be the objective. Spatial models are ill suited to capture the interactions among different sorts of traits, let alone anticipate what happens when a candidate engages in activities (such as tank-riding) that deviate from the configuration of traits associated with his or her putative image.[19]

1986). On the other hand, the inclusion of party identification as a control variable arguably understates the role of policy preferences (Davis et al. 1970; Franklin and Jackson 1983; see, however, Green and Palmquist 1990).

19. Another limitation of the spatial framework has to do with issues that do not lend themselves to representation as a continuous metric dimension (Stokes 1963; compare Davis et al. 1970). A candidate's position on laws restricting abortion may range from favorable to unfavorable, but the gradations in between are likely to involve categories of exceptions, and there may be no simple way to order these exceptions along a single continuum. This problem may be circumvented to some degree by conceptualizing the abortion issue in multidimensional terms, but a further complication remains. If issues are perceived and debated in terms of four or five positions that one might espouse—"finite alternatives," in the parlance of spatial modeling—predicted candidate locations may differ substantially from what might otherwise have been anticipated assuming that candidates can locate anywhere along a continuous dimension. When candidates can choose any point in the space of figure 7.3, point D lies squarely within the uncovered set, but when candidates can only choose from alternatives $\{A, B, C, D,\}$, D turns out to be the one alternative that is covered.

Other neglected aspects of campaign strategy call into question the conclusion that the optimal location for platforms is the center of public opinion. For many foreign and domestic policy issues, one wonders whether candidates who did nothing but endorse milquetoast policies might be sacrificing important opportunities to influence the vote indirectly by garnering campaign contributions, enthusiastic activists, and favorable press attention (Davis et al. 1970). For certain issues on which the median voter feels strongly, following the center of opinion may also expose fissures between mass and elite opinion. A ringing endorsement of prayer in schools places a candidate squarely in agreement with the preponderance of voters, but at what cost in terms of support among the well-educated and influential? Finally, simply taking the stance preferred by the average voter on every issue that arises seems certain to create an ideologically incoherent platform, a mélange of liberal and conservative views that could well be derided as internally contradictory and mercenary.

In sum, to declare, as Erikson and Romero do, that "we should be encouraged about the possibility of global equilibria" seems premature; all the more so the claim that "almost every worry the candidate may have about the possible behavior of the voter is captured by the probabilistic voting model" (Enelow and Hinich 1984a, 477). To those who stand outside the endeavor of searching for optimal campaign strategies, it is by no means apparent that an equilibrium exists; or if it does, whether it is effectively described by an account that focuses attention on policy positioning.

Probabilistic models of this sort also confront some nagging empirical problems inasmuch as actual candidates seem not to be located close to the putative equilibria. In 1988 the presidential nominees were perceived to be ideologically distinct, and neither candidate was particularly close to the center of opinion. The same pattern seems to hold for the 1980 and 1984 contests (Enelow et al. 1993).[20] Erikson and Romero (1990) do not grapple with this anomaly, but Enelow et al. (1993) make it the focus of their revised probabilistic model. Arguing that divergent candidate positions can be explained by variation among voter perceptions of the effectiveness with which candidates are likely to effect their policy platforms, the authors in effect discount each voter's assessment of how the candidate will change the status quo by a competence weight ranging from zero to one. (Again, perceptions of candidate competence are treated as exogenously given.) It turns out that the predicted equilibrium positions tend to be rather close together and only weakly related to the actual stances of the candidates, even after the authors make an ad hoc adjustment to account for the effects of incumbency. Tracing the two issues, domestic and defense spending,

20. Granted, one should be cautious about characterizing differences between candidates by using National Election Study policy measures, as they offer respondents seven-point continua, only the extremes of which are assigned substantive labels. Nonetheless, there seems to be a consistent pattern to these data: on a policy scale that ranged from less (1) to more (7) defense spending, Democratic presidential candidates from 1980 to 1888 were rated on average 3.5, 3.2, and 3.1, while Republicans were rated 5.6, 5.8, and 5.4 (Enelow et al. 1993, 136).

that are examined in each of the three presidential contests reveals little connection between changes in the location of the equilibria and changes in observed locations.

We know of no more successful attempts to corroborate probabilistic models empirically. Thus the question remains open as to whether probabilistic spatial models have contributed to the understanding of American electoral competition. From a theoretical standpoint, the underlying distinction between what falls within the scope of campaign strategy and what is relegated to the stochastic term seems arbitrary. Certainly, the case has yet to be made that nonpolicy evaluations fall outside the purview of candidate strategy. This concern about the rationale for probabilistic theories is compounded by the apparent discrepancy between the predicted equilibria and the actual locations of the candidates, a discrepancy that becomes particularly apparent when one uses a more exacting standard that traces the pattern of candidate positions over time.

Policy-Motivated Candidates   In the basic spatial model, candidates seek to articulate a policy platform that would maximize their chances of election. But as Wittman (1983, 1990) has argued, this portrayal of politicians as single-minded seekers of electoral victory seems to be at variance with evidence indicating that candidates also harbor preferences over the kinds of policies they espouse during the campaign. Several variants of the policy-seeking candidate have been proposed. Some hold that in addition to valuing electoral victory candidates seek to receive an electoral mandate for a given policy stance (Riker and Ordeshook 1973, 353; Wittman 1983). Candidates may be constrained to adopt certain policy positions in order to placate interest groups (Calvert 1985) or uphold promises made during the primary election phase of the campaign (Wittman 1990). Office-seekers may propose policies that will assist them in pursuing their legislative agendas if elected (Cox 1984). Or they may derive utility from expressing what they believe to be a good platform (Mitchell 1987). Each variant suggests a somewhat different formal model, but all create the conditions for a potential trade-off among different objectives.

For example, it may be assumed (Calvert 1985, 72) that candidates, in addition to seeking election, "pursue office as a means to achieving desirable policies."[21] If x and y are the platforms of the two candidates, respectively, then one may write the expected utility of the election outcome in the eyes of candidate R:

$$EU_R(x,y) = u_R(x)P_R(x,y) + u_R(y)[1 - P_R(x,y)] + P_R(x,y)V_R$$

21. As Cox (1984) and others note, the real-world connection between campaign platforms and policy outcomes need not be a close one. The theme of promise-keeping has generated a substantial literature in recent years, as rational choice theorists have attempted to offer accounts of why public officials might be impelled to keep their campaign promises and how voters may use campaign promises to predict future actions in office.

where $u_R(x)$ is the utility derived from an electoral outcome in which x is the victorious platform, $u_R(y)$ is the utility derived from an electoral outcome in which y is the
victorious platform, $P_R(x,y)$ is the probability that candidate R wins the election given
the two platforms, and V_R is the value of winning office per se to candidate R. When
the candidates' ideal points lie on opposite sides of the median voter on each issue,
and voting is probabilistic, candidates whose motives consist of this admixture of
policy and election concerns will adopt platforms that diverge to the degree that they
value policy objectives in relation to electoral victory (Cox 1984, Calvert 1985,
Wittman 1990).

One implication of this model is that a policy-motivated candidate is at a disadvantage when confronted by a pure election-seeking opponent. Another is that when the
intrinsic value of an office goes up—owing to, for example, an increase in salary—
candidates would be expected to shift in the direction of a convergent platform. A
further proposition is that when an exogenous event increases the popularity of a
policy-motivated candidate, the candidate should trade in some of this newfound
electoral support for a platform farther from the center of opinion and closer to his or
her ideal point. Each of these propositions is plausible and, in principle, testable.

In practice, of course, it is difficult to design an empirical test that guards against
confounding influences. Policy-motivated candidates could prove to be less successful for reasons having to do with how they tend to manage campaigns rather than with
their ideological unattractiveness to voters. A growth in the perquisites of office may
lure a less ideological cadre of candidates who might not otherwise run for office, in
which case growing centrism might reflect a composition effect rather than a calcu-
lated shift in campaign tactics. Similarly, candidates who are favored by the winds of
fortune may adopt ever more extreme stances because they mistakenly believe that
their hardline message is responsible for their growing popularity. And in each of
these cases there remains the nagging possibility that the nature of candidate motivation itself varies endogenously with changes in the electoral environment.

Perhaps sensing these difficulties, spatial modelers have seldom applied their
predictions to real-world electoral politics. Wittman (1983, 146–48), to his credit, is
among the few to survey the traditional political science literature in search of evidence that popularity shocks affect candidate platforms, but the findings he turns up
are far from convincing.[22] The closest thing to an essay that combines theory and

22. One defect of the studies Wittman cites is that they are all cross-sectional, that is, they
compare candidates at a single point in time. For example, in relation to the hypothesis that the
prospect of presidential coattails ought to embolden the candidates of the favored presidential
candidate's party, Wittman cites a study that examines the correlation between senators' roll-
call votes and constituent opinion for senators running for reelection in 1972. This study finds a
somewhat higher correlation for Democratic than Republican senators—a statistical finding of
debatable substantive meaning (Achen 1977)—but is this pattern significantly different from
what one would observe during a year such as 1974, when party fortunes were reversed?

original empirical analysis is Londregan and Romer's investigation of the hypothesis that "the degree of ideological polarization between contending candidates for an open congressional seat increases with the salience to voters of service provision ability" (1993, 373). Using the 1978 National Election Study, the authors analyze the bivariate relation between how respondents rated the importance of constituency service and the degree of ideological polarization they perceived between the two House candidates. But with only ten open-seat districts at their disposal, the authors were unable to obtain statistically reliable results. Other than this inconclusive study and some computer simulations of adaptive party strategies (Kollman et al. 1992) and platform adjustment in anticipation of candidate debates (Chappell and Keech 1986), applications of the spatial model in which candidates have policy motives have been confined to the laboratory.[23]

Indeed, when applications are proposed, they tend to beg the question of whether the model offers an accurate depiction of how candidates behave. Cox (1984), for example, suggests that candidates reveal the strength of their underlying policy motivation through their reactions to exogenous improvements in their popularity. Candidates who respond to such external shocks by moving toward their ideal points may be said to have policy motives, while candidates who do not react in this fashion may be said to lack such motives. Notice that candidate traits are in effect measured by the changing locations of their platforms. No pattern of possible candidate actions can be inconsistent with this model unless one brings to bear extrinsic information about the motives of the candidates. The question of how to measure candidate motives apart from interpreting their strategies, however, is not something that rational choice scholarship has taken up.

In sum, spatial theories of candidate competition have in recent years expanded to accommodate the possibility of policy-motivated candidates. This development has often been hailed as a sign that spatial models are moving in the direction of greater realism. This may be true in the sense that these models now take account of new motive-related contingencies, but the question remains whether augmenting the basic model along these lines pays off empirically. Applications testing the consequences of policy motivation have yet to get off the ground; indeed, as we have noted, basic questions of measurement and hypothesis testing remain unresolved. Nonetheless,

23. When experimental candidates were paid not for winning but rather for the distance between their ideal point and that of the winning candidate's platform, as in the experiments reported by Morton (1993), platforms converged over a series of elections provided the candidates were informed about voter preferences. Morton reports that when candidates were both uncertain about voter preferences and assigned ideological preferences of their own, platforms on average tended to remain divergent across eight successive elections. The degree of average divergence under these conditions was less than anticipated, however, a fact that Morton interprets as evidence that subjects valued electoral victory in its own right.

rational choice theorists who are drawn to the topic of candidate motivation believe that their models supply a sufficient account of the divergent platforms they take to be explanandum of two-candidate competition. Chief among the problems with this view is that many other sufficient accounts may be called on to explain the same stylized fact.

OTHER EMBELLISHMENTS

Multidimensional competition, uncertainty, and policy motivation represent but a small set of the proposed revisions of the basic spatial model. As noted earlier, rational choice theorists have become increasingly impressed by a mounting number of empirical studies suggesting that, cynical though the public might be about the two ideologically indistinct major parties, presidential platforms have frequently differed in systematic ways (Page 1978; Tufte 1978), and voters have sensed these differences (Aldrich and McKelvey 1977; Enelow et al. 1993).[24] This generalization about candidate strategy has stimulated considerable post hoc theorizing, the object of which has been to formulate a model predicting that in equilibrium candidates will adopt ideologically distinct platforms.[25]

Even before divergence took root as a stylized fact about American electoral competition, it was apparent how the basic model might be changed in order to make candidate divergence the predicted outcome. Riker and Ordeshook (1973, 348–49) remark, for example:

24. It may be added that, once elected, U.S. senators from the same state but of different party have voted differently (Poole and Rosenthal 1984; Grofman, Griffin, and Glazer 1990), and the parties have generally attended to different policy problems once elected (Hibbs 1977).

25. Some rational choice theorists have resisted this stylized fact, preferring to think of convergent platforms as the rule. Representative of this sentiment is the remark by Kollman et al. (1992, 936), who conclude their essay with the assertion that "extreme candidates rarely emerge as national candidates; and when they do, they lose by a wide margin." It is unclear what these authors regard as extreme or rare, or what to make of presidential elections dating back to 1980. Similar characterizations of moderate presidential politics abound. The central positioning of the candidates is used, for example, by Brams and Straffin (1982) to explain why third-party candidates seldom can locate themselves so as to obtain a plurality of votes. They assert that "in presidential elections in the United States, the candidates of the two major parties usually take positions reasonably close to each other, the elections of 1964 and 1972 notwithstanding" (193). Again, one wonders how close "reasonably close" is. Similarly, Enelow and Hinich (1984b, 221) argue, based on their analysis of National Election Study data, that "even extremist candidates in American elections, such as George Wallace, are relatively close to the middle of the predictive space. No candidate lies anywhere near the horizontal periphery of the electorate." Enelow and Hinich's results should be read with caution, as their analysis also yields the conclusion that Carter and Mondale were perceived to be more socially conservative than Reagan in 1980 (205).

Candidates and parties, nevertheless, do differ significantly on many issues. Should the existence of these differences, then, be interpreted as a refutation of [convergence] results we consider here? Obviously, the validity of the theory can be reasserted by attributing the failure of candidates to adopt similar policies in real campaigns to the violation of the assumptions of the model, such as imperfect information or spatial mobility. Or again, it may be said in excuse that a candidate can find it necessary to advocate policies distant from the mean in order to win the nomination of his party, and later find himself committed to these policies in the campaign. Or, it may be said that candidates possess ideological prejudices which they may be unwilling or unable to forego. Finally, it may be said simply that candidates err. These attempts to resolve an apparent disparity between theory and empirical evidence, nevertheless, are not entirely necessary: conditions can be found in spatial analysis for which the candidates should provide distinct alternatives.

Accordingly, Riker and Ordeshook go on to point out that, with the right combination of assumptions about voter abstention, the distribution of voter preferences, and symmetry of voter utility functions, unvarnished models of spatial competition can predict divergence.

Riker and Ordeshook's list of potential sources of divergence is long but by no means exhaustive. Candidates may attempt the joint maximization of votes and campaign resources, such as funds or activist participation, that can be translated into votes. Wooing donors and activists, who tend to be more ideologically extreme than the voting public, may pull candidates toward their respective backers (Riker and Ordeshook 1973, 361–62). Anticipation of a third-party candidate may drive the two major-party candidates from the center (Palfrey 1984), as might uncertainty about shifts in public sentiment stemming from such events as presidential debates (Chappell and Keech 1986; see also Wittman 1990) or differential degrees of uncertainty about challengers and incumbents (Bernhardt and Ingberman 1985). A party may also swing away from the center of opinion in an effort to lead voters to a new set of policy views (Gerber and Jackson 1993). Finally, candidates may utter extreme positions that may be ignored or discounted by certain segments of the public. Downs, for example, asserts that candidates may "sprinkle" a few extreme stances into their platforms in an effort to curry favor among party activists (1957, 135), while Enelow and Hinich (1984b, 53), rendering the example of Adolf Hitler's electoral platform, argue that candidates can articulate extreme positions to the extent that voters discount their promises for radical change as unlikely to come to fruition in actual policy.

That several of these hypotheses have gone untested may in part reflect their dubious plausibility and empirical tractability. Regarding Palfrey's thesis about anticipation of a third candidate, do contenders in two-candidate races really take more convergent stances on issues that arise after the filing deadline for entry in an election race has passed? And what extreme candidate position could not be rationalized by Enelow and Hinich's thesis about public skepticism?[26]

In other cases, the difficulty lies in choosing among the many competing explanations for why candidates diverge. One standard for winnowing the field of sufficient explanations is the criterion of parsimony. A good example of this approach may be found in the last sentence of the previous quotation from Riker and Ordeshook, who make a point of looking for simple mechanisms that might produce candidate divergence rather than encumbering the theory with one or more admittedly plausible complexities. The problem is that parsimony is not an easy standard to apply to alternative spatial models, each of which embellishes the basic model in a different way.[27] It is not clear, for example, which is more parsimonious: a theory that predicts divergence based on side-payments to interest groups or one that predicts divergence based on primary election competition.

Another criterion might be to judge alternative models according to their degree of verisimilitude with real electoral competition. Like parsimony, realism is an attractive but elusive standard. It is easy to skewer "pure" theories of candidate competition (for example, Ledyard 1984) on the grounds that they fail to take into account one or more of the many strategic complexities associated with particular electoral settings (Austen-Smith 1984), but striving for models that resemble the competitive give-and-take of candidate competition admits a potentially endless series of theoretical embellishments. Furthermore, on theoretical grounds alone one cannot establish which features of a campaign are causally pertinent and which are safely ignored. Whether a realistic model of campaign strategy ought to include a more detailed depiction of such factors as the nature and sequence of announced policy stances, the deployment of campaign resources, or the management of press coverage is ultimately an empirical question. By the same token, the realism of the various sufficient explanations for divergent equilibria leads one to ask: *To what extent* do each of these factors impel candidates to move away from the center of voter opinion?

Performing the systematic inquiry necessary to answer this question leads one into uncharted territory. Empirical studies designed to examine the effects of changes in conditions of uncertainty, policy motivations, costs of altering past policy commitments, primary competition, side-payments from activists or financial backers, and

26. In a rather strained fashion, Enelow and Hinich say of the 1980 election that the public supported Ronald Reagan despite his ideological unattractiveness because they believed him incapable of translating his policy inclinations into action. Presumably Clinton's persistent calls for change in 1992 were similarly discounted.

27. Such models are sometimes described as nonnested alternatives because one model's parameters cannot be written as a subset of another model's. Thus the standard techniques of statistical hypothesis testing do not apply in any direct fashion.

so forth have not been undertaken.[28] One might ask, for example, whether the rise of campaign polling and its attendant reduction in candidate uncertainty has been associated with more centrist (or perhaps cyclical) campaign politics or whether, among candidates with similar ideological profiles, those who run unopposed in primaries pursue more centrist general election campaigns than those who face primary competition. Ideally, one would seek not only a statistical relation between a given variable and the degree of candidate divergence but some evidence that the posited causal mechanism (for example, policy motivation) is responsible for this correlation, perhaps through close observation of the formulation and execution of campaign strategy. Process-tracing of this sort could suggest whether the adoption of predicted campaign strategies reflects conscious maximizing behavior of the principal, maximizing behavior on the part of agents whose interests are harmonized with those of the candidate, or the accidental product of a campaign organization muddling through.

DO SPATIAL MODELS PROVIDE INSIGHT INTO CANDIDATE STRATEGIES?

At present, the elaboration of spatial models has had only a tenuous connection with empirical application. Theorizing occurs within a research environment in which virtually no systematic inquiry links the causal mechanisms posited in spatial models (for example, uncertainty) to the strategic behavior of candidates. Accordingly, few essays proposing novel ways of modeling candidate competition devote more than a paragraph to what the new aspects of the model amount to operationally or to ways that the revised model might be distinguished empirically from competing accounts. One strains to find applications, no matter how abbreviated, that indicate the empirical value of looking at electoral competition through the lens of rational choice theory.

Many of the extant applications take the form of short narratives that weave an interpretation of observed candidate strategies from a loose assortment of analytic principles. Brams (1993), for example, offers a model of presidential election competition in which candidates are of two types (incumbent and challenger) and may adopt one of two types of strategies (risky and safe). The equilibrium to one version of this game suggests that when incumbents face "strong" challengers, both candidates have an incentive to play risky strategies. Dubbing "risky" those campaign strategies that

28. On occasion, researchers have made the case for one particular source of candidate divergence (e.g., Enelow et al. 1993), but these empirical tests have not been constructed in ways that would control for competing explanatory factors. Even the relatively strong empirical study by Gerber and Jackson (1993) goes only so far as to suggest that the parties' capacity to shake the issue positions of voters could contribute to the formulation of divergent campaign platforms.

tend to have "less predictable consequences" (48), Brams asserts that the campaign tactics of the major party nominees in 1976 and 1980 were indeed risky: in 1976, Ford defended his pardon of Nixon while Carter ran against the Beltway; in 1980 Reagan ran against the Beltway while Carter initially ignored his challenger and refused to participate in the first debate. This rendering leads one to question either the porous fashion in which risky is defined or the crude manner in which campaigns are classified. Brams, however, regards this application of game theory to electoral politics as promising. Although quick to concede that the eight presidential elections from 1960 to 1988 do not provide a rigorous test of the model, Brams (1993, 52) nonetheless argues that these cases offer "prima facie evidence that these different . . . games may model, albeit in a highly simplified way, different campaign scenarios that actually occur in elections."

Other applications of spatial models exhibit a similarly diffuse quality. One finds, for example, several discussions of how utility-maximizing candidates might be expected to capitalize on the strategic vulnerability of their opponents. In this scenario it is assumed that an equilibrium exists, as in the case of one-dimensional competition, but that for some reason one candidate is unable or unwilling to adopt the equilibrium platform.[29] In order to visualize a situation of this kind, return to the case of a single issue dimension and deterministic voting without abstention in which candidates seek to maximize their chances of election. The equilibrium strategy for candidates in figure 7.1 is to adopt the preferred position of the median voter. If one candidate should adopt a position to the right of the rightmost voter, however, a vote-maximizing opponent should also shift to the right, stopping just a hair to the left of the opposition. As Tullock (1967, 52) points out, this process of adjustment implies that, holding voter turnout constant, "an extremist candidate can pull a vote-maximizing opponent far off toward the extremist's desires."

This ominous pronouncement implies, for example, that had ex-Klansman David Duke in his 1991 bid for Louisiana governor revealed his plans to expel forcibly all blacks from the South, his opponent might have made the most of the opportunity by announcing his intention to expel only some blacks. Riker and Ordeshook (1973, 353) resist this absurd implication, arguing first that if the more liberal candidate moves too far to the right, his or her activist backers may abstain from voting, resulting in a net loss of electoral support. Furthermore, they suggest that candidates may temper their desire for votes in order to achieve a policy mandate, asserting that Lyndon Johnson limited the extent to which he followed Barry Goldwater rightward

29. Several spatial models depict the incumbent as "stuck" with a set of policy positions adopted while in office and thus vulnerable to defeat by a challenger free to forge a winning coalition (Downs 1957; Wittman 1973; Kramer 1977; Chappell and Keech 1986). This assumption may be applied more generally to situations in which candidates have well-known stances on the issues of the campaign and cannot risk a turnabout.

in the hopes of winning a consensus for a moderate policy agenda (see Kramer 1977 for the contrary assertion). Erikson and Romero (1990) offer a similar strategic prediction, but on the grounds that under probabilistic voting, moves away from the center win few additional votes.

It may be argued, however, that a candidate whose objectives consist of both victory and the articulation of a liberal policy agenda would, under the right proba- bilistic assumptions, trade some of the windfall of votes for a more personally appealing liberal platform (Wittman 1983). Or this candidate might adopt certain sharply liberal positions in order to raise the salience of one or more issues on which the extremist opponent is particularly vulnerable (see Hammond and Humes 1993). Suffice it to say that if one is content to pluck assumptions from a large assortment of potential premises about a specific pair of candidates' objectives or beliefs—few of which are testable in any direct way—potentially any strategic reaction to an oppo- nent's weakness could be characterized in a manner consistent with the predictions of a spatial model. For that matter, strategies could be attributed to a candidate's child- hood experiences (George and George 1956) or to habits acquired early in a candi- date's career (Barber 1977, 241–42; Caro 1990).

What is lacking from rational choice narratives is an underlying foundation of systematic empirical inquiry that would lend credence to interpretations premised on utility maximization. At present, interpretations drawn from spatial models invoke a variety of explanatory factors (for example, candidate objectives, degree of uncer- tainty) for which no measures are offered, while the discussion of optimal candidate strategy presupposes a highly stylized and empirically unsubstantiated characteriza- tion of the strategic options open to candidates. For these reasons, we are not con- vinced that spatial models provide greater insight into the determinants of campaign strategy than do traditional modes of interpretation.

HOW MIGHT SPATIAL MODELS CONTRIBUTE TO THE STUDY OF ELECTIONS?

Early in the development of this literature, when the basic Downsian model predominated, spatial models contained few contingencies and set forth clear- cut predictions. Candidates seek electoral victory; the strategic tools at their disposal consist of policy positions; in order to win, they must go where the voters are—which means articulating centrist platforms. One might dispute this prediction or express concern about its applicability to different domains of American politics, but the implications for empirical inquiry are relatively straightforward. As this model came to be regarded as empirically and theoretically untenable, spatial models grew more elaborate, and the basic model became a special case of more general formulations in which such constructs such as policy motivation, uncertainty, and dimensionality were permitted to vary. No single prediction emerges from encompassing models of this sort unless values are supplied for these variables. Depending on the aims of the actors, information available to them, and constraints on their feasible strategic options, equilibria may be nonexistent, convergent, or divergent.[30]

The development of increasingly general models has made them conceptually richer.[31] Indeed, with the incorporation of such constructs as "nonpolicy utility" the substantive distinctions between spatial models and traditional models have become less pronounced as the former expand to accommodate the objections of traditional students of elections. At the same time, the multiplication of contingencies in spatial modeling have led empirically minded political scientists to question how these models are to guide applied research. Page, one of the few scholars to attempt an empirical assessment of spatial models, laments, for example, that their growing complexity "has brought with it considerable confusion about exactly what, if anything, spatial models predict. Depending on what assumptions are made concerning turnout, the shape of opinion distributions, the nature of voters' utility functions, and candidates' goals, a bewildering variety of contingent predictions can be made" (1978, 18). Theoretical embellishments subsequent to Page's assessment have doubtless added to this confusion, which may explain in part why critics of spatial models have since the 1970s become less inclined to grapple with them empirically.

Contingencies, however, are not an inherently undesirable property of a theoretical account. As Mitchell (1987) notes, only a model that makes contingent predictions affords the possibility of explaining the range of strategic behavior that one observes in electoral politics. A more pointed criticism has to do with contingencies that rest on unobservable terms for which there are either no direct measures or very poor ones. Two implications follow from the abundance of unmeasurable or hard-to-measure constructs—for example, risk aversion, discounting of future outcomes, beliefs

30. Summarizing the literature extant two decades ago, Riker and Ordeshook (1973, 307–51) reviewed the implications of three alternative assumptions about the shape of utility functions, four concerning voter turnout, three on the distribution of voter preferences, and two regarding candidate motivation. These assumptions produced seventy-two combinations, fifty-six of which had at that time been the subject of theorems or reasonable conjectures. This is, to be sure, a large family of spatial theories, but when we add ancillary assumptions that have gained prominence in recent years, the resulting number of combinations achieves Malthusian proportions.

31. That is, conceptually richer if considered as a whole. As Ordeshook (1993, 88) points out, however, "No one pursues a research agenda in which all potentially relevant strategic interaction is studied in the same model. Thus, there is no spatial elections model, for example, that accommodates the strategic decision of voters, candidates, party leaders, and campaign contributors, operating under complex but realistic election rules, while simultaneously taking into account the fact that the election will be followed by a period of legislative-executive interaction, which will be followed by another election, and so on."

about the likely behavior of others, utilities derived from outcomes other than electoral victory—that either figure explicitly in a model or wait in the wings to rescue it.
First, an application to a particular campaign, as we noted above, is likely to be
hopelessly overdetermined. Any number of narratives consistent with rational maximizing might be advanced in a manner consistent with the data, but the same is true
for narratives that highlight the role of strategic shortsightedness or blunder.

Second, it is unlikely that spatial models of candidate competition will be identified, in the sense that their parameters can be estimated statistically given available
data from a sample of electoral races. Consider the hypothesis that some candidates
adopt more extremist platforms than others because of their varying degrees of policy
commitment and uncertainty. Measuring candidates' policy motivations and uncertainty would be hard enough, but to come up with measures of possibly confounding
factors such as risk-aversion or side-payments from activists (which might well
covary with policy motivation) would represent a truly formidable undertaking.[32]
Thus, even if everyone were to accept as uncontroversial the stipulation that candidates adopt equilibrium strategies, drawing inferences about the causal connection
between variation in candidate characteristics and the strategies they adopt would
remain problematic.

One way to mitigate the inference problems created by unobservable entities that
vary across candidates is to focus attention on the effects of shifts in the strategic
environment. If the hypothesis is that the value of policy outcomes relative to the
emoluments of office affects the degree of divergence from the center of opinion
under conditions of uncertainty, then decreases in salary and other nonpolicy rewards
should push candidates away from the center. Tests that track a panel of candidates as
they adjust their strategies to accommodate a new system of incentives are likely to be
informative, particularly if the study compares the strategies adopted over time by a
control group that is not affected by these changes over the same period.[33] This design
does not lay to rest concerns about whether a given environmental change occurred
exogenously, but it does reduce the number of strong assumptions needed to support
empirical inference. The key premise in this kind of analysis is that preferences and
other unobservables remain fixed over the duration of the study, so that the changing
behavior of candidates properly represents adjustment to shifting strategic circumstances and not change in the attributes of the candidates themselves. This assump-

32. To this one adds the complication that the strategic situation confronting different candidates may vary from one race to another in ways that may be difficult to control for.
33. Although the advantage of this design is that it circumvents certain thorny problems of
measurement, it may nevertheless be desirable for researchers using this design to measure the
value candidates place on winning per se so as to check, however crudely, the validity of the
claim that this environmental change affected the evaluations of candidates in the manner
anticipated.

tion is not above suspicion, but it strains credulity to a lesser degree than do the assumptions that undergird alternative research designs, such as comparison of candidate platforms at a given point in time (Londregan and Romer 1993).

Note that a hypothesis tested in this fashion remains contingent in the sense that the degree to which behavior shifts in response to environmental change is left unspecified. On average, candidates may not respond appreciably to a decrease in pay because their policy motivations are centrist or weak or muted by other constraints. These subsidiary hypotheses, however, may be explored in turn by more refined examination of how environmental change affects the behavior of particular types of candidates. With the halting optimism that must accompany any vision of social science research, one might anticipate that as studies of this sort probe each of these contingencies, the pattern of results will supply an empirically grounded depiction of the conditions under which candidates adopt particular campaign strategies.

Informative though it may be, the kind of empirical inquiry just described seldom exposes a model to falsification. A particular model suggests merely that a parameter of unknown magnitude governs the relation between an independent and dependent variable, and unless the data render an estimate with the wrong sign, one would tend to have at most indirect evidence with which to call a model into question. Since one generally wishes to know whether a model explains the data and not merely what the parameters of the model would be were its assumptions true, one must ultimately consider what kinds of behavior a model rules out. For example, spatial models of electoral competition currently make little allowance for the internal divisions that may exist within a campaign effort, the traditional or habitual practices that govern the behavior of campaign managers, or the cognitive biases that affect how candidates and their backers learn about the progress of the campaign. In effect, these influences on campaign strategy are assigned a weight of zero in spatial models. To the extent that the structure and staffing of campaign organizations are found to exert a systematic influence on the kinds of platforms (or other strategies) candidates adopt, these spatial models may be regarded as inadequate. Mounting evidence that these kinds of factors matter greatly would tend to call into question the central premise that electoral competitors pursue equilibrium strategies when they are available.

In sum, the research program that we envision has a very different trajectory from current rational choice scholarship on electoral competition. First and foremost, we place much greater emphasis on the link between theorizing and empirical investigation. The elaboration of spatial theories must be accompanied by much more sustained treatment of how the model in question ought to be translated into operational terms and evaluated empirically. Not only would this make it easier for those outside rational choice circles to participate in this research program (among the benefits of which would be a check against the tendency to seek or project confirming evidence), it would slow the pace of post hoc theorizing by raising the question, What does this embellishment potentially add to the stock of empirically based knowledge about electoral competition?

As for the empirical applications themselves, we advocate replacing case-by-case interpretation of candidate strategy with tests that examine the effects of exogenous changes in the strategic environment. Moreover, we favor tests that probe the limitations of spatial theories by evaluating the effects of variables that these models take to be ineffectual. Putting this suggestion into practice means confronting the tension between, on the one hand, stipulating a narrow set of assumptions about actors' goals and beliefs in an effort to make hypotheses nonobvious and falsifiable, and, on the other hand, introducing ever more nuanced assumptions that render testing difficult and surprises unlikely. As Downs (1957, chap. 1) recognized at the outset of this literature, the success of spatial modeling as a scientific endeavor hinges on striking the right balance between testability and nuance, deliberately omitting from a theory certain factors that, if included, might rescue the assumption of rationality but rob the model of its empirical value.

In essence, spatial models need boundaries in order to preserve a range of phenomena not predicted by the theory. Although most students of American elections would be prepared to accept some version of the proposition that candidates act strategically to achieve their goals, relatively few, we suspect, subscribe to the view that Nash equilibria exist in a competitive environment as complex and open to tactical innovation as campaign politics. Fewer still expect candidates to adopt strategies that are optimal given their tastes, beliefs, and available options. As spatial models evolve from an array of vaguely operationalized and loosely substantiated conjectures to a more viable research agenda, it is imperative that empirical testing allow for the possibility that these skeptical intuitions could be right.

CHAPTER EIGHT

RESPONSES TO LIKELY COUNTERARGUMENTS

In 1979 Clifford Russell noted the existence of a disjunction "between the apparent success of public choice theorems when faced with the tests of casual empiricism and the difficulties discovered when greater specificity is required and actual data are confronted in a rigorous way" (6). Although rational choice theorizing has grown substantially in prestige and influence in the decade and a half since he wrote, the conclusion to be drawn from the last four chapters is that Russell's characterization remains apt. Our reviews of the literatures on voter turnout, collective action, legislative behavior, and electoral competition reveal that the empirical contributions of rational choice theory in these fields are few, far between, and considerably more modest than the combination of mystique and methodological fanfare surrounding the rational choice movement would lead one to expect.

Admittedly, we have restricted our focus to the literatures spawned by the seminal works of Arrow, Downs, and Olson. We justified this selection on the grounds that these are widely regarded as the most important and formidable rational choice literatures. It should be said, however, that a number of other rational choice literatures in political science have been subjected to trenchant critiques. Among the more notable are Barry's analysis (1984) of the electoral business cycles literature and the rational choice–inspired attempts to find a causal link between democracy and inflation, Moe's discussion (1987) of the rational choice literature on congressional oversight, Kelman's review (1988) of rational choice case studies on regulatory agencies, Morton and Cameron's review (1992) of formal theories of campaign contributions, Bendor's analysis (1988) of rational choice theorizing about bureaucracies, and Converse's discussion (1975) of rational choice models of vote choice.

Nor have we taken up the empirical performance of rational choice theorizing in economics. The appeal of rational choice in fields like political science, law, and sociology derives, in part, from its reputation for great success there (Riker 1990,

Abell 1992). Just how well rational actor hypotheses hold up in economics when subjected to empirical scrutiny is debatable, and critiques that parallel ours have been advanced by Thaler (1991), Lane (1991), and Rosenberg (1992). It may be that we are witnessing a curious phenomenon in which rational choice theories are fortified in every discipline by reference to their alleged successes elsewhere, when a more global view of things would reveal the emperor to be, if not entirely naked, somewhat scantily clad.

Whether this larger conclusion is warranted is a question for another day. In this final chapter we respond to ten counterarguments that might be advanced in reply to the case we have developed thus far:

- We are naïve falsificationists, wedded to a view of theory testing that philosophers of science have long since abandoned.
- We formulate no comparable alternative to rational choice theory.
- We are antitheoretical.
- We underestimate the role of advocacy in scientific advance.
- Our criteria for success are so demanding that no theory in political science has ever met them.
- We ignore the fact that all theories simplify empirical reality through the use of abstractions.
- We caricature rational choice as a single monocausal theory of politics.
- We are too impressed by the arbitrary divisions of the social sciences.
- We fail to account for the success that proponents of rational choice models have enjoyed in the discipline of political science.
- We fail to make due allowance for the fact that the rational choice approach is in its infancy.

As we indicate below, these objections are not all compatible with one another. Each nonetheless merits a response on its own terms.

NAIVE FALSIFICATIONISM

The first likely objection turns on the emphasis we have placed on decisive empirical tests of rational choice hypotheses. This might prompt the charge, associated with the philosophies of science popularized by Kuhn (1962) and Lakatos (1970), that we are "naïve falsificationists," committed to a positivist view of the evolution of science that is no longer generally accepted.

Critics of naïve falsificationism contend that there are no decisive falsifying tests of theories. Theories often coexist with empirical anomalies for long periods of time; moreover, they are never decisively falsified by "the facts." They are rejected only when an alternative and more plausible theory is proposed. In Lakatos' memorable example (1970, 100–101), if a planet had "misbehaved" in a way that appeared to disconfirm Newton's law of gravitation, scientists of the pre-Einsteinian era of physics would not have rejected the law. Rather, the conventional Newtonian scientist would have posited the existence of a hitherto undiscovered planet whose gravitational pull would have been presumed to have caused the apparent anomaly. And if attempts to discover this planet failed, it would have been claimed that the undetected planet was hidden by a cloud of cosmic dust or that the measuring instruments were faulty, and so on. The moral of this story, which Lakatos substantiates with many illustrations from the history of science, is that scientists routinely go to great lengths to save established theories in the face of anomalous evidence until an alternative theory becomes available. Crucial falsifying experiments are seldom conducted, and, when they are, they often fail to be recognized as such until long after the fact.

Before confronting his charge squarely, two points should be noted. First, much of the literature we have reviewed here is explicitly devoted to empirical tests of rational choice hypotheses. It would surely be disingenuous to conduct tests and then, on Lakatosian grounds, dismiss results that do falsify as irrelevant to evaluating the theory's truth.[1] Second, since the great majority of rational choice scholarship is conducted by those who believe that genuine advance is possible in science, its proponents are not free to embrace the more extreme critiques of falsificationism. On Kuhn's view, for example, as Lakatos (1970, 177–80) and many others have argued, cumulative scientific advance is impossible because there are no objective criteria by reference to which one paradigm can be judged superior to another. In short, those who accuse us of naïve falsification in the present context must do so from a standpoint like Lakatos' in his defense of "sophisticated methodological falsificationism." It is to that view that we respond here.

We have no quarrel with the Lakatosian account, but we are unconvinced that it undermines the critique of empirical tests of rational choice theory put forward here. Notice, first, that Lakatos' examples of theories that persist in the face of particular anomalies are all taken from highly successful applications in the natural sciences.[2] The explanatory work done in physics by Newton's laws before the Einsteinian revolution was considerable. It is easy to see why scientists would try to account for particular anomalies via auxiliary hypotheses, ceteris paribus clauses, and instrument error; the costs of abandoning so successful a theory in the face of these anomalies would be tremendously high. Rational choice theorists are sometimes inclined to

---

1. Concededly, not all empirical applications of rational choice theory are conceived of as empirical tests. Ferejohn (1991) and Moe (1989) both employ evidence illustratively in the course of developing hypotheses, and they do not describe these ventures as tests.

2. This point applies to Kuhn (1962) as well, since he excluded as preparadigmatic the social sciences from his account of the structure of scientific revolutions.

think of their work in similar ways. For instance, Strom (1990, 11) says the following of spatial models of legislative behavior:

> The theory here is trying to describe the general or central tendency of legislative behavior and is willing, as the price paid for advancement, to ignore for the present factors that cause deviation from the central tendency. As an illustration from a different area of what is meant by this, consider a physicist asked to predict where a given leaf that falls from a tree will land. From the theory of gravity, the physicist knows that the leaf will generally fall downward (the central tendency) and probably not too far from the tree on which it grew. Yet, because of the uncertainties of wind direction and the likelihood of gusts of varying degrees of intensity, the physicist cannot predict precisely where a given leaf will land. Similarly, in developing the spatial rational-actor theory of legis-lative decision-making, theorists have chosen to ignore wind gusts and focus primarily on the central tendency of legislative behavior as determined by the preferences of legislators and the errorless strategies they adopt to maximize the attainment of their preferences.

This begs the question, however, of whether proponents of rational choice models *have* identified "central tendencies" in politics that are analogous to the theory of gravity in physics. In the last four chapters we suggested that there is no comparable track record of success for rational choice theory in the study of politics. Thus, appeals by analogy to successful theories in the physical sciences are misleading. As we have shown, the declarations of success by Lalman, Oppenheimer and Swistak (1993), Kavka (1991), and others are not backed up by empirical results even in the areas in which rational choice is reputed to be most powerful: electoral competition, collective action, and legislative politics. Accordingly, Abell's insistence that despite their failures rational choice models should be granted a "paradigmatic privilege" on account of their numerous unspecified "achievements," which are "barely necessary to mention," rings hollow (1992, 203–4).

The established success argument aside, sophisticated methodological falsifica-tionism does not dispense with the need for empirical testing of proposed theories. Rather, it supplies a standard for appraising hypotheses that differs from Popper's naïve falsificationism (1959, 1963). Whereas for the naïve falsificationist any theory that can be interpreted as experimentally falsifiable may be accepted as scientific, for the sophisticated falsificationist a theory is acceptable only if it exhibits "corroborated excess empirical content over its predecessor (or rival), that is, only if it leads to the discovery of novel facts." For the sophisticated falsificationist, *"no experiment, experimental report, observation statement or well-corroborated low-level falsifying hypothesis alone can lead to falsification. There is no falsification before the emer-gence of a better theory"* (Lakatos 1970, 116, 119).

Proponents of rational choice theory who appeal to this view in order to deal with the theory's failures are apt to misconstrue it as applicable only to their critics. It must, however, be adopted consistently or not at all; in the first instance this means that its strictures must be adhered to in establishing the superiority of rational choice models over earlier or rival alternatives. This places the burden on proponents of rational choice theories to demonstrate that they do indeed contain "corroborated excess empirical content" over predecessor or rival theories. As the preceding chapters have made clear, this requirement is seldom met.

Lakatos points out that unless the proposed new theory explains both what was explained before and new facts as well, there is no scientific basis to prefer it over the existing stock of theory. Without this requirement we would be unable to distinguish degenerative research paradigms, in which endless ad hoc adjustments are engaged in to save a bad theory, from progressive research paradigms, in which empirical understanding is advancing.[3] For the sophisticated falsificationist, "learning about a theory is primarily learning which new facts it anticipated: indeed . . . the only relevant evidence is the evidence anticipated by a theory, and *empiricalness (or scientific character) and theoretical progress are inseparably connected*" (Lakatos 1970, 123).

If rational choice models are to be vindicated on Lakatosian grounds, then, their proponents cannot merely restrict their attention to restating known facts in their preferred theoretical terms. Nor may they legitimately restrict their attention to theory-saving devices to explain away contradictions and anomalous facts. Rather, they must shoulder the burden of demonstrating in particular cases that rational choice theories explain more than do existing or rival theories. Typically, neither burden is carried by proponents of rational choice. Instead, they defend their favored sufficient explanations of known facts, without reference either to credible alternative explanations or to novel predictions.[4]

NO ALTERNATIVE THEORY

A second possible response to our critique is to ask what the alternative is to rational choice. As Elster (1986b, 27) argues, "One can't beat something with

3. "If we put forward a theory to resolve a contradiction between a previous theory and a counterexample in such a way that the new theory, instead of offering a content-increasing (scientific) explanation, offers only a content-decreasing (linguistic) reinterpretation, the contradiction is resolved in a merely semantical, unscientific way. A given fact is explained scientifically only if a new fact is also explained with it" (Lakatos 1970, 119).

4. Notice that Lakatosian criteria cast a shadow on what might otherwise be considered solid empirical work, for example, Lupia's investigation of how California voters with limited information about the provisions of a slew of auto insurance initiatives assimilated cues from the political environment, such as interest group endorsements (1994). Lupia claims support for his rational choice model of information use but makes no effort to distinguish between his model's predictions and those of reference group theory, which has been around for decades in social-psychological interpretations of voting behavior.

nothing." At least we have a theory, this argument runs; what do you propose? This claim need not rely on the appeal to Lakatos just discussed, but the two arguments are mutually reinforcing. Lakatos' insistence that a theory is displaced only by another theory, not by a decisive failure or even a pattern of failures, lends credence to the suggestion that the burden appropriately lies with those who are skeptical of rational choice models to offer something better.

One preliminary point: As we noted in Chapter 3, rational choice theories are sometimes formulated so expansively that they absorb every conceivable alternative hypothesis. In this, the rational choice approach can be reminiscent of Jeremy Bentham's insistence that his brand of utilitarianism be accepted as axiomatic on the grounds that every possible alternative source of human motivation can be re-described in his terms (1960, 124–25). Whatever its particular content, if an empirical theory is formulated in this porous fashion, its defender may not legitimately fault the skeptic for failing to propose an alternative.

In the course of examining different rational choice literatures we have mentioned a variety of alternative hypotheses for particular political phenomena: normative, cultural, psychological, and institutional. The criticism that we offer no alternative theory must be interpreted, therefore, to mean that we offer no theory of comparable generality or range. This raises the question of whether it is reasonable to expect that one general theory can be developed to explain the disparate phenomena that rational choice theorists think of as political. Particularly when politics is conceived of so broadly as to include phenomena as different as spontaneous collective action, coalition formation in legislatures, interest-group activity, and political campaigning, it requires a considerable leap of faith to suppose that a unified deductive theory of the sort aspired to by McKelvey and Riezman (1992, 951) will explain them all. Looking for a general theory of politics may be akin to looking for a general theory of holes; there may be no theory out there waiting to be discovered.

There are two respects in which this point is apt to be misconstrued. First, we are not saying that political behavior is not law governed; to make this claim would be effectively to give up on scientific study of politics.[5] It is one thing, however, to suppose political behavior to be law governed, quite another to suppose that it is all governed by the same laws. Some kinds of political behavior may be irreducibly instrumental, others irreducibly expressive, routinized, or other-directed. If so, there may be no good reason to expect different kinds of politics to be governed by the same causal mechanisms. Roemer (1979b) concedes as much when he urges rational choice theorists to abandon the search for instrumental explanations of such collec-

5. It may of course turn out to be true that political behavior, or some parts of it, are not law-governed; in that case all theories will fail. In this respect politics is no different from any other phenomenon scientists study. We proceed on the assumption that uniform causal processes are at work; in this we can of course be wrong.

tive action as demonstrations or riots, which may often be expressions of bottled-up anger with no instrumental purpose. To concede this is not to embrace the position that such phenomena cannot be studied scientifically, only that they may be governed by causal mechanisms that are qualitatively different from those governing instrumental behavior.

Second, we do not deny that, other things being equal, generality is desirable. The issue is whether the generality in question captures the causal process at work in the politics we observe or whether it comes at the price of verisimilitude. The search for a single set of laws that explains a wide array of political phenomena should not be blind to the possibility that some, but not all, dimensions of politics may be accounted for by the lawlike generalizations in question. Throughout this book we have stressed that empirical research should be designed in ways that might alert us to this possibility. Should it turn out that highly general laws run afoul of the data, this may have nothing to do with the poverty of theory but rather with the recalcitrant complexity of the political world.

WE ARE ANTITHEORETICAL

It is evident from the recommendations of Achen and Snidal (1989), Bueno de Mesquita (1985), Riker (1990), and others that many rational choice theorists believe that predictive hypotheses should be derived from general laws that are validated by theorems. From this vantage point, rational choice theorists might respond to the present critique with the charge that we are antitheoretical.

Riker insists, for example, that valid theoretical explanations must be deduced from equilibrium models. Mere "behavioral laws," he argues, "specify simply that organisms, subjected to a particular treatment, behave in a particular way." Thus the behavioral theory of party identification or the generalization that party proliferation is associated with cabinet instability are not really explanatory because they "cannot be put into a form that allows for interaction among actors that leads to an equilibrium." Such behavioral or sociological laws "may be well supported, sufficiently well, indeed, to provide adequate predictions and justify social engineering; but they cannot, in the absence of an interpretation of a giant social mechanism far too complex for our present understanding, be placed inside a theory of equilibrium. This is why behavioral and sociological laws may be used to predict, but not explain" (Riker 1990, 176).

On this view, behavioral and sociological laws rest on guesswork; rational choice explanations in political science do not. Riker believes this is so because all explanations in the social sciences ultimately rest on presuppositions about preferences and intentions, so that theories that start from these as their primitives begin with what must be the case. Thus Riker dismisses the Skinnerian behaviorist who explains an individual's identification with party A by hypothesizing that the individual's choice of party A over the available alternatives reflects his having been reinforced to approve of party A. "But how can one explain reinforcement?" Riker asks. This, he contends, "must involve some axioms about preferences and, hence, intentions." Because rational choice theory is unique in developing equilibrium models based on individual preferences, it alone can supply the necessary and sufficient conditions to explain political outcomes.

The argument with which Riker confronts the Skinnerian behaviorist can be pressed equally against the rational choice theorist's appeal to the primacy of intentions and preferences. What determines *them*? Perhaps they are products of chemical reactions in the brain or of cultures or of institutional orders. To say that intentions and choices are the building blocks from which explanations of human behavior should be fashioned rests on nothing more than a conjecture that they are in fact the basic determinants.

A subtler version of the claim that only rational choice theorists have a theory worthy of the name has been advanced by Becker (1986) and Elster (1986b). It turns on the *systematic* character of rational choice explanations. The contrast between rational choice theory and other theories becomes most apparent, Becker argues, when rational choice explanations seem to fail and other kinds of explanations are introduced in an ad hoc and "useless" manner:

> Examples abound in the economic literature of changes in preferences conveniently introduced ad hoc to explain puzzling behavior. Education is said to change preferences—about different goods and services, political candidates, or family size—rather than real income or the relative cost of different choices. Businessmen talk about the social responsibilities of business because their attitudes are said to be influenced by public discussions of this question rather than because such talk is necessary to maximize their profits, given the climate of public intervention. . . . With an ingenuity worthy of admiration if put to better use, almost any conceivable behavior is alleged to be dominated by ignorance and irrationality, values and their frequent unexplained shifts, custom and tradition, the compliance somehow induced by social norms, or the ego and the id. (Becker 1986, 117)

Elster echoes these sentiments. He concedes that there "can be little doubt that the appeal to norms sometimes enables us to explain where rational choice fails." Yet he insists that such appeals are typically ad hoc and ex post facto, and that there is no "well confirmed theory specifying the conditions under which, and the limits within which, norms override rationality." Likewise, Elster dismisses Herbert Simon's claim that satisficing behavior is often a better predictor of outcomes than maximizing behavior, contending that it, too, is essentially ad hoc. "The theory does not offer an answer to the crucial question of why people have the aspiration or satisfaction levels they have. . . . These levels must simply be taken as given, which means that the theory offers little more than 'thick description'" (Elster 1986b, 24–26).

The difficulty with the Becker-Elster line of reasoning is that there is little basis for the claim that rational choice explanations are immune to ad hoc and post hoc elaboration. The frequency with which rational choice theorists have explained away anomalies by manipulating the meaning of rationality, restricted arbitrarily the domain in which the theory applies so as to avoid discordant facts, constructed tests that adduce only confirming facts, or ignored competing explanations belies the suggestion that when employed as empirical science rational choice explanations are free from mercurial invention.

Throughout this book we have shown that rational choice theorists devote much of their creative ingenuity to demonstrating that almost any conceivable behavior can be shown to be rational and that almost any conceivable political outcome can be shown to result from acts of individual maximization. The ad hoc character of rational choice hypotheses as they are typically applied may not be evident to those who elaborate the pure theory rather than apply it. If this is so, it tells us something about the pernicious effects of an intellectual division of labor between elaborators and appliers of theory, not about the presumptive merits of rational choice theory. Theory building is necessary for the conduct of empirical analysis, but, as Arrow (1951, 21) cautioned long ago, "it is a means, not an end."

Rational choice theorists sometimes try to establish that their approach is uniquely scientific by virtue of its deductive analytical character. Empirical regularity is never "proof of validity," says Riker, because it "does not reveal the reason for the regularity" (1990, 176). Bueno de Mesquita (1985, 129) warns us in the same spirit that "we must not be lulled by apparent empirical successes into believing that scientific knowledge can be attained without the abstract, rigorous exercise of logical proof." Achen and Snidal (1989, 168) insist that whatever the merits of empirical generalizations, they "are not a substitute for theorizing; empirical laws should not be mistaken for theoretical propositions."

When these theorists insist that demonstrating the existence of an empirical regularity is no proof of validity of an explanation, they are right. Observing an empirical regularity, and even correctly predicting from it, does not amount to an explanation. One might be able to make a correct prediction while lacking an explanation for why an observed regularity occurs (as when a schizophrenic who is given psychotropic drugs ceases to be delusional; pharmacologists know that the drug works and can predict the therapeutic result, but they do not know why it works). One is in possession of an explanation only if one can accurately characterize the causal mechanism involved in producing the relevant regularity; rational choice theorists do not deny this. Too often, however, they fail to appreciate the fact that all such putative characterizations are conjectures; it is never possible to prove that they are correct. Theorems can be proved, theories cannot. All we can ever know of a theory is that it has not been falsified in a Popperian sense or that it has not been superseded in a Lakatosian sense. For an explanation to be accepted as correct for the moment, it is neither necessary nor sufficient that it be derived from a theorem.

In short, the claim that our stance is antitheoretical because the alternative empirical hypotheses we have discussed are not deduced from laws that are supported by theorems turns out on inspection to be more rhetorical than real. Even if rational choice theorists acted on their own methodological rhetoric, their theories would be no more than empirical conjectures, dependent on the extent to which the particular hypotheses they generate conform to the evidence at hand. When we consider rational choice empirical theory as it is conducted in fact, we find that a good deal of ad hoc guesswork characteristically goes on in the fashioning of hypotheses. As we noted in Chapter 2, this is unimportant if one is a Friedman-instrumentalist but, then, so is the charge that we are antitheoretical. From the standpoint of the covering-law model, on the other hand, we have shown that the various manipulations in which rational choice theorists engage to try to develop serviceable empirical hypotheses are no less suspect than anything with which they can legitimately charge others.

Between the extremes of the covering-law theory and Friedman-instrumentalism lies the commonsense enterprise of building middle-level theoretical generalizations. This endeavor involves theorizing about the conditions under which certain types of explanations are likely to be superior to others and about the relations among types of variables in multicausal explanations. Theorizing of this kind has often seemed beneath contempt to rational choice theorists who are impressed by views that link science to the deduction of hypotheses from well-grounded general laws. In the absence of empirically supported general laws about politics, however, the development of middle-level generalizations might be the only theorizing that turns out to be viable.

THE SCIENTIFIC VALUE OF ADVOCACY

A fourth possible response is that our argument undervalues the role of advocacy in scientific advance. Commentators like Mitroff (1972) have suggested that successful scientists typically do not engage in an impartial search for truth. Rather, they become partisans for particular views and advocate them. On this account, scientists in all fields routinely adopt many of the practices that we have identified as pathologies. They search for confirming evidence, they present this evidence so as to put their pet hypotheses in the best light, and they purposely select weak null hypotheses or none at all (Armstrong 1979, 423–24). On the advocacy view, scientific advance is a by-product of competition in the marketplace of ideas, not of impartial hypothesis testing by individual scientists. I make the best case I can for one theory, you make the best case you can for another, and the community of scholars functions as a jury to decide who wins.

On the advocacy account of the evolution of science much of the preceding discussion might seem to be cast in a different light, but there is less to the advocacy view than meets the eye. It is necessary to distinguish the conceded benefits of competition among scientists from the claim that the best way for them to compete is for each to shout as loudly as possible for his or her own theory. When scientists manipulate evidence to make their own arguments look good, their claim to objectivity is compromised, and they become ineffective advocates. Conversely, when they confront the alternatives and problematic cases for their own arguments in a forthright fashion, their credibility as scientists is enhanced. One competes effectively by making a more persuasive case than one's adversary; this can be done only if one subjects one's own hypothesis to rigorous testing and shows that it survives the ordeal and outperforms the credible alternatives. In short, competition may be beneficial and scientists may often be spurred to greater creative effort by pet attachments to the hypotheses they seek to vindicate, but this in no way buttresses the suggestion that systematic testing of proffered hypotheses is dispensable.

IMPOSSIBLY DEMANDING STANDARDS

A fifth possible response to our argument would be to say that the standards to which we have appealed are unrealistically demanding, not in the sense discussed under the heading of naïve falsificationism but in the pragmatic sense that none of the going alternative theories in political science would survive them. If rational choice theories fail tests that every other theory of politics fails as well, what is the force of demonstrating their failure?

We readily concede part of this claim. Certainly it is true that theories of comparable scope and range to rational choice theory have seldom fared well in the social sciences, and never in political science. We do not doubt that such theories as Marxism, elite theory, systems theory, and structural-functionalism could be shown to be as vulnerable as rational choice if they were subjected to the sort of scrutiny to which rational choice models have been subjected in this book. However, by itself this does not establish that the standards are too demanding. It is equally compatible with the suggestion that these theories might be unrealistically ambitious in scope. If a succession of theories designed to explain all political behavior and institutions fails, one may question the wisdom of propounding such theories rather than the definitions of success and failure. Given our discussion of the diversity of political phenomena, it should come as no surprise that this is our earlier recommendation.

When the scientific study of politics is thought of in less architectonic terms, advances can be identified. Indeed, advances can be identified among works within the rational choice tradition. Fiorina (1994), for example, offers a well-tested prediction that the higher salaries and longer legislative sessions that accompanied the "professionalization" of state legislatures increased the number of Democratic representatives. Prior to professionalization, he argues, the occupational stratum from which Democrats were drawn was ill suited to participate in low-paying, part-time legislatures. The hypotheses that changing occupational incentives caused the partisan balance to shift is tested against such alternative hypotheses as the view that liberals are increasingly attracted to government as its spending rises, and the data sustain Fiorina's interpretation. Granted, Fiorina's hypothesis is not obviously counterintuitive; payment for Members of Parliament was defended in the nineteenth century on the grounds that it would help break the stranglehold of the wealthy classes on the House of Commons. Nonetheless, he is able to show not only that the logic of occupational incentives operates in state legislatures, but that it helps account for another phenomenon—divided government—that researchers had sought to explain.

Another example of well-crafted empirical work may be found in Aldrich's study of the dynamics of candidate strategy in presidential primaries (1980). Aldrich's analysis of the strategic options that confronted primary contenders Gerald Ford and Ronald Reagan in 1976 yields some illuminating predictions about how candidates manage campaigns. He argues, for instance, that candidates tend to compete in states where they believe that they have strong support going in; the risks of attracting media attention and raised expectations to a campaign that subsequently fails are thought to be too high, even though this strategy means giving up some delegates that would otherwise be won. This analysis, coupled with other observations about the strategic implications of the ways that delegates are selected under the rules of each state, is then tested against a detailed account of how the candidates in fact competed. The value added of this study, then, is that it is an informative explanation of why primary competition takes the form it does when two evenly matched candidates square off, an analysis derived from reflection on the strategic calculations of rational actors. Again, Aldrich's theory does not purport to be counterintuitive, but in combination with his close empirical work, it contributes to our understanding of campaign politics and lays the foundation for further study of the consequences of changing electoral laws.

Such results advance the production of knowledge about politics, even if they do not deliver on the more grandiose claims with which rational choice theory is sometimes advertised. That praiseworthy empirical scholarship of this kind exists underscores the fact that we are not proposing new and impossibly demanding standards for the discipline of political science. Note, incidentally, that neither of these empirical studies has theorems standing behind it; the hypotheses in question are not obviously deduced from covering laws; and nothing is claimed about whether they are generalizable to other political or strategic environments. They are, in short, similar in kind to conventional forms of social science research.

ALL THEORIES SIMPLIFY VIA ABSTRACTION

A sixth common rational choice argument that might be advanced in response to our critique is the claim that all explanations rest on simplifying abstractions that distort reality. As a result, this argument goes, it is scarcely telling when critics of rational choice theorists like George and Smoke (1974, 503) complain that actual cases exhibit "complexities which in many respects are not addressed" by rational choice models.

Here we partly agree with defenders of the rational choice perspective. No part of our critique has turned on the use of simplifying assumptions as such, or on the abstract character of rational choice theory.[6] However, rational choice theorists go too far when they "postulate that the generality and parsimony of theories should be given primacy over their accuracy," and that "the greater the generality of a theory, the greater the range of phenomena that can be explained" by it (Przeworski and Teune 1970, 17, 21; see also Olson 1965, 61).

If an abstract theory has explanatory power, this is not merely because it is abstract, but because the abstraction in question captures the essence of what is going on causally. We have expressed skepticism as to whether a theoretical approach that abstracts from widely different domains of politics in the same way is likely to be successful, and we have argued that a convincing case has yet to be made for rational choice theories even in the domains where they are reputed to be most successful. But neither of these arguments amounts to a rejection of the heuristic use of simplifying assumptions. The trick is to distill into an explanation the factors that are causally responsible for outcomes; the question, therefore, is not whether to abstract from the complexity of everyday politics but whether one has chosen an appropriate abstraction. As we noted repeatedly in Chapters 6 and 7, that some rational choice models are more realistic than others should not, by itself, commend them to us as superior, because the additional realistic assumptions may be irrelevant to the model's empirical performance. A car that fails to drive because it lacks an engine will not have its problems solved by adding wing mirrors to it, even though it also lacks wing mirrors, which working cars generally have. Adding realistic assumptions to an explanatory

6. The status of simplifying assumptions varies with one's philosophy of science. For instance, simplifying assumptions are of no consequence on the Friedman-instrumental view discussed in Chapter 2, whereas on the covering-law view one should anticipate that the assumptions on which a theory is based will be modified in the direction of greater realism as that theory matures.

model will improve it only if the newly added assumptions are causally pertinent to understanding the problem under study. There is, however, no way to find out which assumptions in explanatory models *are* causally pertinent absent empirical testing.

RATIONAL CHOICE IS NOT ONE THEORY

A seventh possible rational choice response is to say that we caricature rational choice theory by presenting it as a single theory that purports to explain everything when in fact this is not the case. In practice, few rational choice theorists who tangle with empirical questions in a serious way are pure universalists. Rather, they seem to be committed to one or some combination of the less than fully universalist views discussed in Chapter 2: segmented universalism, partial universalism, or the family-of-theories view. Proponents of segmented universalism concede that rational choice theory is successful only in certain domains of politics. Partial universalists insist that rational choice explains some, but not all, behavior in all domains, leaving open just how much is explained by the strategic maximizing of specified interests. Defenders of the family-of-theories view contend that there is no single rational choice theory and that different rational choice theories rely on competing assumptions and generate quite different predictions.

Before getting to the merits of each of the scaled-down universalisms, we should note that commitment to any of them tends to undermine a common strategy of defending the rational choice by reference to the poverty of the alternatives—the failure, that is, of anyone else to come up with an alternative general theory of politics (see p. 184). One cannot have it both ways. Rational choice theorists saw off the branch on which they are perched if they insist that their view be favored because no one has better defended an alternative general theory of politics while at the same time embracing some version of segmented universalism, partial universalism, or the family-of-theories view.

The three less universally ambitious variants of rational choice theory may have much to commend them; it is not our purpose to dismiss any of them. But if any of these subtler universalisms is to be pursued, the burden surely lies with its proponents to specify and test it, not with the skeptic to show that it is untenable. Developing any of these views would require a considerable redirection of energy. It would involve a turn away from proving theorems about what rationality can explain and toward grappling with the empirical complexities that less simplistic views inevitably raise.

If segmented universalism is to be freed of the pathology of arbitrary domain-restriction and vindicated as the way ahead, its advocates should begin systematically to examine the conditions under which rational choice theories have more or less explanatory power. From this would follow empirically testable accounts of which domains of politics rational choice theories can be expected to succeed in and why.

Elster (1986), Brennan and Buchanan (1984), Maoz (1990), Satz and Ferejohn (1993), Aldrich (1993), and others have offered brief conjectures on this point, noted in Chapter 2, but as yet little more has been attempted. To make any variant of this view credible, an account must be developed to explain why rational choice hypotheses should be expected to succeed in some circumstances and not others. More important, this account must be exposed to empirical evaluation. For instance, Satz and Ferejohn (1993, 14–15) advance the theoretical conjecture that rational choice theory is most likely to be successful in the comparatively rare contexts in which choices are tightly constrained, so that it is more likely, for instance, to explain the behavior of parties than of voters. Although this is a reasonable hypothesis, our reviews of the literature in Chapters 4 and 7 revealed that it remains an untested conjecture.

If the way forward is conceived of along the lines of partial universalism, different questions and possibilities present themselves. The challenge is to specify a testable account of the conditions under which strategic incentives influence political behavior and outcomes. One might argue, for example, that instrumental, normative, and affective thoughts compete for a decision maker's limited attention, with the relative salience of each factor being determined by how decisions are framed and the setting in which choices take place (Green 1992). The empirical task would then become one of identifying cognitive or social-psychological factors that affect the degree to which actors follow impulse, habit, or the lead of others to sacrifice some valued political end. To be sure, formulating and testing a partial universalist model in an exacting manner represents a formidable undertaking, but pursuing such a research program seems to us time better spent than proving theorems about optimal strategic behavior, which may in the end account for a small part of political behavior.

If embracing the family-of-theories approach is the wave of the future, then a good deal more work needs to be done on the relations among the family members, on what makes them a family, on what to do when the family contains incompatible members, and on how different interpretations of what rational choice means are to be adjudicated. It is not sufficient, for example, for Ferejohn and Fiorina (1993, 1) to say of their minimax regret model: "We showed that rejection of the Downsian model was not tantamount to rejection of rational choice theory; alternative rational choice models with empirical content—minimax regret among other possibilities—were available." The burden does not appropriately rest with the skeptic to show that there is no interpretation of rationality that could account for the phenomenon under study. It rests with the defender of a particular interpretation to explain why it is more appropriate than competing interpretations of rationality in accounting for the phenomenon in question, what other phenomena the favored interpretation explains (or rules out) that competing interpretations do not, and why it is superior to explanations that do not invoke rationality at all.

An even weaker version of the family-of-theories argument is the claim that rational choice theory is not a theory at all; rather, it is an "approach," a "methodology" or
a "paradigm," and as such it cannot be tested. If this argument is taken seriously, the
question becomes, Why choose the rational choice approach rather than a different
one? The answer, presumably, must rest on an appeal to the predictive success of the
hypotheses that the approach yields. Our appraisal of the rational choice literature
leads to the conclusion that these successes are, for the moment, decidedly limited.
Furthermore, because rational choice theorizing all too easily generates hypotheses
that among them predict both X and Not-X, it is difficult for an outside observer to tell
what credit to assign the approach for any arrivals it produces. The skeptic cannot be
faulted for sensing a disconcerting similarity between the rational choice paradigm
and the psychoanalytic paradigm (see Crews 1993).

THE TYRANNY OF DISCIPLINARY DIVISIONS

An eighth possible rational choice response focuses on our contention
that methods that may have succeeded in economics are not necessarily appropriate
for much of the study of politics. In response to this, rational choice theorists might
claim that we have allowed the division of disciplines in universities to distort our
perception of social reality. Whatever the advantages of an intellectual division of
labor, it must be conceded that the phenomena that social scientists study overlap and
flow into one another. Our disciplinary training and affiliations lead us to carve up the
world in a variety of ways that are often conceptually arbitrary. Like those who
founded the discipline of political economy in the eighteenth century, contemporary
rational choice theorists adopt a unified approach to the social reality. What intellectual grounds do we have to resist this?

None. It is not our claim that political science is necessarily distinctive in its object
or method of study. We do not resist the introduction of approaches or hypotheses
from other disciplines. Nor do we contend that, even within political science, one
type of explanation is always appropriate. It is our impression, however, that much
rational choice theory is method driven rather than problem driven, and that this is
partly responsible for its defects. Empirical science is problem driven when the
elaboration of theories is designed to explain phenomena that arise in the world.
Method-driven research occurs when a theory is elaborated without reference to what
phenomena are to be explained, and the theorist subsequently searches for phenomena to which the theory in question can be applied.

That rational choice theorists cross disciplinary boundaries is not objected to here.
Nor do we reject out of hand the rational choice hypothesis that the complex fabric of
political action and institutions might be explicable by reference to a variant of
rational actor theory that was designed for the different purpose of explaining the

behavior of market prices. Our argument is that much applied rational choice scholarship is method-driven and that method-driven research tends to result in the characteristic errors that we identified in Chapter 3 and documented in Chapters 4 through 7. It would appear to us that those armed with a method in search of applications too often find them. As Abraham Kaplan (1964, 28) once observed, if the only tool in one's possession is a hammer, everything in sight begins to resemble a nail.

THE SUPREMACY OF RATIONAL CHOICE THEORY

A ninth argument that merits attention is the ad hominem contention that if rational choice theory had established as little as we claim, it would not have achieved the status that it enjoys within the discipline of political science. The prominence of rational choice scholars and scholarship can scarcely be disputed, whether gauged by representation at conferences, publications in leading journals, or stature in major departments. How could this have occurred if we are right that rational choice theories have contributed virtually nothing to the empirical study of politics?

If our assessment of rational choice scholarship is on the mark, it would not be the first time that a theory widely accepted at one time is later revealed as mistaken or oversold. Aristotle's physics, the view that the earth is flat or that it is at the center of the universe, and Lamarckian genetics are all cases in point. Nonetheless, the widespread influence of rational choice models in political science calls for an explanation. A variety of possible explanations could be adduced, ranging from the perceived lack of alternatives to ideological explanations that link rational choice to a particular politics to institutional explanations having to do with the availability of resources for political science research that appears rigorous to outsiders.

No doubt factors such as these play a role, but a different, intellectual reason comes to mind based on our reading of the rational choice literature: contrary to the assertions of Riker and others that rational choice theory fares well in political science because the field is theory poor, in fact rational choice theory fares best in environments that are evidence poor. In subfields like mass political behavior and public opinion, where researchers have accumulated a great deal of data, rational choice theories have been refuted or domesticated by this evidence.[7] As we showed in Chapters 4 and 5, the now common contention that turnout is an unusually recalcitrant case of collective action for rational choice theory properly reflects the greater

7. Although one can point to studies that advertise themselves as confirming rational choice theories, this interpretation is often contested by rational choice scholars themselves. Compare, for example, the claims of Abramson et al. (1992) or Enelow and Hinich (1984b) with the respective critiques of Ferejohn and Fiorina (1993) and Brennan and Buchanan (1984).

empirical attention that turnout has attracted. Conversely, in the study of Congress, evidence concerning legislators' beliefs, motives, and strategic options is thin, and rational choice interpretations proliferate. The same appears to hold for the study of international relations, where evidence about the preferences and strategic reasoning of policy makers is difficult to discern even in retrospect (see Zagare 1979; Thakur 1982), and rational choice models abound. If this conjecture turns out to be correct, then it would be reasonable to anticipate that, as the accumulation of empirical knowledge about politics proceeds, the influence of rational choice theory, in its present form at least, will diminish.

WE EXPECT TOO MUCH OF A FLEDGLING THEORY

A final objection—to some extent in tension with the supremacy argument just discussed—is that we fail to make due allowance for the fact that rational choice theories of politics are in their infancy. Granted, variants of rational choice arguments about politics were advanced long ago by Hobbes, Grotius, Condorcet, and others, but these arguments were anecdotal and impressionistic. Systematic attempts to apply the logic of rational choice to politics do not predate the 1940s, and it is only since the 1970s that an appreciable number of scholars have begun working in this tradition. Many of our criticisms might be valid, this line of reasoning goes, but that should not be surprising four decades into the enterprise. Considering the many centuries it took for the mature theories in the physical sciences to develop and the elementary mistakes that attended them in their tender years, what we have identified here should be seen as growing pains rather than anything more serious or fundamental.

Defending this view means conceding the central contention of this book, namely, that little of what has been claimed for rational choice theory is backed up by empirical results. Furthermore, this argument is consistent with our position that there is nothing inherent in rational choice theory that prevents it from advancing scientifically in the future. Where we part company with those who advance this objection has to do with how we envision the future. Implicit in the fledgling theory argument is the notion that mistakes will iron themselves out in time. We are less sanguine about this self-correcting tendency given the deep-seated methodological problems that have persisted to this point.

Significant changes in research style are required, the most basic of which is that a good deal more emphasis should be placed on empirical inquiry itself. As the literatures on collective action and electoral competition discussed in Chapters 5 and 7 reveal, the ratio of theory elaboration to application and testing can be exceedingly one-sided. Rational choice theorists often seem to want to leave what they see as the mundane work of application and testing to unspecified others—who seldom materialize—and concentrate on the intellectual challenges of high theory elabora-tion. But no viable army can consist solely of generals, and even if theorists could really expect to delegate empirical work to others, the question remains whether such a division of labor is desirable. Arguably, mastery of the subject matter under empiri-cal observation is required to guide and inspire innovative theorizing.

On a more optimistic note, it might be said that quality of empirical applications is on the rise. For example, three books—*The Logic of Delegation* (Kiewiet and McCubbins 1991), *Legislative Leviathan* (Cox and McCubbins 1993), and *Informa-tion and Legislative Organization* (Krehbiel 1991)—apply rational choice theories to the committee system of the U.S. Congress. Each work contains a series of innova-tive empirical investigations in which nonobvious hypotheses are pitted against plau-sible alternatives. Viewed against the backdrop of the previous four chapters, these studies are distinguished by the authors' broad knowledge of their subject matter and the clarity with which they link theory to real-world application.

Like those who believe our indictment of rational choice scholarship premature, we hope that works such as these signal a growing commitment to rigorous empirical inquiry. These particular studies of legislative politics do not, however, impel us to retreat from our general contention that little empirically supported knowledge has grown out of rational choice theorizing. Although these works represent a substantial improvement over earlier rational choice applications, their empirical conclusions are, in varying degrees, problematic. Since these acclaimed works may represent something of a model for a new wave of rational choice scholarship, it seems worth-while to lay out our misgivings about these empirical studies.

The thesis of *The Logic of Delegation* grows out of an analogy between the manner in which firms structure organizational incentives to maximize productivity and how party caucuses structure the committee system to achieve desired policy outputs. In contrast to scholars who emphasize committee autonomy and party weakness, Kiewiet and McCubbins contend that this autonomy is more apparent than real: in making committee appointments, parties strive to align their preferences with the policy preferences of pivotal voters on each committee (chaps. 4 and 5). Committees may seem autonomous, even to legislators themselves (60), but that only attests to the success with which the principals (the party caucuses) have harmonized their interests with those of their agents (committee members).[8]

8. This line of argument about the relation between parties and committees immediately raises an important conceptual question. What does it mean to say that the party caucus, a collective entity, functions as a principal? Kiewiet and McCubbins generally treat each caucus as though it were a unitary actor whose preferences reflect those of its median voter. This characterization, however, is premised on the dubious assumption that legislative politics takes place along a single dimension. In addition, it implicitly assumes that committee members, parties, and their respective leaders do not exchange side-payments. One also may ask: By what

The central empirical concern for Kiewiet and McCubbins is the extent to which party caucuses make committee appointments in a strategic fashion, and, if so, whether the committee members behave in the manner anticipated by a principal-agent theory. Kiewiet and McCubbins address this issue with respect to the Appropriations Committee in the House of Representatives and challenge what they regard as Fenno's claim (1966) that Appropriations functions as a "guardian of the Treasury," or an agent of the House as a whole.[9]

Relying on data on the roll-call votes of House members from 1947 to 1984 Kiewiet and McCubbins endeavor to show that party delegations on the Appropriations Committee have historically tended to be representative of their respective party caucuses. But the authors are "troubled" to find substantial differences between Democratic and Republican members of the Appropriations Committee and their respective caucuses, in contrast with their initial expectations (101). Before the mid-1970s committee members from both parties were likely to be disproportionately conservative; afterward, the median Democrat on the committee came into alignment with the caucus median, but the median committee Republican became disproportionately liberal. This setback leads Kiewiet and McCubbins to reformulate the question, "Are the party delegations representative of their respective caucuses?" to read "To what extent did party caucuses fill vacancies so as to make the delegation

---

standard should the rationality of the unitary principal's actions be evaluated? Does this model anticipate that the parties will *maximize* the extent to which committees do the parties' bidding, and, if so, subject to what constraints? Should we expect the majority party caucus, for example, to try to achieve ideological balance on important committees by means of an integrated strategy, one that involves making ideologically congenial new appointments and, if need be, changing the size of committees, altering the ratio of slots assigned to party delegations, or removing recalcitrant committee members? Kiewiet and McCubbins address this question indirectly, through stipulations that the parties must shy away from "all-out assaults on current members' rights to continued service" (107) and alterations to committee sizes and delegation ratios because such arrangements are, in the authors' view, "equilibria to other games" (247). The nature of these other games, however, is not specified. We note, parenthetically, that Kiewiet and McCubbins are by no means alone in stipulating that legislative arrangements represent equilibria. Shepsle and Weingast (1987b, 943), for example, in a "plea for a keener appreciation of equilibrium analysis," assert that a "mature institution," such as Congress, is "an organization in equilibrium."

9. They also question whether the committee resocialized its members to identify with the goals of fiscal responsibility. Using a multivariate analysis, the authors attempt to show that those who served on Appropriations did not become more conservative as a consequence of exposure to committee norms. Unfortunately, the analysis is robbed of some of its persuasiveness in that floor roll-call votes, not committee behavior, is the dependent variable. Perhaps a more minor concern is that socialization is measured by the number of years served on the committee, which fails to highlight the particularly strong socializing forces at work during the initial period of apprenticeship.

more representative?" The data answer the revised question more affirmatively than its predecessor, but important anomalies remain.[10] The Republican caucus, even when it held the majority, continually appointed members in ways that failed to correct the ideological discrepancy between the committee delegation median and caucus median (109). As for the Democrats, the drift in the direction of liberal appointments was so gradual that the authors are forced to grapple with the question of why the party "did not move more decisively against the conservative bias" of their committee contingent (118).[11]

There is much to commend in this study of the indirect ways that parties shape the policy outputs of committees, but the main theoretical conjectures tend to be murky and not well supported by the evidence. Although one cannot rule out the possibility that the hypotheses would have been better supported had the authors been able to study behavior within committees rather than floor roll-call votes, the empirical setbacks may stem from ambiguities in the underlying spatial model. It seems strange, in particular, that the caucuses should seek to align their medians with those of their respective committee contingents. In the usual case in which the Republican (minority) committee members lie to the right of most of their Democratic (majority) colleagues, the committee median will lie to the right of the Democratic caucus median. If the median voter of the majority party caucus is to get his or her way on the committee, appointments will have to be drawn disproportionately from liberal Democrats (compare Cox and McCubbins 1993, 202). This logic would have the parties engaging in a complex game in which the Democrats, for instance, reserve liberals for the key policy committees and exile conservatives to Merchant Marine and Fisheries. It may be said in reply that the internal politics of the parties prevents the adoption of this kind of strategy, but disputes internal to the parties are precisely what is absent from this account.

Legislative Leviathan (Cox and McCubbins 1993) represents an attempt to refine and extend the principal-agent model presented by Kiewiet and McCubbins (1991). The authors discuss a variety of means by which the majority party structures incentives in order to exercise control over policies adopted by the House, among them, the

10. Kiewiet and McCubbins (105–6) replicate their analysis for the Budget Committee, which has fixed terms of appointment, but, against their expectations, find it even less representative of the caucuses than is Appropriations.

11. The answer they offer is that "unless those making committee assignments can accurately forecast changes in the ideological makeup of their party's caucus over the next several Congresses, strategies more aggressive than partial adjustment run the risk of overcompensating, first in one direction and then in the other" (123). Kiewiet and McCubbins seem not to realize that the risk-aversion they impute to the median caucus voter is of a very peculiar sort. In effect, this legislator reasons: "I don't want my policy views to prevail on the committee, lest they come to dominate in years ahead, against the better interests of some new median voter on the caucus."

Speaker's scheduling power (chap. 9) and various ways in which the majority party may reshape committee structure and resources (chap. 10). Their most rigorous empirical extension, however, concerns the hypothesis that committee transfers, especially to the so-called control committees (Appropriations, Rules, and Ways and Means), are granted in return for party loyalty. Tracking nonfreshman members of each Congress from the eightieth to the hundredth, Cox and McCubbins perform a series of probit regressions in which party loyalty is used to predict transfer success net of the effects of region, seniority, and number of available committee vacancies.[12]

Although the authors seem pleased with their findings, the results of the analysis would seem to provide only modest support for the claim that "those whose roll call votes demonstrate loyalty to the leadership are rewarded with committee transfers" (182). According to Cox and McCubbins' estimates (table 20, col. 2, p. 173), the expected probability that a Democrat in the postreform Congress would be transferred to any of twenty openings on a control committee is 18 percent, assuming a loyalty record at the fiftieth percentile of the party. If the same Democrat were to move to the ninety-fifth percentile of party loyalty his or her chances of a transfer would rise to just 26 percent. An incentive of this magnitude hardly seems sufficient to "make committees and their members more responsive to both the party's leadership and goals" (182).[13] It may be said that the weak pattern of results reflects certain econometric problems that, if addressed, might strengthen the case that the majority party caucus structures the behavior of its agents; but for the present, the evidence seems less than convincing.[14]

12. Party loyalty is here defined as the "percentage of times in the previous Congress that a member voted with his party leader and party whip in opposition to the party leader and whip of the opposing party" (170). Hence the exclusion of freshmen from the analysis.

13. Other analyses fare no better. Restricting the analysis to only those Congresses in which data on written transfer requests are available, Cox and McCubbins find that in the postreform era loyalty did not differentiate those representatives whose requests were denied from representatives who neither made a request nor received one. Nor did loyalty discriminate between the latter group and representatives who were granted their transfer requests (table 23, p. 182). The results for the relation between freshman committee assignments and the loyalty scores of their first term are also spotty. Noting that "the bottom line is clear," Cox and McCubbins (185) conclude that "first term loyalty scores correlate positively with higher probabilities of receiving requested assignments for most categories of freshmen and committees." Yet, in contrast to the thrust of the principal-agent thesis, loyalty was not statistically significantly related to appointment to either control committees or other "major" committees (table 24, p. 184).

14. Cox and McCubbins (171–79) are quick to acknowledge the econometric complications that arise when two potentially endogenous variables, transfer requests and number of vacancies, are used as regressors. They could have noted also the possibility of serially correlated disturbances that arises when the same Democratic members of Congress appear repeatedly in a pooled dataset of 4,407 observations, a problem that biases their standard errors and hence significance levels.

Information and Legislative Organization (Krehbiel 1991) interprets the committee system not as an agent of the parties but as a means by which the House gathers information about policy outcomes. To reward members for expending the resources necessary to acquire expertise and, under conditions of great uncertainty, to encourage committee members to divulge their private information, committees are granted closed rules on the floor. By preventing or limiting amendment activity, a closed rule affords the committee the opportunity to report a take-it-or-leave-it proposal. Thus the members of the committee can include pet provisions that, if subject to an open rule, would be amended to the median position of the House floor. This interpretation of the closed rule as an incentive for legislative specialization differs from the conventional distributive politics interpretation, which contends that closed rules function to hold together intra- or inter-committee logrolling (chap. 5).

This line of analysis naturally suggests the empirical question: "Under what circumstances are closed rules assigned to committee proposals?" Krehbiel attempts to address this question with a multivariate analysis of all bills in the ninety-eighth and ninety-ninth Congresses for which a rule was either requested or granted and accepted on the House floor (167–68). Drawing on an assortment of traditional and rational choice literatures, Krehbiel develops a statistical model in which the probability of obtaining a closed rule is said to be a function of several constructs: distributive content, legislative specialization, ideological distance between floor and committee medians, ideological heterogeneity, bipartisanship, and scope and urgency of the proposed legislation. Measures for these constructs are drawn primarily from the keyword index of LEGI-SLATE, an online database. The indicator for distributive content, for example, is "simply the ratio of states listed to the total number of keywords plus the number of states" (170). The central construct, legislative specialization, is measured twice, first by the number of laws cited in the keyword index and second by the average years of seniority on the committee reporting the bill. The rough-and-ready nature of these variables casts a pall over the analysis, since a combination of random error, nonrandom error, and measurement redundancy biases the results in unknown and potentially serious ways.[15] By the same token, one must ask whether seniority properly measures "jurisdiction-specific expertise" alone (171), rather than some combination of expert knowledge, political savvy, horse-trading resources, and informal influence.

---

15. Random measurement error among the independent variables potentially biases regression estimates positively or negatively. Nonrandom error may be present here as well, since the measure of distributive content is a nonlinear function of the variable "scope" (the number of LEGI-SLATE keywords listed under a bill [169]) and since the numbers of Democratic and Republican cosponsors are entered separately in the regression. Krehbiel makes the case for the validity of his measures of distributive content and expertise by noting that bills that rank highly on these measures seem on their face distributive or specialized, respectively. Unfortunately, we are not shown comparable lists for bills scoring low on these measures.

The estimates that Krehbiel derives from his multivariate model—that is, before he "refines" the analysis by discarding statistically insignificant regressors—offer relatively limited support for his thesis that specialization is compensated by the assignment of closed rules. To get a sense of the questionable extent to which expertise pays, consider two bills produced by a committee whose median is identical to the floor median (according to ADA ratings). The first cites three laws, the second, eighteen; otherwise, they are equivalent. If the first has a 10 percent chance of getting a closed rule, the second's chances are expected to be 24 percent (table C.1, col. 1, p. 276). Whether this change in probabilities is of sufficient magnitude to encourage members to invest in expertise is unclear, especially since the marginal effect of this regressor is not statistically distinguishable from zero. The effects of seniority are more reliable statistically but, as we noted, harder to interpret substantively. All told, it is hard to say whether this statistical exercise contributes to the credibility of Krehbiel's claim that information matters while distributive content generally does not.

In sum, although these three works convey a great deal of useful information about Congress, parties, and committees, their central hypotheses are not well supported empirically. One limitation is the difficulty of obtaining reliable measures of constructs such as legislative expertise or policy preferences (Rieselbach 1992). Another is the complexity of using nonexperimental data to test propositions that involve numerous simultaneously determined variables. Whether rational choice scholarship will in the future contribute significantly to the study of legislative politics depends on the degree to which empirical inquiries can overcome methodological infirmities of this kind, which have so often kept traditional students of legislative politics at bay.

CONCLUDING REMARKS

Our central argument in this book has been that empirical applications of rational choice theory in political science since the 1960s have been marred by a syndrome of methodological shortcomings. These defects differ in kind from the pedestrian mistakes that often attend empirical social science; they are rooted in the ambition to come up with a universal theory of politics and the belief that anything less cannot aspire to be genuine science. We remain skeptical that a universal theory of politics could survive systematic empirical scrutiny. Perhaps our skepticism will turn out in the future to have been misplaced; about that one can only speculate. We have shown in this book, however, that to date no empirically credible universal theory has been developed by proponents of rational choice. We do not find it surprising that those rational choice theorists who have grappled with empirical applications have frequently abandoned pure universalist ambitions for more subtle and modest formulations. We have also contended that taking this course need not be thought of as threatening to rational choice theorists' scientific aspirations; on the contrary, if a variant of rational choice theory is to advance our understanding of politics, it is essential. In conclusion, it may be helpful to reiterate some of the ways rational choice scholarship must change if future research is to overcome the problems that have hampered the progress of this form of political science.

The first is that rational choice theorists must resist the theory-saving impulses that result in method-driven research. More fruitful than asking "How might a rational choice theory explain X?" would be the problem-driven question: "What explains X?" This will naturally lead to inquiries about the relative importance of a host of possible explanatory variables. No doubt strategic calculation will be one, but there will typically be many others, ranging from traditions of behavior, norms, and cultures to differences in peoples' capacities and the contingencies of historical circumstance. The urge to run from this complexity rather than build explanatory models that take it into account should be resisted, even if this means scaling down the range of application. Our recommendation is not for empirical work instead of theory; it is for theorists to get closer to the data so as to theorize in empirically pertinent ways.

The injunction to theorize "closer to the data" highlights the tension between theory development and theory testing in any empirical science. On the one hand, the failure of theories to be empirically informed can result in irrelevant theorizing and the mushrooming of controversies driven by little more than the theoretical conjectures out of which they emerged. On the other hand, empirically informed theorizing threatens to collapse into post hoc theory-mending. The only viable way to deal with this tension is never to rest content with revised theoretical conjectures that are designed in response to previous failures of theory. Theories may be revised when they fail to account for the evidence, but the revised theory must then be tested against new evidence, and so on. In sum, rational choice theorists must discover the necessity for systematic empirical testing in the process of theory elaboration.

Second, rational choice theorists should relinquish the commitment to pure universalism and the concomitant tendency to ignore, absorb, or discredit competing theoretical accounts. The hypotheses that flow from rational choice theory would be more insightful were there a clearer distinction between rational action and other modes of behavior, and empirical tests would be more convincing and informative if they were designed to probe the limits of what rational choice can explain. This change in perspective would, among other things, encourage rational choice theorists to be more forthcoming about the conditions under which they are willing to give up their explanations in light of empirical observations.

Since the time of its introduction into political science, rational choice theorizing has hearkened to two contrary impulses: an interdisciplinary spirit that seeks to unify social science explanation and a parochial tendency to interpret all social phenomena through the lens of microeconomics. Downs (1957, 8), for example, explicitly shied away from social-psychological explanations, even in the face of an existing stock of knowledge that pointed him toward them, for fear of losing a distinctive voice: "Empirical studies are almost unanimous in their conclusion that adjustment in primary groups is far more crucial to nearly every individual than more remote considerations of economic or political welfare. . . . Nevertheless, we must assume men orient their behavior chiefly toward the latter in our world; otherwise all analysis of either economics or politics turns into a mere adjunct of primary group-sociology."

In light of Downs's remark, it is not surprising that what rational choice theorists regard as their multidisciplinary perspective is perceived by others as a form of colonization. The impulse to defend rational choice models at all costs and against all comers evokes a dismissive response that, if anything, reinforces disciplinary divisions. If social science were viewed less as a prizefight between competing theoretical perspectives, only one of which may prevail, and more as a joint venture in which explanations condition and augment one another, the partisan impulses that give rise to methodologically deficient research might be held in check. The question would change from "Whether or not rational choice theory?" to something more fruitful: "How does rationality interact with other facets of human nature and organization to produce the politics that we seek to understand?"

REFERENCES

Abell, Peter. 1992. Is Rational Choice Theory a Rational Choice of Theory? In *Rational Choice Theory: Advocacy and Critique,* ed. James S. Coleman and Thomas J. Fararo. Newbury Park, Calif.: Sage.

Abelson, Robert P. 1976. Psychological Status of the Script Concept. *American Psychologist* 36:715–29.

Abelson, Robert P., and Ariel Levi. 1985. Decision Making and Decision Theory. In *Handbook of Social Psychology,* ed. Gardner Lindzey and Elliot Aronson. New York: Random House.

Abramson, Paul R., John H. Aldrich, Phil Paolino, and David W. Rohde. 1992. Sophisticated Voting in the 1988 Presidential Primaries. *American Political Science Review* 86:55–69.

Achen, Christopher H. 1977. Measuring Representation: Perils of the Correlation Coefficient. *American Journal of Political Science* 21:805–15.

———. 1986. *The Statistical Analysis of Quasi-Experiments.* Berkeley: University of California Press.

Achen, Christopher H., and Duncan Snidal. 1989. Rational Deterrence Theory and Comparative Case Studies. *World Politics* 41:143–69.

Aldrich, John H. 1976. Some Problems in Testing Two Rational Models of Participation. *American Journal of Political Science* 20:713–33.

———. 1980. *Before the Convention: Strategies and Choices in Presidential Nomination Campaigns.* Chicago: University of Chicago Press.

———. 1989. Power and Order in Congress. In *Home Style and Washington Work,* ed. Morris P. Fiorina and David W. Rohde. Ann Arbor: University of Michigan.

———. 1993. Rational Choice and Turnout. *American Journal of Political Science* 37:246–78.

Aldrich, John H., and Richard D. McKelvey. 1977. A Method of Scaling with Applications to the 1968 and 1972 Presidential Elections. *American Political Science Review* 71:111–30.

Alt, James E., and Kenneth A. Shepsle. 1990. Editor's Introduction. In *Perspectives on Positive Political Economy,* ed. James E. Alt and Kenneth A. Shepsle. Cambridge: Cambridge University Press.

Andreoni, James. 1988. Why Free Ride? Strategies and Learning in Public Goods Experiments. *Journal of Public Economics* 37:291–304.

Armstrong, Scott. 1979. Advocacy and Objectivity in Science. *Management Science* 25:423–28.

Arrow, Kenneth J. 1951. *Social Choice and Individual Values.* New Haven: Yale University Press.

Asch, S. E. 1958. Effects of Group Pressure upon the Modification and Distortion of Judgment. In *Groups, Leadership, and Men,* ed. H. Guetkow. Pittsburgh: Carnegie Press.

Ashenfelter, Orley, and Stanley Kelley, Jr. 1975. Determinants of Participation in Presidential Elections. *Journal of Law and Economics* 18:695–733.

Austen-Smith, David. 1984. The Pure Theory of Large Two-Candidate Elections: A Comment on the Ledyard Paper. *Public Choice* 44:43–47.

———. 1991. Rational Consumers and Irrational Voters: A Review Essay on Black Hole Tariffs and Endogenous Policy Theory. *Economics and Politics* 3:73–92.

Austen-Smith, David, and William H. Riker. 1987. Asymmetric Information and the Coherence of Legislation. *American Political Science Review* 81:897–918.

———. 1990. Asymmetric Information and the Coherence of Legislation: A Correction. *American Political Science Review* 84:243–45.

Axelrod, Robert M. 1984. *The Evolution of Cooperation.* New York: Basic Books.

Bandura, A. 1977. *Social Learning Theory.* Englewood Cliffs, N.J.: Prentice Hall.

Banks, Jeffrey S. 1984. Sophisticated Voting Outcomes and Agenda Control. *Social Choice and Welfare* 1:295–306.

———. 1989. Agency Budgets, Cost Information, and Auditing. *American Journal of Political Science* 33:670–99.

Banks, Jeffrey S., and D. Roderick Kiewiet. 1989. Explaining Patterns of Candidate Competition in Congressional Elections. *American Journal of Political Science* 33:997–1015.

Barber, James David. 1977. *The Presidential Character: Predicting Performance in the White House.* 2nd ed. Englewood Cliffs, N.J.: Prentice Hall.

Baron, David P., and John A. Ferejohn. 1989. Bargaining in Legislatures. *American Political Science Review* 83:1181–1206.

Barry, Brian M. 1978. *Sociologists, Economists and Democracy.* New York: Macmillan.

———. 1984. Does Democracy Cause Inflation? Political Ideas of Some Economists. In *The Politics of Inflation and Economic Stagnation: Theoretical Approaches and International Case Studies,* ed. Leon N. Lindberg and Charles S. Maier. Washington, D.C.: Brookings Institution.

Bartholdi, John J., Craig A. Tovey, and Michael A. Trick. 1987. The Computational Difficulty of Manipulating an Election. Manuscript, Georgia Institute of Technology.

Barzel, Yoram, and Eugene Silberberg. 1973. Is the Act of Voting Rational? *Public Choice* 16:51–58.

Beck, Nathaniel. 1975. The Paradox of Minimax Regret. *American Political Science Review* 69:918.

Becker, Gary S. 1976. *The Economic Approach to Human Behavior.* Chicago: University of Chicago Press.

———. 1986. The Economic Approach to Human Behavior. In *Rational Choice,* ed. John Elster. New York: New York University Press.

Bell, Colin E. 1978. What Happens When Majority Rule Breaks Down? Some Probability Calculations. *Public Choice* 33:121–26.

Bendor, Jonathan. 1988. Review Article: Formal Models of Bureaucracy. *British Journal of Political Science* 18:353–95.

Benn, Stanley. 1979. The Problematic Rationality of Political Participation. In *Philosophy, Politics, and Society, Fifth Series: A Collection,* ed. Peter Laslett and James Fishkin, 291–312. Oxford: Oxford University Press.

Bentham, Jeremy. 1960. *A Fragment on Government and an Introduction to the Principles of Morals and Legislation.* Oxford: Basil Blackwell.

Bergson, Abram. 1938. A Reformulation of Certain Aspects of Welfare Economics. *Quarterly Journal of Economics* 52:314–44.

Berl, Janet, Richard D. McKelvey, Peter C. Ordeshook, and Mark Winer. 1976. An Experimental Test of the Core in a Simple N-Person Cooperative Nonsidepayment Game. *Journal of Conflict Resolution* 20:453–79.

Bernhardt, M. Daniel, and Daniel E. Ingberman. 1985. Candidate Reputations and the 'Incumbency' Effect. *Journal of Public Economics* 27:47–67.

Bernholz, Peter. 1978. On the Stability of Logrolling Outcomes in Stochastic Games. *Public Choice* 33(3):65–82.

Bettenhausen, Kenneth L., and J. Keith Murninghan. 1991. The Development of an Intragroup Norm and the Effects of Interpersonal and Structural Challenges. *Administrative Science Quarterly* 36:20–35.

Biddle, B. J., and E. J. Thomas, eds. 1966. *Role Theory: Concepts and Research.* New York: John Wiley & Sons.

Black, Duncan. 1958. *The Theory of Committees and Elections.* Cambridge: Cambridge University Press.

Blydenburgh, John C. 1971. The Closed Rule and the Paradox of Voting. *Journal of Politics* 33:57–71.

Bollen, Kenneth A. 1989. *Structural Equations with Latent Variables.* New York: John Wiley & Sons.

Boring, Edwin G. 1954. The Nature and History of Experimental Control. *American Journal of Psychology* 67:573–89.

Bowen, Bruce D. 1972. Toward an Estimate of the Frequency of Occurrence of the Paradox of Voting in U.S. Senate Roll Call Votes. In *Probability Models of Collective Decision Making,* ed. Richard G. Niemi and Herbert F. Weisberg. Columbus, Ohio: Charles Merrill.

Brams, Steven J. 1980. *Biblical Games: A Strategic Analysis of Stories in the Old Testament.* Cambridge: MIT Press.

———. 1993. *Theory of Moves.* Cambridge: Cambridge University Press.

Brams, Steven J., and Philip D. Straffin, Jr. 1982. The Entry Problem in a Political Race. In *Political Equilibrium,* ed. Peter C. Ordeshook and Kenneth A. Shepsle. Boston: Kluwer-Nijhoff.

Brennan, Geoffrey, and James M. Buchanan. 1984. Voter Choice: Evaluating Political Alternatives. *American Behavioral Scientist* 28:185–201.

Brewer, Marilynn B., and Roderick Kramer. 1986. Choice Behavior in Social Dilemmas: Effects of Social Identity, Group Size, and Decision Framing. *Journal of Personality and Social Psychology* 50:543–49.

Brittan, Samuel. 1977. *The Economic Consequences of Democracy.* London: Temple Smith.

Brody, Richard A., and Paul M. Sniderman. 1977. Life Space to Polling Place: The Relevance of Personal Concerns for Voting Behavior. *British Journal of Political Science* 7:337–60.

Brunk, Gregory G. 1980. The Impact of Rational Participation Models on Voting Attitudes. *Public Choice* 35:549–64.

Buchanan, James M., and Gordon Tullock. 1962. *The Calculus of Consent.* Ann Arbor: University of Michigan Press.

Buchanan, James M., and Richard E. Wagner. 1977. *Democracy in Deficit: The Political Legacy of Lord Keynes.* New York: Academic Press.

Budge, Ian, and Dennis Farlie. 1977. *Voting and Party Competition: A Theoretical Critique and Synthesis Applied to Surveys from Ten Democracies.* London: John Wiley & Sons.

Bueno de Mesquita, Bruce. 1985. Toward a Scientific Understanding of International Conflict: A Personal View. *International Studies Quarterly* 29:121–36.

Bueno de Mesquita, Bruce, and David Lalman. 1992. *War and Reason: Domestic and International Imperatives.* New Haven: Yale University Press.

Calvert, Randall L. 1985. Robustness of Multidimensional Voting Model: Candidate Motivations, Uncertainty, and Convergence. *American Journal of Political Science* 29:69–95.

Cameron, David R. 1988. Distributional Coalitions and Other Sources of Economic Stagnation: On Olson's *Rise and Decline of Nations. International Organizations* 42:561–603.

Campbell, Angus, Philip Converse, Warren Miller, and Donald Stokes. 1960. *The American Voter.* New York: John Wiley & Sons.

Campbell, Angus, Gerald Gurin, and Warren E. Miller. 1954. *The Voter Decides.* Evanston, Ill.: Row, Peterson.

Campbell, Donald T., and Julian C. Stanley. 1963. *Experimental and Quasi-Experimental Designs for Research.* Chicago: Rand McNally.

Caplin, Andrew, and Barry Nalebuff. 1988. On 64% Majority Rule. *Econometrica* 56:787–814.

Caro, Robert A. 1990. *Means of Ascent.* New York: Knopf.

Chamberlain, Gary, and Michael Rothschild. 1981. A Note on the Probability of Casting a Decisive Vote. *Journal of Economic Theory* 25:152–62.

Chamberlin, John R. 1979. Comments. In *Collective Decision Making: Applications from Public Choice Theory,* ed. Clifford S. Russell, 161–67. Baltimore: Johns Hopkins University Press

Chamberlin, John R., Jerry L. Cohen, and Clyde H. Coombs. 1984. Social Choice Observed: Five Presidential Elections of the American Psychological Association. *Journal of Politics* 46:479–502.

Chappell, Henry W., and William R. Keech. 1986. Policy Motivation and Party Difference in a Dynamic Spatial Model of Party Competition. *American Political Science Review* 80:881–99.

Cheung, Frederick Hok-Ming. 1983. From Military Aristocracy to Imperial Bureaucracy: Patterns of Consolidation in Two Medieval Empires. Ph.D. diss., University of California, Santa Barbara.

Chong, Dennis. 1991. *Collective Action and the Civil Rights Movement.* Chicago: University of Chicago Press.

Cohen, Linda. 1979. Cyclic Sets in Multidimensional Voting Models. *Journal of Economic Theory* 20:1–12.

Cohen, Linda, Michael E. Levine, and Charles R. Plott. 1978. Communication and Agenda Influence: The Chocolate Pizza Design. In *Coalition Forming Behavior, Contributions to Experimental Economics,* ed. Heinz Saverman. Tubingen, Germany: Mohr.

Coleman, James S. 1986. *Individual Interests and Collective Action: Selected Essays.* Cambridge: Cambridge University Press.

Coleman, James S., and Thomas J. Fararo. 1992. *Rational Choice Theory: Advocacy and Critique.* Newbury Park, Calif.: Sage.

Collier, Kenneth E., Richard D. McKelvey, Peter C. Ordeshook, and Kenneth C. Williams. 1987. Retrospective Voting: An Experimental Study. *Public Choice* 53:101–30.

Connolly, Terry, Brian K. Thorn, and Alan Heminger. 1992. Discretionary Databases as Social Dilemmas. In *Social Dilemmas: Theoretical Issues and Research Findings,* ed. William G. Liebrand, David M. Messick, and Henk A. M. Wilke. Oxford: Pergamon Press.

Converse, Philip E. 1975. Public Opinion and Voting Behavior. In *Handbook of Political Science,* ed. Fred I. Greenstein. Reading, Mass.: Addison-Wesley.

Cook, Thomas D., and Donald T. Campbell. 1979. *Quasi-Experimentation: Design & Analysis Issues for Field Settings.* Boston: Houghton Mifflin.

Coughlin, Peter J. 1984. Probabilistic Voting Models. In *Encyclopedia of Statistical Sciences,* ed. S. Kotz, N. Johnson, and C. Read. Vol. 1. New York: John Wiley & Sons.

———. 1990. Majority Rule and Election Models. *Journal of Economic Surveys* 3:157–88.

———. 1992. *Probabilistic Voting Theory.* Cambridge: Cambridge University Press.

Cox, Gary W. 1984. An Expected-Utility Model of Electoral Competition. *Quality and Quantity* 18:337–49.

———. 1987. The Uncovered Set and the Core. *American Journal of Political Science* 31:408–22.

———. 1988. Closeness and Turnout: A Methodological Note. *Journal of Politics* 50:768–75.

Cox, Gary W., and Mathew D. McCubbins. 1993. *Legislative Leviathan: Party Government in the House.* Berkeley: University of California Press.

Cox, Gary W., and Michael C. Munger. 1989. Closeness, Expenditures, and Turnout in the 1982 U.S. House Elections. *American Political Science Review* 83:217–32.

Crain, W. Mark, Donald R. Leavens, and Lynn Abbot. 1987. Voting and Not Voting at the Same Time. *Public Choice* 53:221–29.

Crenson, Mathew A. 1987. The Private Stake in Public Goods: Overcoming the Illogic of Collective Action. *Policy Sciences* 20:259–76.

Crews, Frederick. 1993. The Unknown Freud. *New York Review of Books,* November 18, 1993, 55–66.

Cyr, A. Bruce. 1975. The Calculus of Voting Reconsidered. *Public Opinion Quarterly* 39:19–38.

Dahl, Robert A. 1971. *Polyarchy: Participation and Opposition.* New Haven: Yale University Press.

Dallek, Robert. 1979. *Franklin D. Roosevelt and American Foreign Policy, 1932–1945.* New York: Oxford University Press.

Davis, Otto A., Melvin Hinich, and Peter Ordeshook. 1970. An Expository Development of a Mathematical Model of the Electoral Process. *American Political Science Review* 64:426–48.

Dawes, Robyn M. 1991. Social Dilemmas, Economic Self-Interest, and Evolutionary Theory. In *Frontiers of Mathematical Psychology: Essays in Honor of Clyde Coombs,* ed. Donald R. Brown and J. E. Keith Smith. New York: Springer-Verlag.

Dawes, Robyn M., Jeanne McTavish, and Harriet Shaklee. 1977. Behavior, Communication, and Assumptions about Other People's Behavior in a Commons Dilemma Situation. *Journal of Personality and Social Psychology* 35:1–11.

Dawes, Robyn M., John M. Orbell, and Randy T. Simmons. 1986. Organizing Groups for Collective Action. *American Political Science Review* 80:1171–85.

Dawes, Robyn M., Alphons J. C. van de Kragt, and John M. Orbell. 1988. Not Me or Thee but WE: The Importance of Group Identity in Eliciting Cooperation in Dilemma Situations: Experimental Manipulations. *Acta Psychologica* 68:83–97.

Dawson, Paul A., and James E. Zinser. 1976. Political Finance and Participation in Congressional Elections. *Annals of the American Academy of Political and Social Science* 425:59–73.

DeCanio, Stephen J. 1979. Proposition 13 and the Failure of Economic Politics. *National Tax Journal* 32:55–65.

Dennis, Jack. 1991. Theories of Turnout: An Empirical Comparison of Alienationist and Rationalist Perspectives. In *Political Participation and American Democracy,* ed. William Crotty. New York: Greenwood Press.

Denzau, Arthur T., and Robert J. Mackay. 1981. Structure-Induced Equilibria and Perfect Foresight Expectations. *American Journal of Political Science* 25:762–79.

Denzau, Arthur T., William H. Riker, and Kenneth A. Shepsle. 1985. Farquharson and Fenno: Sophisticated Voting and Home Style. *American Political Science Review* 79:1117–34.

Dion, Douglas. 1992. The Robustness of the Structure-Induced Equilibrium. *American Journal of Political Science* 36:462–82.

Dobra, John L. 1983. An Approach to Empirical Studies of Voting Paradoxes: An Update and Extension. *Public Choice* 41:241–50.

Dobra, John L., and Gordon Tullock. 1981. An Approach to Empirical Measures of Voting Paradoxes. *Public Choice* 36:193–95.

Downs, Anthony. 1957. *An Economic Theory of Democracy.* New York: Harper & Row.

Easterling, Larry J. 1975. Senator Joseph L. Bristow and the Seventeenth Amendment. *Kansas Historical Quarterly* 41:488–511.

Eavey, Cheryl L. 1991. Patterns of Distribution in Spatial Games. *Rationality and Society* 3:450–74.

———. 1994. Preference-Based Stability: Experiments on Cooperative Solutions to Majority Rule Games. In *Social Choice and Political Economy,* ed. Norman Schofield. Boston: Kluwer-Nijhoff.

Eavey, Cheryl L., and Gary J. Miller. 1984a. Bureaucratic Agenda Control: Imposition or Bargaining? *American Political Science Review* 78:719–33.

———. 1984b. Fairness in Majority Rule Games Without a Core. *American Journal of Political Science* 28: 570–86.

Eckel, Catherine, and Charles A. Holt. 1989. Strategic Voting in Agenda-Controlled Committee Experiments. *American Economic Review* 79:763–73.

Eckstein, Harry. 1991. Rationality and Frustration in Political Behavior. In *The Economic Approach to Politics,* ed. Kristen Renwick Monroe. New York: Harper Collins.

Elster, Jon, ed. 1986a. *Rational Choice.* New York: New York University Press.

———. 1986b. Introduction. In *Rational Choice,* ed. Jon Elster. New York: New York University Press.

Endersby, James W. 1993. Rules of Method and Rules of Conduct: An Experimental Study on Two Types of Procedure and Committee Behavior. Journal of Politics 55:218–36.

Enelow, James. 1981. Saving Amendments, Killer Amendments, and an Expected Utility Theory of Sophisticated Voting. *Journal of Politics* 43:396–413.

Enelow, James, James W. Endersby, and Michael C. Munger. 1993. A Revised Probabilistic Spatial Model of Elections: Theory and Evidence. In *Information, Participation and Choice,* ed. Bernard Grofman. Ann Arbor: University of Michigan Press.

Enelow, James, and Melvin J. Hinich. 1982. Ideology, Issues, and the Spatial Theory of Elections. *American Political Science Review* 76:492–501.

———. 1983. On Plott's Pairwise Symmetry Condition for Majority Rule Equilibrium. *Public Choice* 40:317–21.

———. 1984a. Probabilistic Voting and the Importance of Centrist Ideologies in Democratic Elections. *Journal of Politics* 46:459–78.

———. 1984b. *The Spatial Theory of Voting: An Introduction.* Cambridge: Cambridge University Press.

———. 1989. A General Probabilistic Spatial Theory of Elections. *Public Choice* 61:101–13.

Enelow, James, Melvin J. Hinich, and Nancy R. Mendell. 1986. An Empirical Evaluation of Alternative Spatial Models of Elections. *Journal of Politics* 48:675–93.

Enelow, James, and David H. Koehler. 1979. Vote Trading in a Legislative Context: An Analysis of Cooperative and Noncooperative Strategic Voting. *Public Choice* 34:157–75.

———. 1980. The Amendment in Legislative Strategy: Sophisticated Voting in the U.S. Congress. *Journal of Politics* 42:396–413.

Epple, Dennis, and Michael H. Riordan. 1987. Cooperation and Punishment Under Repeated Majority Voting. *Public Choice* 55:41–73.

Erikson, Robert S., and David W. Romero. 1990. Candidate Equilibrium and the Behavioral Model of the Vote. *American Political Science Review* 84:1103–26.

Fedderson, Timothy J. 1992. A Voting Model Implying Duverger's Law and Positive Turnout. *American Journal of Political Science* 36:939–62.

Feldman, Paul, and James Jondrow. 1984. Congressional Elections and Local Federal Spending. *American Journal of Political Science* 28:147–63.

Fenno, Richard F. 1966. *The Power of the Purse: Appropriations Politics in Congress.* Boston: Little, Brown.

———. 1978. *Home Style: House Members in Their Districts.* Boston: Little, Brown.

Ferejohn, John. 1991. Rationality and Interpretation: Parliamentary Elections in Early Stuart England. In *The Economic Approach to Politics: A Critical Reassessment of the Theory of Rational Action,* ed. Kristen Renwick Monroe. New York: Harper Collins.

———. 1993. The Spatial Model and Elections. In *Information, Participation and Choice,* ed. Bernard Grofman. Ann Arbor: University of Michigan Press.

Ferejohn, John, and Morris P. Fiorina. 1974. The Paradox of Not Voting: A Decision Theoretic Analysis. *American Political Science Review* 68:525–36.

———. 1975. Closeness Counts Only in Horseshoes and Dancing. *American Political Science Review* 69:920–25.

———. 1993. To P or Not to P? Still Asking After All These Years. Manuscript, Stanford University.

Filer, John E., and Lawrence W. Kenny. 1980. Voter Turnout and the Benefits of Voting. *Public Choice* 35:575–85.

Filer, John E., Lawrence W. Kenny, and Rebecca B. Morton. 1993. Redistribution, Income and Voting. *American Journal of Political Science* 37:63–87.

Fiorina, Morris P. 1976. The Voting Decision: Instrumental and Expressive Aspects. *Journal of Politics* 38:390–413.

———. 1979. Public Choice in Practice. In *Collective Decision Making: Applications from Public Choice Theory,* ed. Clifford S. Russell. Baltimore: Johns Hopkins University Press.

———. 1990. Information and Rationality in Elections. In *Information and Democratic Processes,* ed. John A. Ferejohn and James H. Kuklinski. Urbana: University of Illinois Press.

———. 1994. Divided Government in the American States: A By-Product of Legislative Professionalism? *American Political Science Review* 88:304–16.

Fiorina, Morris P., and Charles R. Plott. 1978. Committee Decisions Under Majority Rule: An Experimental Study. *American Political Science Review* 72:575–98.

Fiorina, Morris P., and Kenneth A. Shepsle. 1982. Equilibrium, Disequilibrium, and the General Possibility of a Science of Politics. In *Political Equilibrium,* ed. Peter C. Ordeshook and Kenneth A. Shepsle. The Hague: Kluwer-Nijhoff.

Fireman, Bruce, and William A. Gamson. 1988. Utilitarian Logic in the Resource Mobilization Perspective. In *The Dynamics of Social Movements,* ed. Mayer N. Zald and John D. McCarthy. Cambridge, Mass.: Winthrop.

Fischhoff, Baruch. 1991. Value Elicitation: Is There Anything There? *American Psychologist* 46:835–47.

Fishburn, Peter C. 1988. *Nonlinear Preference and Utility Theory.* Baltimore: Johns Hopkins University Press.

Fleishman, John A. 1988. The Effects of Decision Framing and Others' Behavior on Cooperation in a Social Dilemma. *Journal of Conflict Resolution* 32:162–80.

Foster, Carroll B. 1984. The Performance of Rational Voter Models in Recent Presidential Elections. *American Political Science Review* 78:678–90.

Frank, Robert H. 1988. *Passions Within Reason: The Strategic Role of the Emotions.* New York: W. W. Norton.

Franklin, Charles H., and John E. Jackson. 1983. The Dynamics of Party Identification. *American Political Science Review* 77:957–73.

Fraser, John. 1972. Why Do High Income People Participate More in Politics? The Wrong Answer. *Public Choice* 13:115–18.

Frey, Bruno. 1971. Why Do High Income People Participate More in Politics? *Public Choice* 11:101–05.

Friedman, Milton. 1953. The Methodology of Positive Economics. In *Essays in Positive Economics,* ed. Milton Friedman. Chicago: University of Chicago Press.

Frohlich, Norman, and Joe A. Oppenheimer. 1978. *Modern Political Economy.* Englewood Cliffs, N.J.: Prentice Hall.

Frohlich, Norman, Joe A. Oppenheimer, Jeffrey Smith, and Oran R. Young. 1978. A Test of Downsian Voter Rationality: 1964 Presidential Voting. *American Political Science Review* 72:178–97.

Frohlich, Norman, Joe A. Oppenheimer, and Oran R. Young. 1971. *Political Leadership and Collective Goods.* Princeton, N.J.: Princeton University Press.

Fudenberg, Drew, and Eric Maskin. 1986. The Folk Theorem in Repeated Games with Discounting or with Incomplete Information. *Econometrica* 54:533–54.

George, Alexander L., and Juliette L. George. 1956. *Woodrow Wilson and Colonel House: A Personality Study.* New York: J. Day.

George, Alexander L., and Richard Smoke. 1974. *Deterrence in American Foreign Policy: Theory and Practice.* New York: Columbia University Press.

Gerber, Elisabeth R., and John E. Jackson. 1993. Endogenous Preferences and the Study of Institutions. *American Political Science Review* 87:639–56.

Godwin, R. Kenneth, and Robert C. Mitchell. 1984. The Implications of Direct Mail for Political Organizations. *Social Science Quarterly* 65:829–39.

Goetze, David, and Peter Galderisi. 1989. Explaining Collective Action with Rational Models. *Public Choice* 62:25–39.

Gosnell, Harold F. 1927. *Getting Out the Vote.* Chicago: University of Chicago Press.

Gould, Stephen Jay. 1992. The Confusion over Evolution. *The New York Review of Books,* November 19, 1992, 47–55.

Grafstein, Robert. 1991. An Evidential Decision Theory of Turnout. *American Journal of Political Science* 35:989–1010.

Gray, Virginia. 1976. A Note on Competition and Turnout in the American States. *Journal of Politics* 38:153–58.

Green, Donald Philip. 1992. The Price Elasticity of Mass Preferences. *American Political Science Review* 86:128–48.

Green, Donald Philip, and Jonathan Cowden. 1992. Who Protests: Self-Interest and White Opposition to Busing. *Journal of Politics* 54:471–96.

Green, Donald Philip, and Jonathan S. Krasno. 1988. Salvation for the Spendthrift Incumbent: Reestimating the Effects of Campaign Spending in House Elections. *American Journal of Political Science* 32:884–907.

Green, Donald Philip, and Bradley L. Palmquist. 1990. Of Artifacts and Partisan Instability. *American Journal of Political Science* 34:872–902.

Greenstein, Fred I. 1982. *The Hidden-Hand Presidency: Eisenhower as Leader.* New York: Basic Books.

Grofman, Bernard. 1993a. Is Turnout the Paradox that Ate Rational Choice Theory? In *Information, Participation and Choice,* ed. Bernard Grofman. Ann Arbor: University of Michigan Press.

———. 1993b. On the Gentle Art of Rational Choice Bashing. In *Information, Participation and Choice,* ed. Bernard Grofman. Ann Arbor: University of Michigan Press.

———. 1993c. Toward an Institution-Rich Theory of Political Competition with a Supply Side Component. In *Information, Participation and Choice,* ed. Bernard Grofman. Ann Arbor: University of Michigan Press.

Grofman, Bernard, Robert Griffin, and Amihai Glazer. 1990. Identical Geography, Different Party: A Natural Experiment on the Magnitude of Party Differences in the U.S. Senate, 1960–1984. In *Developments in Electoral Geography,* ed. R. J. Johnston, Peter Taylor, and J. F. Shelley. London: Croom Helm.

Grofman, Bernard, and Carole Uhlaner. 1985. Metapreferences and the Reasons for Stability in Social Choice: Thoughts on Broadening and Clarifying the Debate. *Theory and Decision* 19:31–50.

Gross, Bertram M. 1953. *The Legislative Struggle: A Study in Social Combat.* New York: McGraw-Hill.

Hammond, Thomas H., and Brian D. Humes. 1993. "What This Campaign Is All about Is . . . ": A Rational Choice Alternative to the Downsian Spatial Model of Elections. In *Information, Participation and Choice,* ed. Bernard Grofman. Ann Arbor: University of Michigan Press.

Hammond, Thomas H., and Gary J. Miller. 1987. The Core of the Constitution. *American Political Science Review* 81:1155–74.

Hampton, Jean. 1987. Free-Rider Problems in the Production of Collective Goods. *Economics and Philosophy* 3:245–73.

Hansen, John Mark. 1985. The Political Economy of Group Membership. *American Political Science Review* 79:79–96.

Hardin, Garrett. 1968. The Tragedy of the Commons. *Science* 162:1243–48.

Hardin, Russell. 1971. Collective Action as an Agreeable N-Person Prisoner's Dilemma. *Behavioral Science* 16:472–81.

———. 1979. National Environmental Lobbies and the Apparent Illogic of Collective Action: A Comment. In *Collective Decision Making: Applications from Public Choice Theory,* ed. Clifford S. Russell. Baltimore: Johns Hopkins University Press.

———. 1982. *Collective Action.* Baltimore: Johns Hopkins University Press.

Harsanyi, John C. 1986. Advances in Understanding Rational Behavior. In *Rational Choice,* ed. Jon Elster. New York: New York University Press.

Hartley, Richard, and D. Marc Kilgour. 1987. The Geometry of the Uncovered Set in the Three-Voter Spatial Model. *Mathematical Social Sciences* 14:175–83.

Harvard Law Review. 1991. Environmental Activism and the Collective Action Problem. *Harvard Law Review* 104:1705–10.

Haynes, George H. 1938. *The Senate of the United States.* Boston: Houghton Mifflin.

Hechter, Michael. 1987. *Principles of Group Solidarity.* Berkeley: University of California Press.

Hedges, Roman B. 1984. Reasons for Political Involvement: A Study of Contributors to the 1972 Presidential Campaign. *Western Political Quarterly* 37:257–71.

Herzberg, Roberta, and Rick Wilson. 1988. Results on Sophisticated Voting in an Experimental Setting. *Journal of Politics* 50:471–86.

———. 1991. Costly Agendas and Spatial Voting Games: Theory and Experiments on Agenda Access Costs. In *Laboratory Research in Political Economy,* ed. Thomas R. Palfrey. Ann Arbor: University of Michigan Press.

Hibbs, Douglas A., Jr. 1977. Political Parties and Macroeconomic Policy. *American Political Science Review* 71:1467–87.

Hinich, Melvin J., John Ledyard, and Peter C. Ordeshook. 1972. Nonvoting and Existence of Equilibrium Under Majority Rule. *Journal of Economic Theory* 4:144–53.

———. 1981. Voting as an Act of Contribution. *Public Choice* 36:135–40.

Hirsch, Eric Donald. 1987. *Cultural Literacy: What Every American Needs to Know.* Boston: Houghton Mifflin.

Hochshild, Jennifer L. 1981. *What's Fair? American Beliefs about Distributive Justice.* Cambridge: Harvard University Press.

Hoenack, Stephen A. 1983. On the Stability of Legislative Outcomes. *Public Choice* 41:251–60.

Hoffman, Elizabeth, and Edward W. Packel. 1982. A Stochastic Model of Committee Voting with Exogenous Costs: Theory and Experiments. *Behavioral Science* 27:43–56.

Hoffman, Elizabeth, and Charles R. Plott. 1983. Pre-Meeting Discussions and the Possibility of Coalition-Breaking Procedures in Majority Rule Committees. *Public Choice* 40:21–39.

Hoffman, Elizabeth, and Matthew L. Spitzer. 1982. The Coase Theorem: Some Experimental Tests. *Journal of Law and Economics* 25:73–98.

———. 1985. Entitlements, Rights, and Fairness: An Experimental Examination of Subjects' Concepts of Distributive Justice. *Journal of Legal Studies* 14:259–97.

Hotelling, Harold. 1929. Stability in Competition. *Economic Journal* 39:41–57.

Imig, Douglas R. 1992. Resource Mobilization and Survival Tactics of Poverty Advocacy Groups. *Western Political Quarterly* 45:501–21.

Isaac, R. Mark, K. F. McCue, and Charles Plott. 1985. Public Goods Provision in an Experimental Environment. *Journal of Public Economics* 26:51–74.

Isaac, R. Mark, and Charles Plott. 1978. Cooperative Game Models of the Influence of the Closed Rule in Three-Person Majority Rule Committees: Theory and Experiment. In *Game Theory and Political Science,* ed. Peter C. Ordeshook. New York: New York University Press.

Isaac, R. Mark, James H. Walker, and Susan H. Thomas. 1984. Divergent Evidence on Free-Riding. *Public Choice* 43:113–49.

Jackman, Robert W. 1993. Rationality and Political Participation. *American Journal of Political Science* 37:279–90.

Jacobson, Gary C. 1993. Deficit-Cutting Politics and Congressional Elections. Political Science Quarterly 108:375–403.

Jenkins, J. Craig, and Charles Perrow. 1977. Insurgency of the Powerless: Farm Worker Movements (1946–1972). *American Sociological Review* 42:249–68.

Johnson, James D. 1991. Rational Choice as a Reconstructive Theory. In *The Economic Approach to Politics: A Critical Reassessment of the Theory of Rational Action,* ed. Kristen Renwick Monroe. New York: Harper Collins.

Kahneman, Daniel, and I. Ritov. 1994. Determinants of Stated Willingness to Pay for Public Goods: A Study in the Headline Method. *Journal of Risk and Uncertainty.* 9:1–38.

Kahneman, Daniel, and Amos Tversky. 1979. Prospect Theory: An Analysis of Decision Under Risk. *Econometrica* 47:263–91.

———. 1984. Choices, Values, and Frames. *American Psychologist* 39:341–50.

Kalisch, G., J. W. Milnor, J. Nash, and E. D. Nering. 1954. Some Experimental N-Person Games. In *Decision Processes,* ed. R. M. Thrall, C. H. Coombs, and R. L. Davis. New York: John Wiley & Sons.

Kaplan, Abraham. 1964. *The Conduct of Inquiry.* San Francisco: Chandler.

Kaplowitz, Stan, and Bradley Fisher. 1985. Revealing the Logic of Free-Riding and Contributions to the Nuclear Freeze Movement. *Research in Social Movements* 8: 47–64.

Kau, James B., and Paul H. Rubin. 1976. The Electoral College and the Rational Vote. *Public Choice* 27:101–07.

Kavka, Gregory S. 1991. Rational Maximizing in Economic Theories of Politics. In *The Economic Approach to Politics: A Critical Reassessment of the Theory of Rational Action,* ed. Kristen Renwick Monroe. New York: Harper Collins.

Kelman, Mark. 1988. On Democracy Bashing: A Skeptical Look at the Theoretical and 'Empirical' Practice of the Public Choice Movement. *Virginia Law Review* 74:199–273.

Kerr, Norbert L. 1989. Illusions of Efficacy: The Effects of Group Size on Perceived Efficacy in Social Dilemmas. *Journal of Experimental Social Psychology* 25:287–313.

Key, V. O., Jr. 1965. *Public Opinion and American Democracy.* New York: Knopf.

Kiewiet, Roderick D., and Mathew D. McCubbins. 1991. *The Logic of Delegation.* Chicago: University of Chicago Press.

Kim, Oliver, and Mark Walker. 1984. The Free Rider Problem: Experimental Evidence. *Public Choice* 43:3–24.

Klosko, George. 1987. Rebellious Collective Action Revisited. *American Political Science Review* 81:557–61.

Knack, Stephen. 1992. Civic Norms, Social Sanctions, and Voter Turnout. *Rationality and Society* 4:133–56.

———. 1993a. Political Participation and American Democracy. *Public Choice* 75:297–300.

———. 1993b. The Voter Participation Effects of Selecting Jurors from Registration Lists. *Journal of Law and Economics* 36:99–114.

———. 1994. Does Rain Help the Republicans? Theory and Evidence on Turnout and the Vote. *Public Choice.* Forthcoming.

Knight, Jack. 1992. Social Norms and Economic Institutions. *American Political Science Review* 86:1063–64.

Knoke, David. 1988. Incentives in Collective Action Organizations. *American Sociological Review* 53:311–30.

———. 1990. *Organizing for Collective Action: The Political Economies of Associations.* New York: Aldine de Gruyter.

Kollman, Ken, John H. Miller, and Scott E. Page. 1992. Adaptive Parties and Spatial Elections. *American Political Science Review* 86:929–37.

Komorita, Samuel S., and Joan M. Barth. 1985. Components of Reward in Social Dilemmas. *Journal of Personality and Social Psychology* 48:364–73.

Kormendi, Roger C., and Charles R. Plott. 1982. Committee Decisions Under Alternative Procedural Rules. *Journal of Economic Behavior and Organization* 3:175–95.

Kramer, Gerald H. 1972. Sophisticated Voting over Multidimensional Choice Spaces. *Journal of Mathematical Sociology* 2:165–80.

———. 1973. On a Class of Equilibrium Conditions for Majority Rule. *Econometrica* 41:285–97.

———. 1977. A Dynamical Model of Political Equilibrium. *Journal of Economic Theory* 12:472–82.

Kramer, Roderick, and Marilynn B. Brewer. 1984. Effects of Group Identity on Resource Use in a Simulated Commons Dilemma. *Journal of Personality and Social Psychology* 46:1044–57.

———. 1986. Social Group Identity and the Emergence of Cooperation in Resource Conservation Dilemmas. In *Experimental Social Dilemmas*, ed. Henk A. M. Wilke, David Messick, and Christel G. Rutte. Frankfurt am Main: Verlag Peter Lang.

Krehbiel, Keith. 1987. Institutional Erosion of Committee Power. *American Political Science Review* 81:929–35.

———. 1988. Spatial Models of Legislative Choice. *Legislative Studies Quarterly* 13:259–319.

———. 1991. *Information and Legislative Organization*. Ann Arbor: University of Michigan.

Krehbiel, Keith, and Douglas Rivers. 1990. Sophisticated Voting in Congress: A Reconsideration. *Journal of Politics* 52:548–78.

Kuhn, Thomas S. 1962. *The Structure of Scientific Revolutions*. Chicago: University of Chicago Press.

Laing, J. D., and S. Olmstead. 1978. An Experimental and Game-Theoretic Study of Committees. In *Game Theory and Political Science*, ed. Peter C. Ordeshook. New York: New York University Press.

Laing, J. D., and Benjamin Slotznick. 1987. Viable Alternatives to the Status Quo. *Journal of Conflict Resolution* 31:63–85.

———. 1991. When Anyone Can Veto: A Laboratory Study of Committees Governed by Unanimous Rule. *Behavioral Science* 36:179–95.

Lakatos, Imre. 1970. Falsification and the Methodology of Scientific Research Programmes. In *Criticism and the Growth of Knowledge*, ed. Imre Lakatos and Alan Musgrave. Cambridge: Cambridge University Press.

Lalman, David, Joe Oppenheimer, and Piotr Swistak. 1993. Formal Rational Choice Theory: A Cumulative Science of Politics. In *Political Science: The State of the Discipline II*, ed. Ada W. Finifter. Washington, D.C.: American Political Science Association.

Lane, Robert E. 1991. *The Market Experience*. New York: Cambridge University Press.

Laver, Michael. 1980. Political Solutions to the Collective Action Problem. *Political Studies* 28:195–209.

———. 1981. *The Politics of Private Desires: The Guide to the Politics of Rational Choice*. New York: Penguin.

Ledyard, John O. 1981. The Paradox of Voting and Candidate Competition: A General Equilibrium Analysis. In *Essays in Contemporary Fields of Economics*, ed. G. Horwich and J. Quirk. West Lafayette, Ind.: Purdue University Press.

———. 1984. The Pure Theory of Large Two-Candidate Elections. *Public Choice* 44: 7–41.

Lindbeck, Assar. 1976. Stabilization Policy in Open Economies with Endogenous Politicians. *American Economic Review* 66:1–19.

Linder, D. E. 1982. Social Trap Analogs: The Tragedy of the Commons in the Laboratory. In *Cooperation and Helping Behavior, Theories and Research,* ed. K. J. Derlage and J. Grzlak. New York: Academic Press.

Lipset, Seymour Martin, and William Schneider. 1983. *The Confidence Gap: Business, Labor, and Government in the Public Mind.* New York: Free Press.

Londregan, John, and Thomas Romer. 1993. Polarization, Incumbency, and the Personal Vote. In *Political Economy: Institutions, Competition, and Representation,* ed. William A. Barnett, Melvin J. Hinich, and Norman J. Schofield. Cambridge: Cambridge University Press.

Lowenstein, Daniel H. 1982. Campaign Spending and Ballot Propositions: Recent Experience, Public Choice Theory and the First Amendment. *UCLA Law Review* 29:505–641.

Lowenstein, George F., Max H. Bazerman, and Leigh Thompson. 1989. Social Utility and Decision Making in Interpersonal Contexts. *Journal of Personality and Social Psychology* 57:426–41.

Lowi, Theodore J. 1992. The State in Political Science: How We Become What We Study. *American Political Science Review* 86:1–8.

Luce, Duncan R., and Howard Raiffa. 1957. *Games and Decisions.* New York: John Wiley & Sons.

Lupia, Arthur. 1994. Shortcuts Versus Encyclopedias: Information and Voting Behavior in California Insurance Reform Elections. *American Political Science Review* 88: 63–76.

McCubbins, Mathew D. 1991. Government on Lay-Away: Federal Spending and Deficit Under Divided Party Control. In *The Politics of Divided Government,* ed. Gary W. Cox and Samuel Kernell. Boulder, Colo.: Westview.

McCubbins, Mathew D., and Thomas Schwartz. 1984. Congressional Oversight Overlooked: Police Patrols versus Fire Alarms. *American Journal of Political Science* 28:165–79.

———. 1985. The Politics of Flatland. *Public Choice* 46:45–60.

McDaniel, William C., and Frances Sistrunk. 1991. Management Dilemmas and Decisions. *Journal of Conflict Resolution* 35:21–42.

McKelvey, Richard D. 1976. Intransitivities in Multidimensional Voting Models and Some Implications for Agenda Control. *Journal of Economic Theory* 12:472–82.

———. 1986. Covering, Dominance, and Institution Free Properties of Social Choice. *American Journal of Political Science* 30:283–315.

———. 1991. An Experimental Test of a Stochastic Game Model of Committee Bargaining. In *Laboratory Research in Political Economy,* ed. Thomas R. Palfrey. Ann Arbor: University of Michigan Press.

McKelvey, Richard D., and Peter C. Ordeshook. 1976. Symmetric Spatial Games Without Majority Rule Equilibria. *American Political Science Review* 70:1172–84.

———. 1979. An Experimental Test of Several Theories of Committee Decision-Making Under Majority Rule. In *Applied Game Theory,* ed. S. Brams, A. Schotter, and G. Schwodiauer. Wurzburg: Physica Verlag.

———. 1980. Vote Trading: An Experimental Study. *Public Choice* 35:151–84.

———. 1981. Experiments on the Core: Some Disconcerting Results for Majority Rule Voting Games. *Journal of Conflict Resolution* 25:709–24.

———. 1982. An Experimental Test of Solution Theories for Cooperative Games in Normal Form. In *Political Equilibrium,* ed. Peter C. Ordeshook and Kenneth A. Shepsle. The Hague: Kluwer-Nijhoff.

———. 1983. Some Experimental Results That Fail to Support the Competitive Solution. *Public Choice* 40:281–91.

———. 1984a. An Experimental Study of the Effects of Procedural Rules on Committee Behavior. *Journal of Politics* 46:182–205.

———. 1984b. Rational Expectations in Elections: Some Experimental Results Based on a Multidimensional Model. *Public Choice* 44:61–102.

———. 1986. Sequential Elections with Limited Information: A Formal Analysis. *Social Choice and Welfare* 3:199–211.

———. 1987. Elections with Limited Information: A Multidimensional Model. *Mathematical Social Sciences* 14:77–99.

———. 1990a. A Decade of Experimental Research on Spatial Models of Elections and Committees. In *Advances in the Spatial Theory of Voting,* ed. James M. Enelow and Melvin J. Hinich. Cambridge: Cambridge University Press.

———. 1990b. Information and Elections: Retrospective Voting and Rational Expectations. In *Information and Democratic Processes,* ed. John A. Ferejohn and James H. Kuklinski. Chicago: University of Illinois Press.

McKelvey, Richard D., Peter Ordeshook, and Mark D. Winer. 1978. The Competitive Solution for N-Person Games Without Transferable Utility, with an Application to Committee Games. *American Political Science Review* 72:599–615.

McKelvey, Richard D., and Raymond Riezman. 1992. Seniority in Legislatures. *American Political Science Review* 86:951–65.

McKelvey, Richard D., and Howard Rosenthal. 1978. Coalition Formation, Policy Distance, and the Theory of Games Without Sidepayments: An Application to the French *Apparentement* System. In *Game Theory and Political Science,* ed. Peter C. Ordeshook. New York: New York University Press.

McKenzie, Richard. 1976. Politics, Learning, and Public Goods Literacy. *Frontiers of Economics.* Blacksburg, Va.: Center for the Study of Public Choice.

Maoz, Zeev. 1990. *National Choices and International Processes.* Cambridge: Cambridge University Press.

Margolis, Howard. 1977. Probability of a Tie Election. *Public Choice* 31:134–37.

———. 1982. *Selfishness, Altruism, and Rationality: A Theory of Social Choice.* Chicago: University of Chicago Press.

Markus, Gregory B. 1982. Political Attitudes During an Election Year: A Report on the 1980 NES Panel Study. *American Political Science Review* 76:538–60.

Marsh, David. 1976. On Joining Interest Groups: An Empirical Consideration of the Work of Mancur Olson, Jr. *British Journal of Political Science* 6:257–71.

Marwell, Gerald, and Ruth E. Ames. 1979. Experiments on the Provision of Public Goods. I: Resources, Interest, Group Size, and the Free Rider Problem. *American Journal of Sociology* 84:1335–60.

———. 1980. Experiments on the Provision of Public Goods. II: Provision Points, Stakes, Experience, and the Free Rider Problem. *American Journal of Sociology* 85:926–37.

Marwell, Gerald, and Pamela Oliver. 1993. *The Critical Mass in Collective Action: A Micro-Social Theory.* Cambridge: Cambridge University Press.

Matsunga, Spark M., and Ping Chen. 1976. *Rulemakers of the House.* Urbana: University of Illinois Press.

Matthews, Donald R. 1960. *U.S. Senators and Their World.* New York: Vintage.

Mayhew, David R. 1974. *Congress: The Electoral Connection.* New Haven: Yale University Press.

———. 1991. *Divided We Govern.* New Haven: Yale University Press.

Meehl, Paul E. 1977. The Selfish Citizen Paradox and the Throw Away Vote Argument. *American Journal of Political Science* 71:11–30.

Meltzer, Allan H., and Scott F. Richard. 1978. Why Government Grows (and Grows) in a Democracy. *Public Interest* 52:111–18.

———. 1981. A Rational Theory of the Size of Government. *Journal of Political Economy.* 89:914–27.

Messick, David, and Christol G. Rutte. 1992. The Provision of Public Goods by Experts: The Gronigen Study. In *Social Dilemmas: Theoretical Issues and Research Findings,* ed. Wim Liebrand, David Messick, and Henk Wilke. New York: Pergamon.

Mezey, Susan Gluck. 1992. *In Pursuit of Equality: Women, Public Policy, and the Federal Courts.* New York: St. Martin's Press.

Michelson, Melissa R. 1994. The Effect of Presidential Approval on Presidential Power. Ph.D. diss., Yale University.

Michener, H. Andrew, and Kenneth Yuen. 1982. A Competitive Test of the Core Solution in Side-Payment Games. *Behavioral Science* 27:57–68.

Miller, Arthur H., Martin P. Wattenberg, and Oksana Malanchuk. 1986. Schematic Assessments of Presidential Candidates. *American Political Science Review* 80:521–40.

Miller, Gary J., and Thomas H. Hammond. 1990. Committees and the Core of the Constitution. *Public Choice* 66:201–27.

Miller, Gary J., and Joe A. Oppenheimer. 1982. Universalism in Experimental Committees. *American Political Science Review* 76:561–74.

Miller, Nicholas R. 1980. A New Solution Set for Tournaments and Majority Voting. *American Journal of Political Science* 21:769–803.

———. 1983. Pluralism and Social Choice. *American Political Science Review* 77: 734–47.

Miller, Richard. 1987. *Fact and Method*. Princeton, N.J.: Princeton University Press.

Mitchell, D. W. 1987. Candidate Behavior Under Mixed Motives. *Social Choice and Welfare* 4:153–60.

Mitchell, Robert C. 1979. National Environmental Lobbies and the Apparent Illogic of Collective Action. In *Collective Decision-Making,* ed. C. Russell. Baltimore: Johns Hopkins University Press.

Mitchell, Robert C., and R. T. Carson. 1989. *Using Surveys to Value Public Goods: The Contingent Valuation Method*. Washington D.C.: Resources for the Future.

Mitroff, Ian. 1972. The Myth of Objectivity or Why Science Needs a New Psychology of Science. *Management Science* 18:B613–B618.

Moe, Terry M. 1979. On the Scientific Status of Rational Choice Theory. *American Journal of Political Science* 23:215–43.

———. 1980. *The Organization of Interests: Incentives and the Internal Dynamics of Political Interest Groups*. Chicago: University of Chicago Press.

———. 1987. An Assessment of the Positive Theory of Congressional Dominance. *Legislative Studies Quarterly* 12:475–520.

———. 1989. The Politics of Bureaucratic Structure. In *Can the Government Govern?* ed. John Chubb and Paul Peterson. Washington, D.C.: Brookings Institution.

Monroe, Kristen R. 1991. The Theory of Rational Action: What Is It? How Useful Is It for Political Science? In *Political Science: Looking to the Future,* ed. William Crotty. Evanston, Ill.: Northwestern University Press.

Morton, Rebecca B. 1991. Groups in Rational Turnout Models. *American Journal of Political Science* 35:758–76.

———. 1993. Incomplete Information and Ideological Explanations of Platform Divergence. *American Political Science Review* 87:382–92.

Morton, Rebecca B., and Charles Cameron. 1992. Elections and the Theory of Campaign Contributions: A Survey and Critical Analysis. *Economics and Politics* 4:79–108.

Mosca, Gaetano. 1939. *The Ruling Class*. New York: McGraw-Hill.

Mueller, Dennis C. 1979. Public Choice in Practice: A Comment. In *Collective Decision Making: Applications from Public Choice Theory,* ed. Clifford S. Russell. Baltimore: Johns Hopkins University.

———. 1989. *Public Choice II*. Cambridge: Cambridge University Press.

Muller, Edward, and Karl-Dieter Opp. 1986. Rational Choice and Rebellious Collective Action. *American Political Science Review* 80:471–87.

———. 1987. Controversy: Rebellious Collective Action Revisited. *American Political Science Review* 81:561–64.

Myerson, Roger B. 1991. *Game Theory: Analysis of Conflict*. Cambridge: Harvard University Press.

Nagler, Jonathan. 1991. The Effect of Registration Laws and Education on U.S. Voter Turnout. *American Political Science Review* 85:1393–1406.

Nash, John F., Jr. 1950. The Bargaining Problem. *Econometrica* 18:155–62.

Neuman, Russell W. 1986. *The Paradox of Mass Politics: Knowledge and Opinion in the American Electorate*. Cambridge: Harvard University Press.

Niemi, Richard G. 1976. Costs of Voting and Nonvoting. *Public Choice* 27:115–19.

———. 1983. Why So Much Stability?: Another Opinion. *Public Choice* 41:261–70.

Niemi, Richard G., and Herbert F. Weisberg, eds. 1972. *Probability Models of Collective Decision Making*. Columbus, Ohio: Charles Merrill.

Noll, Roger G. 1989. The Economic Theory of Regulation After a Decade of Deregulation: A Comment. In *Brookings Papers on Economic Activity: Microeconomics,* ed. Martin Neil Baily and Clifford Winston. Washington D.C.: Brookings Institution.

Noll, Roger G., and Barry R. Weingast. 1991. Rational Actor Theory, Social Norms, and Policy Implementation: Applications to Administrative Processes and Bureaucratic Culture. In *The Economic Approach to Politics: A Critical Reassessment of the Theory of Rational Action,* ed. Kristen Renwick Monroe. New York: Harper Collins.

Nordhaus, William D. 1975. The Political Business Cycle. *Review of Economic Studies* 42:169–90.

Nozick, Robert. 1974. *Anarchy, State, and Utopia*. New York: Basic Books.

Oberschall, Anthony. 1980. Loosely Structured Collective Conflict: A Theory and an Application. In *Research in Social Movements, Conflicts, and Change,* ed. Louis Kriesberg. Greenwich, Conn.: JAI Press.

O'Brien, David. 1974. The Public Goods Dilemma and the 'Apathy' of the Poor Toward Neighborhood Organization. *Social Service Review* 48:229–44.

Oliver, Pam. 1984. 'If You Don't Do It, Nobody Else Will': Active and Token Contributors to Local Collective Action. *American Sociological Review* 49:601–10.

Olsen, Marvin E. 1968. Perceived Legitimacy of Social Protest Actions. *Social Problems* 15:297–310.

Olson, Mancur, Jr. [1965] 1971. *The Logic of Collective Action*. Cambridge: Harvard University Press.

———. 1979. Group Size and Contributions to Collective Action: A Response. *Research in Social Movements, Conflicts and Change* 2:149–50.

———. 1982. *The Rise and Decline of Nations: Economic Growth, Stagflation, and Social Rigidities*. New Haven: Yale University Press.

———. 1990. Is Britain the Wave of the Future? How Ideas Affect Societies. In *The Rise and Decline of the Nation State,* ed. Michael Mann. Cambridge, Mass.: Blackwell.

———. 1991. Can We Still Get Rid of Saddam? *Washington Post,* May 26, 1991, p. D2.

Ordeshook, Peter C. 1982. Political Disequilibrium and Scientific Inquiry. In *Political Equilibrium,* ed. Peter C. Ordeshook and Kenneth A. Shepsle. Boston: Kluwer-Nijhoff.

———. 1986. *Game Theory and Political Science,* Cambridge: Cambridge University Press.

———. 1992. *A Political Theory Primer*. New York: Routledge.

———. 1993. The development of contemporary political theory. In *Political Economy: Institutions, Competition, and Representation,* ed. William A. Barnett, Melvin J. Hinich, and Norman J. Schofield. Cambridge: Cambridge University Press.

Ordeshook, Peter C., and Thomas Schwartz. 1987. Agendas and the Control of Political Outcomes. *American Political Science Review* 81:179–99.

Ordeshook, Peter C., and Kenneth A. Shepsle, eds. 1982. *Political Equilibrium*. Boston: Kluwer-Nijhoff.

Ostrom, Elinor, and James Walker. 1991. Communication in a Commons: Cooperation Without External Enforcement. In *Laboratory Research in Political Economy*, ed. Thomas R. Palfrey. Ann Arbor: University of Michigan Press.

Ostrom, Elinor, James Walker, and Roy Gardner. 1992. Covenants With and Without a Sword: Self-Governance Is Possible. *American Political Science Review* 86:404–17.

Ostrosky, Anthony L. 1984. The Electoral College and Voter Participation Rates: A Comment. *Public Choice* 43:99–100.

Owen, Guillermo, and Bernard Grofman. 1984. To Vote or Not to Vote: The Paradox of Nonvoting. *Public Choice* 42:311–25.

Page, Benjamin I. 1977. Elections and Social Choice: The State of Evidence. *American Journal of Political Science* 21:639–68.

———. 1978. *Choice and Echoes in Presidential Elections*. Chicago: University of Chicago Press.

Page, Benjamin I., and Robert Y. Shapiro. 1983. Effects of Public Opinion on Policy. *American Political Science Review* 77:175–90.

Palfrey, Thomas R. 1984. Spatial Equilibrium with Entry. *Review of Economic Studies* 51:139–56.

———. 1991. Introduction. In *Laboratory Research in Political Economy*, ed. Thomas R. Palfrey. Ann Arbor: University of Michigan Press.

Palfrey, Thomas R., and Howard Rosenthal. 1983. A Strategic Calculus of Voting. *Public Choice* 41:7–53.

———. 1985. Voter Participation and Strategic Uncertainty. *American Political Science Review* 79:62–78.

———. 1988. Private Incentives in Social Dilemmas. *Journal of Public Economics* 35:309–32.

Palmquist, Bradley L. 1993. Ecological Inferences, Aggregate Data Analysis of U.S. Elections, and the Socialist Party of America. Ph.D. diss., University of California, Berkeley.

Panning, William H. 1982. Rational Choice and Congressional Norms. *Western Political Quarterly* 35:193–203.

Parsons, Talcott, and Robert F. Bales. 1955. *Family*. Glencoe, Ill.: Free Press.

Patterson, Samuel C., and Greg A. Caldeira. 1983. Getting Out the Vote: Participation in Gubernatorial Elections. *American Political Science Review* 77:675–89.

Paulos, John Allen. 1988. *Innumeracy: Mathematical Illiteracy and Its Consequences*. New York: Hill & Wang.

Peltzman, Sam. 1980. The Growth of Government. *Journal of Law and Economics* 23:209–88.

Plott, Charles R. 1967. A Notion of Equilibrium and Its Possibility Under Majority Rule. *American Economic Review* 57:787–806.

———. 1979. The Application of Laboratory Experimental Methods to Public Choice. In

Collective Decision Making: Applications from Public Choice Theory, ed. Clifford S. Russell. Baltimore: Johns Hopkins University Press.

Plott, Charles R., and Michael E. Levine. 1978. A Model of Agenda Influence on Committee Decisions. *American Economic Review* 68:146–60.

———. 1991. A Comparative Analysis of Direct Democracy, Two-Candidate Elections, and Three-Candidate Elections in an Experimental Environment. In *Laboratory Research in Political Economy,* ed. Thomas R. Palfrey. Ann Arbor: University of Michigan Press.

Plott, Charles R., and Vernon L. Smith. 1979. Further Comments. In *Collective Decision Making: Applications from Public Choice Theory,* ed. Clifford S. Russell. Baltimore: Johns Hopkins University Press.

Polsby, Nelson W., and Aaron Wildavsky. 1991. *Presidential Elections: Contemporary Strategies of American Electoral Politics.* 8th ed. New York: Free Press.

Poole, Keith T., and Howard Rosenthal. 1984. The Polarization of American Politics. *Journal of Politics* 46:1061–79.

Popkin, Samuel L. 1991. *The Reasoning Voter.* Chicago: University of Chicago Press.

———. 1993. Information Shortcuts and the Reasoning Voter. In *Information, Participation and Choice,* ed. Bernard Grofman. Ann Arbor: University of Michigan Press.

Popper, Karl. 1959. *The Logic of Scientific Discovery.* New York: Lisher.

———. 1963. *Conjectures and Refutations: The Growth of Scientific Knowledge.* London: Routledge and Kegan Paul.

Posner, Richard A. 1972. A Theory of Negligence. *Journal of Legal Studies* 1:29–96.

———. 1979. Some Uses and Abuses of Economics in Law. *University of Chicago Law Review.* 46:281–306.

———. 1980. The Ethical and Political Basis of the Efficiency Norm in Common Law Adjudication. *Hofstra Law Review* 8:487–551.

———. 1985. An Economic Theory of the Criminal Law. *Columbia Law Review* 85:1193–1231.

Presser, Stanley, and Michael Traugott. 1992. Little White Lies and Social Science Models: Correlated Response Errors in a Panel Study of Voting. *Public Opinion Quarterly* 56:77–86.

Przeworski, Adam. 1991. *Democracy and the Market.* Cambridge: Cambridge University Press.

Przeworski, Adam, and Henry Teune. 1970. *Logic of Comparative Social Inquiry: Comparative Studies in Behavioral Science.* New York: Wiley-Interscience.

Quattrone, George A., and Amos Tversky. 1988. Contrasting Rational and Psychological Analyses of Political Choice. *American Political Science Review* 82:719–36.

Ragsdale, Lyn, and Timothy E. Cook. 1987. Representatives' Actions and Challengers' Reactions: Limits to Candidate Connections in the House. *American Journal of Political Science* 31:45–81.

Rapoport, Anatol. 1985. Provision of Public Goods and the Minimal Contributing Set Experimental Paradigm. *American Political Science Review* 79:148–55.

Rieselbach, Leroy N. 1992. Purposive Politicians Meet the Institutional Congress: A Review Essay. *Legislative Studies Quarterly* 17:95–111

Riker, William H. 1958. The Paradox of Voting and Congressional Rules for Voting on Amendments. *American Political Science Review* 52:349–66.

———. 1965. Arrow's Theory and Some Examples of the Paradox of Voting. In *Mathematical Applications in Political Science,* ed. John M. Claunch. Vol. 1. Dallas: Southern Methodist University Press.

———. 1980. Implications from the Disequilibrium of Majority Rule for the Study of Institutions. *American Political Science Review* 74:432–47.

———. 1982. *Liberalism Against Populism.* San Francisco: Freeman.

———. 1986. *The Art of Political Manipulation.* New Haven: Yale University Press.

———. 1990. Political Science and Rational Choice. In *Perspectives on Positive Political Economy,* ed. James E. Alt and Kenneth A. Shepsle. Cambridge: Cambridge University Press.

———. 1992. The Justification of Bicameralism. *International Political Science Review* 13:101–16.

Riker, William, and Peter C. Ordeshook. 1968. A Theory of the Calculus of Voting. *American Political Science Review* 62:25–42.

———. 1973. *Introduction to Positive Political Theory.* Englewood Cliffs, N.J.: Prentice Hall.

Riker, William, and Barry Weingast. 1988. Constitutional Regulation of Legislative Choice: The Political Consequences of Judicial Deference to Legislatures. *Virginia Law Review* 74:373–401.

Robinson, W. S. 1950. Ecological Correlations and the Behavior of Individuals. *American Sociological Review* 15:351–517.

Roemer, John E. 1979a. Continuing Controversy on the Falling Rate of Profit: Fixed Capital and Other Issues. *Cambridge Journal of Economics* 3:379–98.

———. 1979b. Mass Action Is Not Individually Rational: Reply. *Journal of Economic Issues* 13:763–67.

Rosenberg, Alexander. 1992. *Economics: Mathematical Politics or Science of Diminishing Returns?* Chicago: University of Chicago Press.

Rosenstone, Steven J., and Raymond E. Wolfinger. 1978. The Effect of Registration Laws on Voter Turnout. *American Political Science Review* 72:22–45.

Roth, Alvin E. 1988. Laboratory Experimentation in Economics: A Methodological Overview. *Economical Journal* 98:974.

Rothschild, K. W. 1946. The Meaning of Rationality. *Review of Economic Studies* 14:50–52.

Rubenstein, Ariel. 1979. A Note About the 'Nowhere Denseness' of Societies Having an Equilibrium Under Majority Rule. *Econometrica* 47:511–14.

Russell, Clifford S. 1979. Applications of Public Choice Theory: An Introduction. In *Collective Decision Making: Applications from Public Choice Theory,* ed. Clifford S. Russell. Baltimore: Johns Hopkins University Press.

Russell, Keith. 1972. Why Do High Income People Participate More in Politics? A Response. *Public Choice* 13:113–14.

Russett, Bruce. 1994. Processes of Dyadic Choice for War and Peace. *World Politics*. Forthcoming.

Salant, Stephen W., and Eban Goodstein. 1990. Predicting Committee Behavior in Majority Rule Voting Experiments. *The Rand Journal of Economics* 21:293–313.

Salovey, Peter, John D. Mayer, and David L. Rosenhan. 1991. Mood and Helping: Mood as a Motivator of Helping and Helping as a Regulator of Mood. *Review of Personality and Social Psychology* 12:215–37.

Samuelson, Charles D., David Messick, Henk A. M. Wilke, and Christel Rutte. 1986. Individual Restraint and Structural Change as Solutions to Social Dilemmas. In *Experimental Social Dilemmas*, ed. Henk A. M. Wilke, David M. Messick, and Christel G. Rutte. Frankfurt am Main: Verlag Peter Lang.

Samuelson, Paul A. 1954. The Pure Theory of Public Expenditure. *Review of Economics and Statistics* 36:387–90.

Sanders, Elizabeth. 1980. On the Costs, Utilities and Simple Joys of Voting. *Journal of Politics* 42:854–63.

Sandler, Todd. 1992. *Collective Action: Theory and Applications*. Ann Arbor: University of Michigan Press.

Satz, Debra, and John Ferejohn. 1993. Rational Choice and Social Theory. Manuscript, Stanford University.

Schlozman, Kay Lehman, and Sidney Verba. 1979. *Injury to Insult: Unemployment, Class, and Political Responses*. Cambridge: Harvard University Press.

Schofield, Norman. 1978. Instability of Simple Dynamic Games. *Review of Economic Studies* 45:575–94.

———. 1983. General Instability of Majority Rule. *Review of Economic Studies* 50:695–705.

Schofield, Norman, Bernard Grofman, and Scott L. Feld. 1988. The Core and the Stability of Group Choice in Spatial Voting Games. *American Political Science Review* 82:195–212.

Schram, Arthur J. H. C. 1991. *Voter Behavior in Economic Perspective*. Berlin: Springer-Verlag.

Schroeder, David A., Thomas D. Jensen, Andrew J. Reed, Debra K. Sullivan, and Michael Schwab. 1983. The Actions of Others as Determinants of Behavior in Social Trap Situations. *Journal of Experimental Social Psychology* 19:522–39.

Schumpeter, Joseph A. 1942. *Capitalism, Socialism and Democracy*. New York: Harper & Row.

Schwartz, Thomas. 1987. Your Vote Counts on Account of the Way It is Counted. *Public Choice* 54:101–21.

Schwartz-Shea, Peregrine, and Randy T. Simmons. 1990. The Layered Prisoners' Dilemma: Ingroup versus Macro-Efficiency. *Public Choice* 65:61–83.

Sears, David O., Richard R. Lau, Tom R. Tyler, and Harris M. Allen, Jr. 1980. Self-

Interest vs. Symbolic Politics in Policy Attitudes and Presidential Voting. *American Political Science Review* 74:670–84.

Selten, Reinhard, and Rolf Stroecker. 1986. End Behavior in Sequences of Finite Prisoner's Dilemma Supergames. *Journal of Economic Behavior and Organization* 7: 47–70.

Settle, Russell F., and Burton A. Abrams. 1976. The Determinants of Voter Participation: A More General Model. *Public Choice* 27:81–89.

Shapiro, Ian. 1993. Democratic Innovation: South Africa in Comparative Context. *World Politics* 46:121–50.

Shepsle, Kenneth A. 1972a. The Paradox of Voting and Uncertainty. In *Probability Models of Collective Decision Making,* ed. Richard G. Niemi and Herbert F. Weisberg. Columbus, Ohio: Charles Merrill.

———. 1972b. The Strategy of Ambiguity: Uncertainty and Electoral Competition. *American Political Science Review* 66:555–68.

———. 1979. Institutional Arrangements and Equilibrium in Multidimensional Voting Models. *American Journal of Political Science* 23:27–59.

———. 1986. The Positive Theory of Legislative Institutions: An Enrichment of Social Choice and Spatial Models. *Public Choice* 50:135–78.

Shepsle, Kenneth A., and Ronald N. Cohen. 1990. Multiparty Competition, Entry, and Entry Deterrence in Spatial Models of Elections. In *Advances in the Spatial Theory of Voting,* ed. James Enelow and Melvin Hinich. Cambridge: Cambridge University Press.

Shepsle, Kenneth A., and Barry R. Weingast. 1981. Structure-Induced Equilibrium and Legislative Choice. *Public Choice* 37:503–19.

———. 1984. Unconverted Sets and Sophisticated Voting Outcomes with Implications for Agenda Institutions. *American Journal of Political Science* 28:49–74.

———. 1987a. The Institutional Foundations of Committee Power. *American Political Science Review* 81:86–108.

———. 1987b. Reflections on Committee Power. *American Political Science Review* 81:935–45.

Silberman, Jonathan, and Garey Durden. 1975. The Rational Behavior Theory of Voter Participation: The Evidence from Congressional Elections. *Public Choice* 23:503–19.

Simon, Herbert A. 1955. A Behavioral Model of Rational Choice. *Quarterly Journal of Economics* 69:99–118.

———. 1956. Rational Choice and the Structure of the Environment. *Psychological Review* 63:129–38.

———. 1993. The State of American Political Science: Professor Lowi's View of Our Discipline. *PS: Political Science and Politics* 26:49–51.

Sinclair, Barbara. 1986. The Transformation of the U.S. Senate. In *Home Style and Washington Work,* ed. Morris P. Fiorina and David W. Rohde. Ann Arbor: University of Michigan Press.

Smith, Darlene Branningan, and Paul N. Bloom. 1986. Is Consumerism Dead or Alive?

Some Empirical Evidence. In *The Future of Consumerism,* ed. Paul N. Bloom and Ruth B. Smith. Lexington, Mass.: Lexington Books.

Smith, Jeffrey W. 1975. A Clear Test of Rational Voting. *Public Choice* 23:55–68.

Smith, Vernon. 1976. Experimental Economics: Induced Value Theory. *American Economic Review* 66:274–79.

Snyder, James M., Jr. 1990. Campaign Contributions as Investments: The U.S. House of Representatives, 1980–1986. *Journal of Political Economy* 98:1195–1227.

Sorauf, Frank J. 1988. *Money in American Elections.* Glenview, Ill.: Scott, Foresman.

Spiller, Pablo T., and Matthew L. Spitzer. Judicial Choice of Legal Doctrines. *Journal of Law, Economics, and Organization* 8, no. 1, 8–44.

Stevens, Stephen V. 1975. The Paradox of Not Voting: Comment. *American Political Science Review* 69:914–15.

Stigler, George. 1972. Economic Competition and Political Competition. *Public Choice* 13:91–106.

———. 1975. Determinants of Participation in Presidential Elections: Comment. *Journal of Law and Economics* 18:743–44.

Stigler, George, and Gary S. Becker. 1977. De Gustibus Non Est Disputandum. *American Economic Review* 67:76–90.

Stokes, Donald. 1963. Spatial Models of Party Competition. *American Political Science Review* 57:368–77.

Strom, Gerald S. 1975. On the Apparent Paradox of Participation: A New Proposal. *American Political Science Review* 69:908–13.

———. 1990. *The Logic of Lawmaking: A Spatial Theory Approach.* Baltimore: Johns Hopkins University Press.

Swenson, Peter. 1991a. Bringing Capital Back In, or Social Democracy Reconsidered. *World Politics* 43:513–44.

———. 1991b. Labor and the Limits of the Welfare State. *Comparative Politics* 23:379–99.

Tajfel, Henri, ed. 1978. *Differentiation Between Social Groups: Studies on the Social Psychology of Intergroup Relations.* London: Academic Press.

Taylor, Michael. 1987. *The Possibility of Cooperation.* Cambridge: Cambridge University Press.

Teixeira, Ruy A. 1987. *Why Americans Don't Vote: Turnout Decline in the United States, 1960–1984.* New York: Greenwood Press.

Thakur, Ramesh C. 1982. Tacit Deception Reexamined: The Geneva Conference of 1954. *International Studies Quarterly* 26:127–39.

Thaler, Richard H. 1991. *Quasi-Rational Economics.* New York: Russell Sage.

Thompson, Fred. 1982. Closeness Counts in Horseshoes and Dancing . . . and Elections. *Public Choice* 38:305–16.

Tideman, T. Nicolaus. 1985. Remorse, Elation, and the Paradox of Voting. *Public Choice* 46:103–6.

Tillock, Harriet, and Denton E. Morrison. 1979. Group Size and Contribution to Collective Action: A Test of Mancur Olson's Theory on Zero Population Growth, Inc. *Research in Social Movements, Conflict, and Change* 2:131–58.

Tollison, Richard D., and Thomas D. Willett. 1973. Some Simple Economics of Voting and Not Voting. *Public Choice* 16:59–71.

Tootle, Deborah M., and Sara Green. 1989. The Effect of Ethnic Identity on Support for Farm Worker Unions. *Rural Sociology* 54:83–91.

Tovey, Craig A. 1993. Some Foundations for Empirical Study in the Euclidean Spatial Model of Social Choice. In *Political Economy: Institutions, Competition, and Representation,* ed. William A. Barnett, Melvin J. Hinich, and Norman J. Schofield. Cambridge: Cambridge University Press.

Traugott, Michael Wolfe. 1974. An Economic Model of Voting Behavior. Ph.D. diss., University of Michigan.

Tufte, Edward R. 1978. *Political Control of the Economy.* Princeton, N.J.: Princeton University Press.

Tullock, Gordon. 1962. Theoretical Forerunners. In *The Calculus of Consent,* ed. James M. Buchanan and Gordon Tullock. Ann Arbor: University of Michigan Press.

———. 1967. *Toward a Mathematics of Politics.* Ann Arbor: University of Michigan Press.

———. 1971. The Paradox of Revolution. *Public Choice* 11:89–99.

———. 1975. The Paradox of Not Voting for Oneself. *American Political Science Review* 69:919.

———. 1976. *The Vote Motive.* London: Institute for Economic Affairs.

———. 1979. Public Choice in Practice. In *Collective Decision Making: Applications from Public Choice Theory,* ed. Clifford S. Russell. Baltimore: Johns Hopkins University Press.

———. 1981. Why So Much Stability? *Public Choice* 37:189–202.

Tversky, Amos, and Daniel Kahneman. 1981. The Framing of Decisions and the Psychology of Choice. *Science* 211:453–58.

———. 1986. Rational Choice and the Framing of Decisions. *Journal of Business* 59:S251–78.

Uhlaner, Carole J. 1989. Rational Turnout: The Neglected Role of Groups. *American Journal of Political Science* 33:390–422.

United States Commission on Civil Rights. 1965. *Voting in Mississippi.* Washington, D.C.: U.S. Commission on Civil Rights.

United States Commission on Civil Rights. 1968. *Political Participation: A Study of Political Participation by Negroes.* Washington, D.C.: U.S. Commission on Civil Rights.

Van de Kragt, Alphons J. C., Robyn M. Dawes, and John M. Orbell. 1988. Are People Who Cooperate 'Rational Altruists?' *Public Choice* 56:233–47.

Van Parijs, Philippe. 1980. The Falling-Rate-of-Profit Theory of Crisis: A Rational Reconstruction by Way of Obituary. *The Review of Radical Political Economics* 12:1–16.

Verba, Sidney, and Norman Nie. 1972. *Participation in America*. New York: Harper & Row.

Von Neumann, John, and Oskar Morgenstern. 1947. *Theory of Games and Economic Behavior*. 2nd ed. Princeton: Princeton University Press.

Walsh, Edward J., and Rex H. Warland. 1983. Social Movement Involvement in the Wake of a Nuclear Accident: Activists and Free Riders in the TMI Area. *American Sociological Review* 48:764–80.

Weingast, Barry. 1979. A Rational Choice Perspective on Congressional Norms. *American Journal of Political Science* 23:245–62.

———. 1984. The Congressional-Bureaucratic System: A Principal-Agent Perspective (With Applications to the SEC). *Public Choice* 44:147–91.

———. 1989. Floor Behavior in the U.S. Congress: Committee Power Under the Open Role. *American Political Science Review* 83:795–815.

Weingast, Barry, and William Marshall. 1988. The Industrial Organization of Congress. *Journal of Political Economy* 96:132–63.

Weisberg, Herbert F., and Richard G. Niemi. 1972. Probability Calculations for Cyclical Majorities in Congressional Voting. In *Probability Models of Collective Decision-Making,* ed. Richard G. Niemi and Herbert F. Weisberg. Columbus, Ohio: Charles Merrill.

Weiss, Richard M. 1991. Alternative Social Science Perspective on 'Social Dilemma' Laboratory Research. In *Social Norms and Economic Institutions,* ed. Kenneth Koford and Jeffrey Miller. Ann Arbor: University of Michigan.

Williams, Kenneth C. 1991. Candidate Convergence and Information Costs in Spatial Elections: An Experimental Analysis. In *Laboratory Research in Political Economy,* ed. Thomas R. Palfrey. Ann Arbor: University of Michigan Press.

Wilson, Rick K. 1986. Forward and Backward Agenda Procedures: Committee Experiments on Structurally-Induced Equilibrium. *Journal of Politics* 48:390–409.

Wilson, Rick K., and Roberta Herzberg. 1987. Negative Decision Powers and Institutional Equilibrium: Experiments on Blocking Coalitions. *Western Political Quarterly* 40:593–609.

Wilson, Rick K., and Anne Pearson. 1987. Evidence of Sophisticated Voting in a Committee Setting: Theory and Experiments. *Quality and Quantity* 21:255–73.

Wittgenstein, Ludwig. 1963. *Philosophical Investigations*. Trans. G. E. M. Anscombe. Oxford: Basil Blackwell.

Wittman, Donald. 1973. Parties as Utility Maximizers. *American Political Science Review* 67:490–98.

———. 1975. Determinants of Participation in Presidential Elections: A Comment. *Journal of Law and Economics* 18:735–41.

———. 1983. Candidate Motivation: A Synthesis of Alternative Theories. *American Political Science Review* 77:142–57.

———. 1990. Spatial Strategies When Candidates Have Policy Preferences. In *Advances in the Spatial Theory of Voting,* ed. James M. Enelow and Melvin Hinich. New York: Cambridge University Press.

Wolfinger, Raymond E. 1993. The Rational Citizen Faces Election Day, or What Rational Choice Theorists Don't Tell You About American Elections. In *Elections at Home and Abroad: Essays in Honor of Warren E. Miller,* ed. M. Kent Jennings and Thomas E. Mann. Ann Arbor: University of Michigan Press.

Wolfinger, Raymond E., and Stephen J. Rosenstone. 1980. *Who Votes?* New Haven: Yale University Press.

Yamagashi, Yoshio. 1988. Seriousness of Social Dilemmas and the Provision of a Sanctioning System. *Social Psychology Quarterly* 51:32–42.

Zagare, Frank C. 1979. The Geneva Conference of 1954: A Case of Tacit Deception. *International Studies Quarterly* 23:390–411.

———. 1984. *Game Theory: Concepts and Applications.* Beverly Hills, Calif.: Sage.

INDEX